HONDA'S GLOBAL LOCAL CORPORATION

Honda's Global Local Corporation

Andrew Mair

St. Martin's Press

First published in Great Britain 1994 by
THE MACMILLAN PRESS LTD
Houndmills, Basingstoke, Hampshire RG21 2XS
and London
Companies and representatives
throughout the world

A catalogue record for this book is available
from the British Library.

ISBN 0–333–58683–2

Printed in Great Britain by
Antony Rowe Ltd
Chippenham, Wiltshire

First published in the United States of America 1994 by
Scholarly and Reference Division,
ST. MARTIN'S PRESS, INC.,
175 Fifth Avenue,
New York, N.Y. 10010

ISBN 0–312–10668–8

Library of Congress Cataloging-in-Publication Data
Mair, Andrew.
Honda's global local corporation / Andrew Mair.
p. cm.
Includes index.
ISBN 0–312–10688–8
1. Honda Giken Kōgyō Kabushiki Kaisha. 2. Automobile industry and
trade—Japan. 3. Industrial management—Japan. I. Title.
HD9710.J34H65435 1994
338.8' 87292' 0952—dc20
93–31246
CIP

To Sybil Hyacinth and Alexander Joseph

Contents

List of Tables

List of Figures

List of Boxes

Part I

The Japanese Firm
Goes Global

Introduction: Underestimating the Japanese

In 1962, the Honda Motor Co., a Japanese motorcycle manufacturer founded fourteen years previously, made its first automobile. Entering the four-wheeler business had been a hurried affair, rushed along because it looked as if the Japanese Ministry of Trade and Industry (MITI) would try to prevent new firms from joining Japan's small automobile industry. MITI's fear was that the sector's international competitiveness would be undermined by a plethora of small producers unable to reap economies of scale. Between 1958 and 1962 Honda had moved fast, and its engineers came up with a small truck and a small sports car so that Honda could claim already to have joined the ranks of the automobile producers.

Thirty years later Honda has become one of Japan's leading automobile manufacturers, and its products are respected and feared the world over by competitors who have much longer pedigrees in the business. Far from hurting Japan's competitiveness, Honda is leading the world in creating a new kind of multinational enterprise. The *global local corporation* heralds an industrial revolution in global-scale manufacturing with profound economic, political, technological and social consequences for the countries where it operates. Honda's success has become a model for manufacturers everywhere.

This book is about Honda's coming of age as a multinational enterprise. It tells the story of a new kind of global organization and what it means for the world's economy, political structures and citizens. The competition has been watching and studying Honda for several years to see what they can learn. Companies in difficulty, like Chrysler, have made detailed analyses of Honda, on which to model their own restructuring. Toyota, widely seen as the world's most successful automobile company in recent decades, built a close copy of Honda's American operations when it set up its own manufacturing plants there. The equally successful BMW has lured away top Honda managers in North America to teach it how to set up its own new 'transplant'. Honda's European partner Rover has had over a decade

3

to study Honda and internalise the lessons. But this is the first published in-depth analysis of how the pioneer and most innovative among Japan's multinational automobile producers has carved out its distinctive niche globally.[1]

In many ways this is all rather unexpected. Just a decade ago, many thought that Japan's major manufacturers would never dare to operate outside Japan because they would not be able to repeat their home-base successes. When some Japanese companies did invest abroad, their overseas activities soon became subject to a great deal of interest and speculation. Could Japanese manufacturers really function abroad as well as in Japan? What strategies would they follow? Would this mean the spread of 'Japanization'? What would that mean for Western societies?

In Honda's case we are going to see how a Japanese firm can indeed succeed abroad as well as it does in Japan, and what the strategies it has adopted to ensure this happens mean for the people and for the social institutions of North America and Europe. There are some surprises in store.

In taking an in-depth look at Honda's multinational operations we will be forced to overturn many commonly shared assumptions about the Japanese firm. This is no bad thing, because there is much that remains ambiguous and confusing. By studying Honda for five years, I have discovered that our ingrained ways of thinking, so natural to us in the West, have led us to make lots of mistakes. It is well past the time to get to grips with the Japanese firm, and especially its overseas operations.

We have often underestimated the capacity of the Japanese firm to innovate and transform itself, and neglected to learn both how to react and how we might learn from it to transform ourselves. This is true whether we are rival businesses, labour union leaders, employees, managers, or local and national governments. We can use this opportunity of a close look at Honda's global operations to discover how to really make sense of the Japanese multinational enterprise, and Japanese economic success in general, and to dispense with many of the enigmas and myths that have left so many so confused and perplexed.

This is primarily a management book. I hope that it will be read by managers of other firms in the competitive world of manufacturing who want to understand leading edge multinational corporate practice. But this is a management book with a difference; several differences in fact. For a start, it avoids the well-worn path of the 'easy read' explanations of corporate success, the ones full of great men and little anecdotes, of tiny seeds that all seem to become oak trees. Inspirational as these books might be, useful as they are for getting a grip on mindsets – and as we will see the importance of corporate philosophy to firms like Honda cannot be overestimated – they tend to be entertaining but not entirely convincing, because we all know at heart that you don't really organize giant corporations and their global operations on the basis of this kind of stuff.[2]

Compared with the 'easy read' book, this book is going to be hard-nosed. It adopts a serious analytic perspective on corporate strategy. However, this definitely does not require an academic textbook that descends into a morass of abstract theories accompanied by masses of tables and equations. Even the best of management textbooks tend to teach ideas in principle – whether complex theories or simple 'management manual' notions – and then illustrate them with examples taken from diverse case studies to show 'how the best firms do it'. The texts can sometimes seem long, dry and arduous, and the examples can seem isolated and lacking the contextual information about decision-making and implementation that would let us judge whether the theories and notions are in fact transportable from one company to another.

The easy read and the academic text are two opposite ways of studying business management. Too often, the text loses out on interest value because the author thinks that 'serious' analysis has to be abstract and dry; all too easy to put down! But while the easy read can be as much fun as a light novel, it can also leave you unsatisfied.

I think I've found an answer, and I hope you'll agree. By following and studying a single innovative and pioneering firm at the cutting edge of multinational corporate practice we can have the best of both worlds, getting behind its decision-making analytically, seeing how its strategies are implemented in practice, and painting a total picture, including context, that promises a deeper understanding. And as well as gaining analytical depth, we can maintain a real interest as the story builds up and as the parts of Honda's operations all begin to fit together for us (which they have to do since Honda does function, and how!).

Another way this is a management book with a difference is that I have written it not solely for practising business managers, but also for the many other people who deal with management and managers. I hope that it will also be read by international and national government officials concerned over new world trade and investment patterns, by local politicians dealing with the bewildering fragments of the new global economy that have selected their backyards in which to make their products, by labour union officials and employees uncertain how to react to new ideas and unclear what their future holds, by small business owners confronting daunting new realities in their relations with big firms, and by citizens who want to know more about what is happening at the cutting edge of business practice. And while my primary audience is in the Western world, I sincerely hope that this book will also help readers in Japan to understand better what Japan's manufacturing enterprises are doing in their overseas activities.

As well as a book *for* management, then, this is a book *about* management for all those who need to know more. I hope it will help those involved in industry and with industry – Japanese industry in particular – communicate with each other better.

The idea of the *global local corporation* which Honda is pioneering and others are copying raises many significant and novel economic, social and political issues. All the players involved are being forced to confront what is essentially a new kind of animal in the world's economic and political system, one that is rewriting the rule-book on corporate behaviour. But it has been evident to me for some time that many key players are having difficulty adjusting themselves, their perspectives, their actions and their reactions. This is true regardless of whether they need to accommodate themselves to the new phenomenon or to defend themselves against it.

In fact, for managers, politicians, officials, union leaders, employees at various levels, ordinary citizens, whether in the West or in Japan, understanding and dealing with the Japanese multinational manufacturing enterprise over the past few years has sometimes proved to be a source of immense difficulty and considerable institutional and personal conflict. Faced with many surprises and unexpected events, people have not always known what to do, nor even what to think. Lack of understanding has influenced debates over the 'local content' of 'transplant' automobiles, discussions of if and how labour unions can gain worker representation at the transplants, plans to sell auto parts to the Japanese, and government policies towards economic development and international trade. The result is that too many players have remained ill-informed and unable to face up to their tasks as they should and could.

This is where I want to try to help. The Honda case is not of course the whole story of the Japanese multinational manufacturer. But we can use its example as a leader to learn a great deal about what's going on. This doesn't mean that I'm going to tell people precisely what they should and should not do. After all, each player is in a different situation and I can't pretend to know exactly what these situations are. But I am going to try to teach people, in principle and through the outstanding example of Honda, how to think – for I really believe a new way of thinking is needed – so that they can now work out for themselves what they need to do to face up to the challenges that firms like Honda present.

'There's something wrong with the way we have been analysing the Japanese firm.' Let us consider this statement for a moment. Japan's rise to global prominence since the mid-1970s has been accompanied by study after study of what makes the Japanese firm different from its Western counterpart. While some analysts asked why the Japanese firm was so successful, only a decade ago many were suggesting that the Japanese firm had already reached its pinnacle. They said, sure, the Japanese have done well in Japan, but they will fall on their faces if they venture to North America or Europe.

So ingrained was this view that American business and political leaders publicly invited Japanese automobile producers to open manufacturing plants in the United States, in full expectation that doing so would effectively sabotage their competitiveness. After all Americans knew best how to deal with the very difficult American business environment; the insulated Japanese, dependent upon all sorts of special advantages in Japan, wouldn't stand a chance. So the theory went. Ten years later, Japanese-owned plants are the most efficient, and make some of the best-selling automobiles, in North America, and Americans have been falling over themselves in a desperate attempt to learn how the Japanese do it before it is too late.

There have been a whole series of similar errors of judgement in recent years:

- We said 'Don't worry, the Japanese only make little cars: let them, we'll keep the profitable upper segments.' Honda broke this mould in 1985 when it launched its Acura marque in North America. Nissan and Toyota followed suit. A few years on, and Mercedes is more than a little nervous about the coming competition from Toyota's Lexus marque.
- We said 'Don't worry, Japanese products are all "low- tech" copies, so we can maintain the technology edge.' Honda's engines won the Formula 1 constructors' championships every year between 1986

and 1991. A string of other technical innovations have emerged from Japan in recent years.

- **We said 'Don't worry, the Japanese are "reluctant multinationals" so we can keep them at bay with trade restrictions.'**[3] But all of a sudden, during the 1980s, Japan's automobile makers had produced an enormous wave of multinational manufacturing investment when they swooped into North America to build their 'transplants', to be followed by 300 Japanese automotive industry suppliers. More slowly, they are now building up a substantial production capacity in Europe.

- **We said 'Don't worry, the Japanese only operate "screwdriver plants" abroad so we can defeat them by arousing public indignation.'** But now, hundreds of Japanese-owned parts makers manufacture their products in North America too, providing the assembly firms with locally made components. And the 'transplants' in Europe dampen criticism by purchasing parts from European firms across the continent.

- **We said 'Don't worry, our powerful labour unions will prevent them from using their manufacturing techniques at the transplants, so their factories in the West will turn out no better than ours.'** In fact, the tables have been completely turned: labour unions only represent workers at transplants if the Japanese let them, and then only under strict conditions. In Europe the unions have been forced to line up in 'beauty contests' so that Japanese managers – not the workers – can choose the most suitable. Now many Western firms are trying to reduce union power to a level matching the transplants.

Certainly, fewer people are underestimating the Japanese today. (Although there has been a disturbing tendency to view the difficulties of Japanese companies in Japan, due to the early 1990s recession there, with a sense of satisfaction: once more some seem tempted to think 'that will put a stop to them!'). Yet, for the most part, increased respect – and fear – has not been accompanied by a deeper understanding. Look at how Westerners have chopped and changed their ideas as they search for the key to Japan's success. At first we argued that the Japanese were doing essentially the same thing as our firms, but more of it. Their workers worked faster, they worked longer hours, their components suppliers were cheaper, their government helped more, they used more robots. Then we reversed ourselves and argued that the Japanese were doing something quite different from us, something fundamentally unique to Japanese firms (for example, they had the special *Toyota Production System*).

Either way, it followed logically that neither the Japanese firm nor the Western firm would be able to achieve the same results outside Japan, where the whole operating environment was different. But recently our ideas have switched again: now we're being told that Japanese management techniques can be applied anywhere we want! What are we supposed to believe?[4]

Little by little the curtain has of course been lifted on Japan. But little by little isn't quick enough when we have to make decisions here and now. I believe it is fair to say that most of us remain quite unclear about the fundamentals of the Japanese firm and how it operates, especially how it operates abroad. While we know its results all too well, the strategic development of the Japanese firm remains something of an enigma.

This state of affairs has far-reaching consequences, because it influences our own actions and reactions. Matters have come to a head as Japanese firms move massively and decisively to launch overseas manufacturing operations in the very heartlands of their global rivals. Western players are faced with all sorts of new decisions to make, and those decisions are bound to be based upon our understanding of how Japanese firms function.

Competitor firms need to analyse their relative strengths and weaknesses. Taking advantage of your own strengths depends upon correctly estimating the strengths of the opposition. Some firms have to decide whether to collaborate with Japanese firms. Who will gain most from collaboration? How can the Western firm learn quickly and effectively from a Japanese partner, or will it simply be exploited?

Governments have to make policy decisions, how to protect their domestic industries, whether to invite Japanese investment with subsidies, whether to keep pushing for trade restrictions. What is the best way to protect and support an existing industrial base? Which is best, inviting the Japanese in or shutting them out? Will Japanese investment undermine existing firms or help restore their competitiveness?

Local and regional governments also have to weigh up the costs and benefits of trying to attract Japanese investments: there are questions over subsidies and spin-offs, over how to form close relationships with the Japanese. Do local and regional governments need new strategies for economic development? Is it true that Japanese firms want closer relationships with their local communities? Does this mean a greater role for local and regional governments?

Labour unions want to devise strategies to maintain their important social roles, to be able to represent workers in Japanese firms, and to have something to offer those workers. Moreover, they find themselves challenged in their existing power bases as their accustomed positions in domestic firms are measured against 'the Japanese model'. Is it best to form a cooperative relationship with managers? Or is a more adversarial approach more appropriate to gain the support of employees?

Workers, managers and engineers employed by the Japanese need to understand what their future holds. It helps to see the big picture beyond everyday tasks and relationships. What is the Japanese approach to work and career in reality? Is the individual subordinated to the group? Is the Japanese multinational intent upon 'Japanizing' its Western workforce? Can the Westerner advance, or are the best seats in the career bus reserved for the Japanese? Is work in the Japanese firm more challenging and interesting or is it more stressful? Can you really expect lifetime employment? Do you want to?

Finally, let's not forget that the Japanese themselves are hardly immune to our beliefs about how they operate, since our views affect our reactions to them. And there can be no doubt that the Japanese remain under intense scrutiny. What do we think of Japanese firms? What do we praise them for, what do we criticize them for? What kinds of political and public relations pressure are they under? Our reactions form an important part of the context in which they make their own decisions. Can we influence those decisions? What should we try to achieve?

How can we give our understanding of the Japanese multinational manufacturing enterprise the shot in the arm it needs? The approach I am advocating results from in-depth study of Honda's multinational operations over several years. It has developed step by step through dozens of interviews and factory visits conducted in North America and Europe. I asked people simple questions: 'tell me how you make a car (or a component)', 'tell me what people in this part of the factory do', 'what is the difference between this process and that process?'. I kept reading: magazine interviews, industry trade journals, newspapers. I stared at countless Honda Accords, Civics, Preludes, Legends, on the streets and thought about their design. I visited and talked to other automobile industry manufacturers, American, British, French, German, Dutch, to place Honda in perspective. Towards the end of the research, I tried my ideas out on people to check that I was on the right track.

But at the same time I read and listened to what other people were writing and saying about Japanese firms in North America and Europe: journalists, politicians, academics, trade unionists, managers at competing firms. This began to prove rather disturbing. Frequently, other people's accounts didn't seem to tally with my own investigations.[5] It slowly dawned on me that the root of the discrepancies was that Westerners kept insisting upon a certain philosophical approach to analysing the Japanese firm, but Honda and other Japanese firms didn't make their decisions or organize themselves according to this approach, and so there was a continual mismatch between theory and practice, ideas and reality.

I don't think many people outside Japanese firms have pieced it all together. But I know that a growing number will recognize precisely the approach we are going to adopt here, because they have begun to understand it for themselves. I think you'll find the process of discovery well worth the challenge.[6]

In the next chapter we pause to reflect a little before embarking on the empirical study of Honda's rise to global manufacturing. What is the philosophical approach we tend to adopt towards the Japanese firm in the West, and how does it let us down in the case of firms like Honda? How do we conventionally think about the way the multinational manufacturing enterprise is organized? What ideas have we had about whether Japanese management techniques can be applied outside Japan? A survey of these issues will prepare us for the analysis to follow.

Notes

1. Earlier parts of the Honda story, including the first days of multinationalism, are discussed in Setsuo Mito, *The Honda Book of Management*, London: Kogan Page, 1990; Tetsuo Sakiya, *Honda Motor: The Men, the Management, the Machines*, Tokyo: Kodansha International, 1987 (2nd edn.); Sol Sanders, *Honda: The Man and His Machines*, Boston, Mass.: Little, Brown, 1975; Robert L. Shook, *Honda: An American Success Story*, New York: Prentice Hall, 1988.

2. Honda has already received its fair share of this kind of treatment (the book by Shook in note 1 is a good instance). While there are revealing insights into ideas and philosophies, and plenty of good stories, there tends to be little about the material side of actually organizing how to make automobiles.
3. This was actually the title of one book published in 1983: M. Trevor, *Japan's Reluctant Multinationals: Japanese Management At Home and Abroad*, London: Pinter.
4. On this last viewpoint there are many professional consultants, including those who have 'de-Japanized' the model and re-named it 'lean production': see, for example, James P. Womack, Daniel T. Jones and Daniel Roos, *The Machine that Changed the World*, New York: Rawson Associates, 1990.
5. However, an outstanding study of working life at Mazda's plant near Detroit is Joseph Fucini and Suzy Fucini, *Working for the Japanese*, New York: The Free Press, 1990.
6. The goal of this book is to offer a coherent analysis of how Honda has created a global automobile production network. Concentration on this task precludes us from placing the Honda case fully within the context of business and management theory, and so from direct comparison of the following analysis with potentially relevant contributions by other writers. Likewise, no effort is made here to place Honda management philosophy within the context of Japanese thought in general. A final lacuna should be mentioned, that is, that the activities of Honda's competitors, Japanese and Western, are touched on only in passing. If these are 'gaps', this is the result of the author's starting point, studying Honda directly, from its own perspective and from the perspective of implicated employees, partner companies, and other directly connected institutions (unions, governments). Clearly, there remains more to be written on this subject.

1 Thinking About the Japanese Firm

In the previous chapter we suggested that there is a difference between the philosophical approach we tend to use in the West and how firms like Honda think and act. In this chapter we're going to pursue this difference further, to sharpen up our ideas before we proceed. The discussion is divided into three parts.

In the first part we look at that basic Western philosophical approach, 'dualism'. Dualism means thinking about things in terms of pairs of ideas that we think are opposites. Examples in business and management are individual and group, cost and quality, labour intensity and capital intensity, thinking work and doing work, efficient work and humane work, vertical organization and horizontal organization. In the West we tend to think you have to choose one or the other in each pair, or that if you gain on one side you must lose on the other side, so you have to trade off the opposites against one another. For instance, we might think that efficient work is inhumane, and that humane work tends to be inefficient: work cannot be both. Or that an organization is either vertical and pyramidal or horizontal and flat, but not both.

Western organizations, business firms especially, tend to be set up along dualist lines, choosing to be efficient, low-cost, vertical, labour-intensive, for instance, or humane, high-quality, capital-intensive (or any combination of one side from each pair). But Honda does not think like this. It does recognize the pairs of opposites, but it refuses to choose between them or lose one as it gains the other.

Honda's corporate strategy, its ideology, is based upon systematically seeking to retain both sides of each pair: work that is humane *and* efficient, both capital- *and* labour- intensive, organization that is both vertical *and* horizontal, and so on. In retaining both elements, the goal is make the elusive '*best of both worlds*' a reality. Rather than a problem of trade-offs, recognition of dualisms implies finding solutions. It is often said that the Japanese are mysteriously able to turn adversity into advantage. Here we'll see how they do it.

The second topic of this chapter is the multinational manufacturing enterprise and how it is organized; or has been up to now. The global local corporation that Honda is pioneering is organized quite differently from the conventional multinational enterprise. In fact a new theory of multinational manufacturing is needed that can accommodate the new model, and in this book we'll help to develop that theory.

The third topic is this: why did so many people believe that Japanese firms would never be able to implement their special management techniques outside Japan? All sorts of features of Western society were expected to sabotage Japanese methods: national cultures, manufacturing practices, labour unions, management values. A decade ago, Europeans, Americans and Japanese alike were agreed on how difficult it would be for Japanese manufacturers to operate in the West. But Honda was not.

There are two issues wrapped up in this last topic. First, how would operating in the West interfere with Japanese management techniques? The normal question to ask is whether the techniques could be transferred intact or would have to be hybridized and watered down. Second, how does introducing Japanese management techniques affect Western society? Will some kind of 'Japanization' of business life inevitably follow?

IMPROVING OUR PHILOSOPHICAL APPROACH

How does Honda get the best of both worlds when we tend to think it's impossible? It treats dualisms like puzzles to be solved.

Let's start with an example that many will already recognize. In the past, Western firms often saw product quality and production cost as a dualist opposite pair. The ideal would have been to have low cost and high quality, but in practice lower costs meant inferior quality and increasing quality increased costs: a trade-off.

But the Japanese discovered a better way, captured in the phrase 'right first time'. If you ensure that the components and the manufacturing process are of superior quality in the first place you can actually reduce costs, because there is less wastage, less machine downtime with inferior parts getting caught up in machines, less demand for special quality control workers. Not only that, but customers will be more satisfied because there is less chance of defective products reaching them. Adopting and pursuing this perspective, many Western manufacturers have been learning that you don't have to trade off quality and cost, you can have both.

It is this kind of puzzle-solution that forms the backbone of the Honda corporate structure; it is an essential ingredient of 'the Honda Way'. In this book we'll see how the Honda Way pervades many other aspects of corporate strategy. We'll provide lots of practice in looking at the world the Honda Way, so that you can begin to tackle some of your own puzzles.

Let's look more closely at the dualist approach, at the Honda method of puzzle-solving, and at why Westerners don't usually do it very well.

Dualism is a basic conceptual or philosophical approach that many of us take for granted but which gets in the way of fully understanding firms like Honda. Dualism underlies a lot of our thinking. We take it for granted, implicitly, that the best way to approach problems is in terms of choosing from pairs of opposite ideas.

So when we look at Japan and Japanese firms we look through dualist eyes. Some dualisms are purely Western in origin. Then we ask 'on which side of the fence does the Japanese firm sit?'. Is it robotized or labour intensive? Do Japanese workers make a mental input or do they just obey orders? Is decision-making a group or individual responsibility? The problem is that we often can't decide (because the answer is 'on both sides'). In other dualisms we set up a 'West versus Japan' opposition: we do it one way, they do it the other way. But this often gives a misleading impression, because firms like Honda do it the 'Japanese way' *and the 'Western way'* at the same time.

Let's look at some examples. It is well worth reflecting for a while, because we will return later in the book to see how Honda has dealt with each dualism to award itself the best of both worlds in many different situations.

Dualisms involving Big Ideas

Big Ideas are grand theories that try to explain everything at once. 'Lean production' is a very popular Big Idea these days, promoted by the best-selling book *The Machine that Changed the World*.[1] The analysis in that book is profoundly dualist. Lean production is set in contrast to mass production. We are given a clear choice: become lean and prosper, or remain mass and disappear. In this kind of approach, adopting lean production means rejecting mass production entirely, just as in the past, the authors tell us, automobile manufacturers rejected craft production in favour of mass production.

There are plenty of other dualisms about among today's Big Ideas. In each case proponents are suggesting that there is an inevitable switch under way from one way of doing things to another. I have collected a list, some of which you may have come across. There is mass production/flexible specialization, mass production/beyond mass production, Fordism/post-Fordism, Fordism/flexibility. In each case you, your organization, your country, are supposed to let go of the old as you grasp the new, a bit like Tarzan swinging from tree to tree it would seem.

But where are the Japanese situated with respect to these opposites? What happens is that the Japanese are currently such important and innovative players in the world economy that the authors of each new Big Idea want to claim Japan as exemplary of the new trend they have identified. So Japan is lean, Japan is flexible specialization, Japan is beyond mass production, and Japan is post-Fordist. In short, Japan is everything we are not. But the question I found myself asking during my research on Honda was: 'how can you say that companies which churn out hundreds of thousands of nearly identical automobiles each year are not involved in *mass production*?'. It maybe lean, flexible, and so on, but it is still mass production surely.

Dualisms in Manufacturing

Taylorism/Post-Taylorism

In this dualism the detailed division of labour of the archetypal Western assembly line, in which individuals are assigned to particular tasks, is frequently contrasted with a less rigid approach involving far more cooperation among workers, as in the case of Swedish-style group-work. According to some, the Japanese are 'post-Taylorist' with groups – or teams – rather than individuals at the centre of production. Others, however, argue that the Japanese are simply better at Taylorism.

Machines Control Workers/Workers Control Machines

How much control does the worker have over technology? Our view of Western factories is that machines tend to dominate workers, all too often leading to numbing alienation. One view of Japanese manufacturing is that the worker also has no control, but is a highly disciplined cog (a human robot, even) in a larger machine. An alternative view is that the worker can control his/her own pace, stop the production line when necessary, and so on.

Manual Labour/Mental Labour

This dualism appears in several other forms, including 'do worker/ think worker' and 'bee worker/architect worker'. Conventionally, Western companies divide up their work on this basis; thus engineers design the work process (architects) and workers do as they are told (bees). Managers used to frankly admit that they preferred it if workers didn't think, which was a further source of alienation for the production worker.

But is the production worker at the Japanese firm simply a hard-driven, highly disciplined and equally alienated version of his Western counterpart? Or does his employer rely upon his mental capabilities and ideas, giving him dignity and worth as a person? Both views can be found in the West.

Unskilled Worker/Skilled Worker

This dualism is a real Pandora's box, which has different contents in different countries, where the word 'skilled' takes on various meanings. In some cases skill is defined by long apprenticeships, in others by formal qualifications, in others again by certain tasks undertaken in the factory. Whichever way we do it though, in the West we all make the distinction between unskilled and skilled workers. The skilled worker has one of the attributes above. By contrast, the unskilled worker could literally be brought in off the streets and set to work straight away.

So is the Japanese worker, who often neither possesses qualifications nor serves an apprenticeship nor specializes in certain tasks, but is nevertheless able to undertake a variety of tasks seemingly efficiently, a skilled or an unskilled worker? It is hard to decide.

Meetings with Workers: The Different Views from Labour Relations/ Production Engineering

In many Western firms labour relations specialists have long taken a back seat to production engineers. To put it crudely, the task of the former was simply to get the workers to agree to what the production engineers wanted, by paying the necessary money and smoothing the feathers the engineers had ruffled.

People-oriented labour relations specialists would hold meetings to 'involve' workers. But production engineers viewed meetings and discussions involving workers as more or less a complete waste of time, as taking the workers away from work, productivity and achieving output goals. After all, the production engineers had done all the thinking and talking needed, designing the best possible production process and telling the factory manager to tell the foreman to tell the workers what to do. With these attitudes coming from higher up, little surprise that workers also viewed meetings and discussions as merely a respite from work, rather than part of work itself.

The Japanese are well-known for their meetings. There are meetings before work, during work, and after work. So how can they be so productive? How can 'not working' make you work better?

Dedicated Capital Equipment/Flexible Automation

In this dualism it is suggested that Western companies use capital equipment that is dedicated to a single task, and so has to be scrapped when the product changes (or at best requires a lengthy tool or die change). Japanese firms, by contrast, are supposed to use flexible automation that can make several different products and so can be reused when the product changes, and to have perfected quick tool and die changes (QTD). But is this gulf between the West and Japan an accurate view?

Push Production/Pull Production

Here the distinction is between a Western style of production logistics that is supply-driven, a push system, and a Japanese-style demand-driven, pull system. Again, is it accurate to say that Japanese firms, in contrast to Western firms, use the 'pull' system?

Economies of Scale/Economies of Scope

Mass production, Fordism, Western manufacturing systems in general, are said to be based upon economies of scale, whereas flexible, post-Fordist production is based on economies of scope. The idea behind the latter approach is basically that ability to make a variety of products can also lead to reduced unit costs.

The Japanese are supposed to be masters of economies of scope. But does this mean that economies of scale are no longer meaningful to them?

Organizational Dualisms

Individual/Group in Decision-Making

The typical Western organization emphasizes individual authority and responsibility in decision-making. The conventional Western view of Japan is of shared decision-making where the individual is subordinated to the group. If the Japanese organization is characterized by meetings, the Western organization is characterized by memos. Is this an accurate portrayal? Is the individual really subordinated to the group in the Japanese firm?

Vertical/Horizontal Structures

Western management theories allow for either vertical, pyramidal organizations (with top-down management authority and information flow), or horizontal, flat, structures (with less authority and more sideways information flow). With horizontal flows the organization becomes more self-managing, no longer needing continual instruction from above.

The horizontal structure may embody 'single status' characteristics in which a large measure of equality is observed among employees, in contrast to authority- and status-symbol-ridden vertical structures in which each pyramidal layer tries to distinguish itself from those below by labels and superficial signs. The horizontal structure with 'single status' is increasingly associated with Japan and with Japanese firms abroad. But just how Japanese is it?

Product and Marketing Dualisms

Model Change/Facelift or Freshening Up

In the Western view a company either completely changes an automobile model, say, every eight years, or it gives a model a facelift, perhaps after four years. A facelift is fairly superficial. There is new trim but the basic car is left untouched. The Japanese firm tends to change the versions of the models it offers much more often, every four years. But the Westerner finds this hard to believe, is sceptical about whether there is a 'real' model change or just a facelift, and asks how much 'carryover' there is between the models. So we want to know what the Japanese do every four years: complete changeover or facelift?

Mass Products/Niche Products

In the West a clear distinction is made between mass and niche markets, so much so that different firms tend to concentrate on each. Japanese firms are seen to offer many different variants of their models, each one often 'tailored to individual specifications' and individually ordered by customers. This certainly looks like a niche strategy. But they also make hundreds of thousands of automobiles per year. So which are the Japanese, mass producers or niche specialists?

Price Competition/Product Innovation

In the conventional Western view, two separate ways for a firm to compete are on the basis of price and on the basis of innovative product. Low price implies low research and development costs to recover. Innovative products mean higher prices because of the expensive research and development which is necessary. When Japanese automobiles were first exported to the West in large numbers, they seemed to compete on price with their Western competitors. But they also seemed to be of higher quality, to last longer without repair, and to offer interesting features not generally available in the West. Now the Japanese have moved upmarket and offer all sorts of innovative features. But they are no more expensive than their Western rivals, and their luxury models are often significantly cheaper than their closest Western rivals.

Can the Japanese be competing on both cost and innovative product?

Parts-Purchasing Dualisms

Several dualist ideas frame discussion of the relationship between assembly companies and parts makers in Japan.

Dual Sourcing/Single Sourcing

Dual sourcing is a Western practice that means simultaneously purchasing the same component from different parts makers, as a means of keeping pressure on each of them and of reducing risk. By contrast, it is widely believed that Japanese firms usually purchase each part from a single parts maker.

Conflict/Cooperation

The Western automobile producer and its parts makers have all too often found themselves locked in continuing battle, often over price, and tend to distrust each other. Japanese firms, it is thought, cooperate more harmoniously with their parts makers: relationships are characterized by trust, exchange of personnel, cooperation in product design with parts makers playing key roles.

Short Term/Long Term

In the West, short-term relationships prevail, with contracts renewed or (quite frequently) cancelled on an annual basis. Japanese companies, by contrast, are thought to maintain almost permanent relationships with their traditional parts makers, whom they favour over any outsiders. Even when the product made by a parts maker is no longer needed, the parts maker may be kept on and start an entirely new line (for example, shifting from steel to plastics).

Market Relationships/Vertical Integration

Western relationships are either driven purely by market concerns, or by ownership of the parts maker as a subsidiary (vertical integration). Which is the prevalent model in Japan? On the one hand Japanese producers are known to have low levels of vertical integration, buying in a large proportion of their components from other companies. On the other hand, they do not put contracts out to tender in search of the lowest bidder. They don't seem to have chosen either Western model. Resourceful Western analysts have come up with various new names, like 'quasi-integration' to describe Japanese inter-firm relationships.

Relatedly, there is a dualism which compares (a) a Japanese organizational hierarchy or pyramid of parts-makers up to 10 companies deep, with an extensive inter-firm division of labour, to (b) a shallow Western hierarchy in which the assembly firm deals directly with a very large number of parts makers.

Spatial Dispersal/Spatial Concentration

In this dualism the Western firm takes little account of the geographical location of its parts makers, buying the cheapest possible parts from anywhere in the world, whereas the Japanese firm demands geographical proximity from its parts makers, to ensure regular deliveries of components at precise times on 'just-in-time' schedules. The example of Toyota City, where Toyota has most of its factories and many parts makers concentrated in a small area, is frequently evoked.

Once more, the question is whether these dualist ideas accurately characterise the behaviour of the Japanese firm.

Dualisms in Labour Relations

Confrontation/Cooperation with Labour Unions

In this dualism the Western style is said to be confrontation between employers and labour unions representing workers. Unions are organized on industrial, craft or political lines. The Japanese system also has labour unions, but they are organized at the level of the firm, as enterprise unions, and they always seem to cooperate with management, especially when the company appears to be in trouble.

Limited Job Security/Job for Life

Western employers can in principle lay off their employees if they wish to, and employees require labour union or legislative protection to ensure a certain minimum level of rights. At big firms in Japan, by contrast, there is a 'job for life' until retirement. When you join a firm, the company will not lay you off, and neither will you quit and go elsewhere.

As above, the question is whether these dualist ideas really help us to understand the Japanese firm.

The kinds of dualist ideas and questions posed above have confronted a lot of Westerners faced with making sense of Japan and of the Japanese firm. We react in different ways. One approach is to say 'We don't seem to be able to label them A or B: frankly, the Japanese are ambiguous.' But try explaining to your colleague – worse still your boss – who wants to know all about Japan, that the explanation is that the Japanese are ambiguous! A second approach is to blame 'language differences' for misunderstandings, to talk of the 'inscrutable' Japanese, and then get (privately) annoyed with the Japanese who 'refuse' to tell us whether it is A or B. Communication collapses.

A third approach is simply to impose our ideas on Japan and the Japanese firm, to decide for ourselves that the Japanese are B, not A. In fact, it is precisely this dualist approach that has given us a supposedly 'Japanese' model of industrial organization. This 'Japanese model' is composed of a list of features regarding work, technology, organization, marketing, interfirm relations and labour relations. These features, well-known in the West by now, map out an industrial model that seems to be quite the opposite of the Western model. The conclusion of the exercise that derives from the third approach is that this divergence explains why the Japanese are more successful than we are.

The funny thing is that the Japanese have difficulty recognizing the 'Japanese model' as their own. It is in fact a very Western construct, full of Western interpretations, already several steps removed from how the Japanese see their own system. Take the concept of *team work*, for instance, that is frequently associated in the West with the Japanese model. One searches in vain for references to team work in literature on Japanese industry written by Japanese observers.[2] Likewise, the 'lean production' concept, supposedly based on the Japanese example, is viewed with a kind of silent curiosity in Japan. Why? Because translated into Japanese the word 'lean' has several negative connotations (the word 'slim' would have been more appropriate). So in creating a 'de-nationalized' version of the Japanese production system the authors of 'lean production' have come up with a concept that may work globally; everywhere, that is, except Japan!

These are the kinds of difficulties it is high time we surmounted. If the Japanese sometimes seem ambiguous, I believe it's because our ideas aren't up to the task. The barrier to understanding isn't just a language barrier, it's a barrier of ideas. Perhaps we can use the opportunity of a close look at Honda, at home and abroad, to change our philosophy about the Japanese firm.

UNDERSTANDING THE MULTINATIONAL ENTERPRISE

The multinational enterprise has occupied a unique role in the world economy during the second half of the twentieth century. Multinational enterprises are:

- economically, the most powerful institutions in our global society, controlling a large part of society's productive forces;
- politically, rival powers to most of the world's governments, in the resources they command and in their ability to move those resources out of reach of national governments, giving multinational enterprises the power to potentially escape from government regulation;
- technologically, the most important vehicles for the waves of innovation that spread economic growth around the globe, bringing new products and new production methods with them wherever they choose to operate;
- socially, one of the world's key instruments of social change: when new ways of producing new products diffuse from country to country, so too do new social systems, ways of relating to other people, new social institutions.

For these reasons the multinational enterprise is one of the most closely studied phenomena in the modern business, political, technological and social world. It becomes essential to keep abreast of the latest developments.

The Conventional Ladder to Multinational Enterprise:

Close scrutiny of American and European multinational enterprises has given us a typical picture of the ladders a firm climbs as it becomes a multinational enterprise. While this picture is a bit of an over-simplification, it does capture the essence of the typical Western multinational manufacturer. It also gives us a good benchmark from which to observe the new global local corporation in action.

   As we will see later, many observers are wrongly assuming that the global local corporation is climbing a conventional ladder.

Ladder 1: The Go-It-Alone Route

When a firm acts by itself, without overseas partners, the process of becoming multinational is seen as a linear progression that may stop at any stage. The influence of national governments, which can restrict access to overseas markets, plays a powerful role in pushing the budding multinational enterprise further at each step. The foreign government's ability to do this depends upon whether the firm considers the particular overseas market important enough to deepen its involvement.

Step 1: *Export strategy*: only sales and service, possibly also market research, are located overseas:

Step 2: *Knocked-down kit production develops overseas*: only an assembly plant is built and nearly all the components are sent from the home base in kits to be unwrapped and assembled (in the car industry there may also be welding and painting abroad because welded, painted bodies are hard to transport securely and cheaply). Step 2 can be reconciled with limited local political pressure but there may be problems of economies of scale if the firm is pushed to manufacture components in small overseas markets too.

Step 3: *Stand-alone production*: the overseas factory builds up a local supply network and the capacity to design and develop products itself, becoming essentially an overseas subsidiary independent from the parent in a manufacturing sense, with 100 per cent or close to 100 per cent 'local content'. The subsidiary can be very responsive to local market needs, but Step 3 does depend upon an adequate market to support all the activities necessary. In some cases the overseas subsidiaries continue to make products outmoded in the parent market, according to a 'product life cycle' idea in which 'lesser' markets are given less innovative products.

At Step 3 the overseas operation is linked to the parent by: (a) financial ties, allowing losses in one market to be balanced by gains in others, and (b) top executives, who are often sent out from the parent operation for tours of duty. Step 3 does not, however, mean creation of a truly global manufacturing firm, because product development, products, components sourcing and manufacturing processes in the different operations are run largely independently of one another.

Ladder 2: The Quick Route Through Partnership and Purchase

When a firm links up with firms in other countries there are two types of relationship, one more developed than the other:

Step 1:   *Technology licensing*: a firm accepts a fee for allowing an
            independent overseas firm to use a process or make a product
            it has developed.
Step 2:   *Takeover*: a short cut to Step 3 on the first ladder is to
            purchase control over an independent overseas firm, which
            then becomes a foreign subsidiary.

Extending the Multinational Ladder

Over the past twenty years, American and European automobile
producers have been trying to add further rungs to the multinational
ladder, beyond Step 3, in order to create properly global *manufacturing*
enterprises, in which production itself (rather than merely finance and
top personnel) is organized on a world scale. Western firms have
attempted two routes to this summit, but in each case they have been
forced down again.

The World Car

The favoured solution of the 1970s and 1980s was to make the same
vehicle for several world markets. There would be big cost reductions
due to economies of scale in R&D and in manufacturing operations
through the use of lowest-cost sites to make each vehicle. Critically, the
world car idea assumes a 'convergence of tastes' across the world's
markets. The pioneer was Ford of Europe's unified model range,
introduced during the 1970s.

   However, at the global level the world car ran into bad weather,
especially when Ford and General Motors tried to make a single car to
sell in both Europe and North America. The principal problem was
that while tastes had indeed begun to converge – especially after the
1973 oil crisis in North America when smaller cars became popular –
they simply had not converged enough. Not even the design engineers,
let alone the customers, could reach agreement on what the world car
should be like. The relics of failed attempts at creating a world car can
still be seen on the streets in many countries, in the model names
'Escort' (Ford), 'Chevette', and 'Cavalier' (General Motors). Besides
their common name, all they shared was a general styling theme.[3]

Global Sourcing

During the early 1980s, global sourcing was expected to be one of the key Western responses to the Japanese challenge. Like the world car, global sourcing was a means of reducing costs though economies of scale by manufacturing at the global level, this time components rather than finished automobiles. One of the novel aspects of global sourcing would be to turn existing knocked-down kit assembly sites built in various countries into factories able to produce massive numbers of single components. These would then be exported for use at assembly sites all over the world. Governments in third-world countries would welcome the boost to their exports. In a variant of global sourcing, whole vehicles (especially cheap small cars whose quality could afford to be lower) would be sourced from third-world countries for sale in North America and Europe.[4]

Global sourcing was particularly favoured by the American producers, but it has run into a number of problems:

(a) product technology changes: more complex technologies, demands for higher quality, production of modular parts (that is, substantial subassembly before a part reaches the assembly plant) means that fewer parts are susceptible to the kind of cheap, low-quality, large-scale mass production envisaged in global sourcing;

(b) adoption of just-in-time manufacturing militates against long-distance sourcing;

(c) currency fluctuations (for example, for American firms the decline of the US dollar) made the strategy very risky: global sourcing requires a stable international framework for trade and investment, including stable currency values, a framework which did not exist during the 1970s and 1980s; moreover, the actions of American automobile producers in shifting their sourcing overseas actually helped to undermine the dollar by weakening the US economy, thus making imports more expensive and counteracting the firms' own strategy.

Is Truly Global Manufacturing Possible?

Based upon the steps of the multinational ladder and attempts to extend it upwards, the conventional Western view of how a multi-

national manufacturing enterprise should be organized has two –
dualist – versions: decentralized and centralized. On the one hand there
is decentralization into a 'bottom up' multinational composed of
separate subsidiaries that are basically independent companies (that
is, Step 3). These are locally responsive but tend to take limited
advantage of the resources that might be available from corporate
subsidiaries in other countries. On the other hand there is tight central
control with top-down decision-making designed to reap global
economies of scale through standardization.

It is this second version of multinational organization that the world
car and global sourcing have attempted to construct. And their failure
reflects the fact that the Western firms concerned began to lose their
ability to respond to changing local circumstances. The result is that we
have yet to see truly global corporations that successfully operate
worldwide in all their aspects, from R&D through to sales, including
manufacturing.

Can a truly global manufacturing enterprise be organized? How do
you achieve global economies of scale while also taking local market
differences into account? And how do you operate a unified production
system that simultaneously takes account of different societies and
their different ways of doing things? This is the essential goal of the
global local corporation.

'Stateless Corporations' in a 'Borderless World', or 'Nothing New Under the Rising Sun'?

The appearance of the global local corporation has not escaped the
attention of other observers. But current ideas about it are still
formulated in dualist fashion. They jump from one extreme to its
opposite, from the national firm to a firm which apparently pays no
heed at all to the world's nation-states. Thus we read increasingly
about the 'post-national' firm or 'stateless corporation' that operates in
a 'borderless world'.[5]

The case of Honda is uniformly quoted by advocates of such ideas as
exemplifying the emergence of the post-national, stateless corporation.
We'll see if this is true, or if it's another case of people with Big Ideas
inaccurately claiming that examination of the most innovative companies provides ample evidence that their ideas are correct.

A common alternative view is to claim that Japanese multinational
manufacturers are no different from American and European ones in
reality, except for being based in another part of the world. While

superficially different, at root they behave just like their Western counterparts (albeit more efficiently). There is nothing new under the rising sun.

This second view is in fact the most widespread interpretation among politicians and lay commentators in the West. Multinational Japanese enterprises are discussed with the same theories used to discuss American and European ones, and are measured against the same ladders we looked at a moment ago. What stage are the Japanese at? How can we push them further up?

As we shall see, Honda and other Japanese firms have been attacked by political critics first because they were only exporting from Japan, and were 'reluctant multinationals' (that is, at Step 1), and then because they were knocked-down kit producers exporting to mere 'screwdriver plants' (that is, at Step 2). Western critics have wanted the North American and European branches of Japanese firms to become independent subsidiaries (that is, move to Step 3). Moreover, when Japanese firms launch collaborative ventures with Western partners, host-country politicians worry whether Step 1 (technology transfer) will soon become Step 2 (purchase of complete control), and with that, disappearance of the Western partner's independence.

The application of conventional theory thus undergirds a great deal of political commentary on the 'transplants'. Ironically, such issues attract public attention in part precisely because of the poor past records of multinational enterprises based in North America and Europe, which have sometimes climbed the multinational ladder from exports to full local production only after considerable resistance and accompanied by considerable political pressure, or, if they have taken over existing local firms, have not always behaved responsibly towards their new assets.

TRANSFERABILITY OF JAPANESE MANAGEMENT TECHNIQUES AND JAPANIZATION

The management techniques used in the Japanese automobile industry have been widely recognized to be currently the world's best. But can they really be implemented outside Japan itself? If they can be, does this mean we shall all have to start adopting Japanese behaviours and habits? These twin questions weave a thread that runs throughout this book. First, though, I want to look at how they have been answered up to now.

A decade ago it was widely argued in the West (and in Japan too) that Japanese management techniques simply could not be properly reproduced outside Japan. This explained most of the reluctance of Japanese manufacturers to go multinational. There were all kinds of reasons why Japanese management techniques were supposedly unique to Japan. Taken together, they seemed to present a formidable, apparently insurmountable, obstacle to Japanese manufacturing firms that might wish to invest overseas, as well as to Western firms that wanted to learn Japanese methods.[6]

These were some of the arguments that were commonly heard:

The Japanese Business Environment

The continued existence of 'feudal' social structures in Japan is used to great advantage by Japanese firms, but they no longer exist in the West:

1. Groupism

In Japan, a culturally rooted mentality ties Japanese employees to each other and to the firms like serfs were tied to masters. The leading firms play their part in the bargain by offering lifetime employment in exchange for loyalty. However, as in feudalism, lifetime employment is a double-edged sword: you have to stick with the firm you started with because there is no external employment market among the big firms.

By contrast, in the West, individualism prevails. Employees show little deference to their employer, and receive little assurance of long-term employment. External job markets allow people to change their employer several times during their work-life.

What was the practical obstacle to the transferability of Japanese management techniques? It was that the kinds of employees that Japanese firms might want – group-oriented employees who could be trusted to work for the good of the company without leaving after receiving substantial training – would be in very short supply in the West.

Moreover, the types of organizational structures that function well in Japan might not work in the West. In Japan a great deal of the knowledge that glues an organization together is implicit, in people's heads, as distinct from the formalized and codified knowledge that works reasonably well in the West alongside Western individualism. Could Westerners cope with learning the implicit knowledge? Would it not take an awfully long time to teach them?

2. Work Ethic at Large Firms

In Japan, the employee's commitment to his employer results in very long normal work hours, willingness to stay at work after normal hours at short notice, and unwillingness to take even those holidays contractually due.

In the West, the work ethic is much less strong: 'the Japanese live to work, we work to live', is the refrain that was frequently heard. Absenteeism is relatively high. Workers are protected by labour unions and national legislation from long hours and short-notice overtime, and they are guaranteed a certain number of days off work each year.

The practical obstacle here was that Japanese firms could expect substantially higher labour costs in the West, and could not be sure that enough of their employees would come to work on any given day.

3. Exploitation of the Small Firm

In Japan, thousands of little firms based upon extended families form the roots of components-supply pyramids with an extensive vertical division of labour, and with up to ten layers of firms. These firms are very low cost, their workers are unprotected, and they can be discarded at will.

In most Western countries the components sector is different. Most industrial firms are larger and obey normal capitalist rules even if family-run.

What's more, in Japan, many parts makers are located in very close proximity to their customers, which makes it easier to deliver components 'just-in-time': Toyota City's concentration of assembly and parts making activities is said to be exemplary. In North America and Europe supply chains often stretch over very long distances that would make it difficult to deliver parts to assembly lines on a true just-in-time basis.

What was the practical obstacle here? Outside Japan, Japanese firms would lose the benefit of having a low-wage, low-cost, and malleable group of parts makers, located close to the plants they supply.

The Institutional Advantages of Japan

There were said to be various institutional advantages for Japanese firms of operating in a Japanese environment.

Japan's Ministry of International Trade and Industry (MITI) provides an institutional cohesion and direction that dampens internal competition, keeps it within manageable limits and protects firms from external competition. Several Western countries possessed no effective counterpart.

The Japanese financial system offers long-term frameworks for business decision-making that protect firms from the short-termism inflicted upon Western firms by stock-market concerns. Unlike in most Western countries, Japanese banks permit recovery plans for troubled firms that allow sufficient time for deep-rooted restructuring to take place, leaving the firms stronger in the long run.

Keiretsu relationships (that is, 'family' structures of linked enterprises) form the basis of whole industrial groups and their activities, from research to sales via raw materials, finance, making parts and components, final manufacture, trade and transport. Moreover, cross-holding of shares by *keiretsu* members provides mutual protection against hostile takeover bids, keeping corporate frameworks stable and free from upheaval.

A long-term business atmosphere pervades, which allows development of a certain trust so that separate firms can work closely together without fear of proprietary information leaking out. Firms may also be linked more loosely in associations such as the *kyoryokukai* that group components firms supplying a particular assembly company.

Distribution systems for finished products in Japan are often built on an individualized approach in which sales people develop long-term relationships with particular customers. This model of close relationships would be difficult to adopt in the West where a 'supermarket' or 'quick sale' approach more often prevails.

The Role of Labour Unions

Labour unions in the West were expected to greatly interfere with Japanese management techniques. In the first place, Western-style unions raise the financial costs due to labour inputs – shorter hours, more holidays, higher overtime pay, higher indirect benefits – and curtail certain management options like use of overtime at very short notice.

Second, and perhaps more fundamental, in recent decades Western-style labour unions had often come to play an important role in deciding how workers are assigned to particular tasks in the factory, both long-term and on a daily basis. All sorts of classification systems in the West (that vary according to the country in question) determine which employees should do which tasks. Classification may be based on formal qualifications, membership of certain skilled trades, or seniority.

Moreover, typical Western graded pay structures are often linked, with union support, to the particular job a person undertakes (which itself is determined by the above considerations). Unions might therefore be expected to object to a Japanese-style pay structure linked very much to the individual person, which implies that two people doing the same job could receive different pay: 'unfair' in Western eyes.

From a managerial perspective Western-style classifications and rules hamper work-place flexibility. From a union perspective they protect workers from managerial caprice. Changing the system of task assignments in a factory can result in sometimes arduous negotiations. As a result, it makes sense for managers not to try to change the production process except in big steps every few years. This runs counter to the Japanese desire to frequently alter and improve the production process.

Finally, labour unions might have objected to all sorts of practices like daily warm-up exercises and the wearing of company uniforms. These they might interpret as an alien imposition of 'regimentation'. With memories of the Second World War still strong amongst the old guard, and racism against Japanese people easy to stir up, it would be an easy matter to set off a 'clash of cultures' that would undermine the authority of Japanese managers.

In all these aspects Japanese unions organized at the company level (enterprise unions) operate more flexibly from a managerial perspective. The practical implication here was that Western labour unions would stymie the Japanese penchant for utilizing workers flexibly, moving them around without demarcations, and changing the production process in regular short steps.

A decade ago these doubts about the transferability of Japanese management techniques seemed to be shared by everybody, whether they were Japanese or Western, whether they were thinking about Japanese firms operating abroad or Western firms adopting the Japanese methods.

The Japanese themselves were some of the biggest doubters. Here is Taiichi Ohno, author of Toyota's famous just-in-time manufacturing techniques, expressing himself gently but firmly in 1983:

> We have a slight doubt whether our just-in-time system could be applied to the foreign countries where the business climates, industrial relations, and many other social systems are different from ours.[7]

So confident were most Americans that factors due to a peculiar business environment lay behind Japanese success, that American business and political leaders positively invited the Japanese to build factories in North America, assuming either that they would not come (hence justifying increased protectionist barriers) or that if they did come their competitiveness would be severely undermined. Here is Roger Smith, Chairman of General Motors, in 1985, even after Japanese investment was well under way:

> GM can't match Japanese costs in Japan, but if the Japanese really try to build new empires in the US that means a new ball game, on a level playing field. It's a game we think GM could win. When they start doing the castings and engines and transmissions here in the US – oh, come on in – then we'll give them a different story.[8]

European experts shared the view that the different operating environment for companies in the West would prevent transfer of Japanese techniques.

> Is the Japanese alternative the result of more sophisticated management of the universal production functions (production control, personnel allocation, and so on) that can be adopted irrespective of the cultural and social context, or is the Japanese management system dependent on a special social context and therefore not transferable to other countries merely by learning management techniques?
>
> In the following, we shall demonstrate that the Japanese organizational model is *not* primarily a more sophisticated and hence transferable management system. Rather, it is rooted in a system of labor relations that for a number of reasons is unacceptable for trade unions in Europe and the United States.[9]

These questions of the transferability of Japanese management techniques had very significant implications. If the techniques were so tied in with Japan itself, as many believed, then either the West was destined to be a perpetual economic laggard unless it discovered something even better, or a wholesale Japanization of the West would accompany the international diffusion of Japanese management techniques.

But was there not a third way? The stark contrast presented in the previous paragraph smacks of a rather dualist approach. Could the puzzle be solved with a different outcome? Could Japanese management techniques be somehow married to Western society to result in the best of both worlds with no trade-offs? What would such a marriage look like? What aspects of Western society would it incorporate? What kinds of social changes would be necessary? Would Japanese management techniques survive unscathed? Would they be watered down: or, dare we venture, might they even be improved?

This became Honda's challenge when it set out on what company president Kiyoshi Kawashima called its 'voyage of discovery' to America.[10] But before we discover for ourselves what Honda found – or created – let's cast an eye over Honda in Japan, to see if we can discern why this firm, in particular, was destined to play such a pioneering role in the development of the global local corporation.

Notes

1. James P. Womack, Daniel T. Jones and Daniel Roos, *The Machine that Changed the World*, New York: Rawson Associates, 1990.
2. Thanks to Dr Ben Dankbaar, MERIT, University of Maastricht, The Netherlands, for this point.
3. The less known story of General Motors' Cavalier 'world car' is told by Brock Yates, *The Decline and Fall of the American Automobile Industry*, New York: Harper and Row, 1983.
4. The global sourcing strategy and how it was overtaken by (Japanese) events is analysed by Kurt Hoffman and Raphael Kaplinsky, *Driving Force: The Global Restructuring of Technology, Labour, and Investment in the Automobile and Components Industries*, Boulder Colo: Westview Press/ UNCTC, 1988.
5. On the 'post-national' firm, see James P. Womack, 'A post-national auto industry by the year 2000', *JAMA Forum* 8.1, 1988, pp. 3–7; Womack *et al.*, *The Machine That Changed the World*. On the 'stateless corporation' see Amy Borrus with Wendy Zellner and William J. Holstein, 'The stateless corporation', *Business Week* 14 May 1990, pp. 52–60. On the

'borderless world' see Kenichi Ohmae, 'Managing in a borderless world', *Harvard Business Review*, 89.3, 1989, pp. 152–61; Ohmae, *The Borderless World: Power and Strategy in the Interlinked Economy*, New York: Collins, 1990.

6. For a cross-section of the widespread doubts see: Robert H. Ballance and Stuart W. Sinclair, *Collapse and Survival: Industry Strategies in a Changing World*, London: George Allen & Unwin, 1983; Karel O. Cool and Cynthia A. Legnick-Hall, 'Second thoughts on the transferability of Japanese management style', *Organization Studies*, 6.1, 1985, pp. 1–22; Michael A. Cusumano, *The Japanese Automobile Industry: Technology and Management at Nissan and Toyota*, Cambridge, Mass: Council on East Asian Studies, Harvard University, 1985; Knuth Dohse, Ulrich Jürgens and Thomas Malsch, 'From "Fordism" to "Toyotism"? The social organization of the labor process in the Japanese automobile industry', *Politics and Society*, 14.2, 1985, pp. 115–46; George Maxcy, *The Multinational Motor Industry*, London: Croom Helm, 1981; Stuart Sinclair, *The World Car: The Future of the Automobile Industry*, London: Euromonitor, 1983.

7. In Yasuhiro Monden, *The Toyota Production System: Practical Approach to Production Management*, Atlanta, Ga: Institute of Industrial Engineers, 1983, pp. i–ii.

8. Cited in Hoffman and Kaplinsky, *Driving Force*, p. 325.

9. Dohse, Jürgens and Malsch, 'From "Fordism" to "Toyotism"? The social organization of the labor process in the Japanese automobile industry', p. 117.

10. Setsuo Mito, *The Honda Book of Management*, London: Kogan Page, 1990. p. 102

2 Honda at Home Base

Honda is an interesting example of what small companies can do.[1]

In this chapter we are going to take a good look at Honda in Japan, at its factories, at its people, at its organization. We have to be as objective as we can about Honda in its Japanese context. This means steering clear of two tempting approaches, either trying to show how typically 'Japanese' Honda is – a view from the West – or alternatively, noting how 'un-Japanese' Honda is – precisely the view many Japanese observers have taken of the firm.

At some points we will show how Honda fits the conventional Japanese model and in what respects it differs. But I do hope that as you read this chapter, you'll try not to think – let's say you are a Western automotive industry engineer – 'oh, that shows how Japanese Honda is', or alternatively, 'oh, we do the same thing, so Honda's no better than us'. These are the kinds of errors that Honda's British partner Rover used to make. Later we'll see how Rover has learned better. Anyway, what we're going to see is how Honda is both Japanese and un-Japanese. And it's grasping the combination of 'opposites' that is the key to understanding how Honda has solved the puzzle of the Japan – West dualism in constructing its global local corporation.

This is not the place to tell Honda's history in Japan. That tale's been told before.[2] Our goal is to understand Honda as a multinational enterprise. But we do need to get as clear a picture as we can of how Honda functions in Japan, because it is out of the Japanese home base that Honda's multinationalism has emerged, and that home base remains the most important pillar of the multinational enterprise even as new pillars are being erected in other countries on other continents.

We concentrate in this chapter as throughout the book on Honda the automobile producer. Honda is also a world leader in other products: motorcycles and a variety of power products from lawn mowers to outboard motors. But it is the automobile activities that are central to Honda and to us.

However, this is the place to point out that on many occasions Honda has pioneered the way for its automobile business with motorcycles, both in Japan and overseas. Much that has later emerged in automobile production was first seen, in embryo, in making motorcycles. Unfortunately, to analyse that process in detail would complicate our story too much, and certainly by the period we're most interested in, the years since 1980, automobile production was increasingly important for Honda, accounting for 56 per cent of total company sales by value in 1983, and 82 per cent by 1992.

We start with a brief word about Honda's founders. Then it is straight on to analyse the factories, Honda's links to its parts makers, the importance of geography. From there to questions of technology and organization, of research and development, and of markets in Japan and overseas. For each aspect of Honda's operations, we will distil the essence of what has made Honda so successful.

MR HONDA'S COMPANY

Soichiro Honda founded the Honda Motor Co. at Hamamatsu, near the southern coast of Japan between Tokyo and Nagoya. That was in 1948. For the first fifteen years, Honda was a motorcycle producer, selling its products in Japan and the world over. The first automobile for sale came in 1963. And yet only 26 years later, in 1989, Soichiro Honda became the first Japanese to be honoured in Detroit's prestigious 'Automotive Industry Hall of Fame'. When he died in 1991, he was compared to Henry Ford as perhaps the last great individual pioneer in the industry.

This book is not the story of Mr Honda and how he built up his company. But it is the story of that company and how it became a world innovator multinational enterprise, and that story builds on the foundation and legacy Mr Honda left behind. He was known as an engineer of enormous determination, who pushed his employees hard and drove them to succeed. He was known for his lack of formality, his lack of interest in participating in Japan's political scene as a member of 'Japan Inc'. He was known for his focus on making his products equal to the best in the world, even at a time when Japan viewed itself, and was widely viewed from outside, as inferior to the best as far as industry and technology were concerned.

But Mr Honda's company was also known for Takeo Fujisawa. It was Mr Fujisawa who actually ran the Honda Motor Co. as a business until he retired in 1973 (and appears to have persuaded the founder that he should step down then too). It was Mr Fujisawa who left his stamp on the organization side of the business. His willingness to take

risks and his ability to solve puzzles on the business front matched Mr
Honda's approach to technology. So really, this book continues the
story of Mr Honda's and Mr Fujisawa's company.

FACTORIES AND PARTS MAKERS

Honda runs two main automobile factories in Japan, at Sayama, north
of Tokyo, and Suzuka, west of Nagoya. Sayama is Honda's original
automobile plant, and by the early 1990s it manufactured the larger
mainline models, like Accord, Prelude and Legend. Suzuka was
originally a motorcycle factory that gradually added, then changed
to, automobile production, and it makes the smaller automobiles, like
Civic, Concerto, Integra, Today and City. Both factories are now high-
output plants by any standards. Sayama's twin assembly lines have a
capacity of 540 000 vehicles per year, Suzuka's three can make up to
735 000.

Honda makes its niche-oriented four-wheel vehicles elsewhere. Since
production started in 1990, the NSX luxury sports car has been
produced in a special plant at Honda's Tochigi proving grounds
northeast of Tokyo. The Acty series of small vans, originally made
by Honda itself, has been outsourced to 40 per cent Honda-owned
subsidiary and parts maker Yachiyo Industries (located close to
Suzuka) since 1984, and Yachiyo has also made the Beat mini sports
car introduced for the Japanese market in 1991.

Other important manufacturing sites are: the Wako engine plant
located near Sayama; Hamamatsu, the birthplace, where power
products are made; Mohka, near Tochigi; and Kumamoto, now the
main motorcycle plant, on the island of Kyushu. Honda Engineering
(EG), the subsidiary responsible for engineering manufacturing
systems, is situated next to the Sayama plant, while Honda Research
and Development (HRD) is located at the Tochigi proving grounds,
and also at Wako, near the engine plant. Honda's headquarters is in
central Tokyo (Table 2.1).

Honda's ratio of value added in-house *v* bought in from suppliers is
low even by Japanese standards, and is estimated to be only 25–7 per
cent. This means that most of the value of the automobiles Honda
makes is actually added in by the companies which supply materials
and components. Honda itself concentrates its activities largely on
developing and making mechanical components, engines and other
drive-train elements especially, and on producing the final automobile.

Table 2.1   Honda's Main Facilities in Japan

Site	Employment (1992)	Main activities (1992)
1. Suzuka	11000	Manufacture of smaller cars
2. Sayama	6700	Manufacture of larger cars
3. Hamamatsu	4300	Power products motorcycles, automatic transmissions
4. Tochigi	3400 (1990)	Automobile R&D centre
5. Sayama	2700	Honda Engineering headquarters
6. Kumamoto	2400	Motorcycles power products
7. Asaka	1800	Motorcycle R&D
8. Wako	1800	Engines
9. Wako	1600	Engine R&D centre
10. Mohka	970	Engine parts
11. Tochigi	310	NSX sports car
12. Tokyo	N.A.	Headquarters

Source: Honda Annual Reports.

Yet it outsources such important activities as the stamping of major body panels and the production of prototype models.

In keeping with Japanese practice, Honda has spun off a number of companies that make parts for it, including body stampings, door locks, carburettors, and parts for power steering. Several of these firms were established during the 1970s, and Honda retains either 100 per cent or majority ownership even though the subsidiaries are run separately and the value of the parts they make is counted as bought in.

However, Honda's formal relationship with most of its parts suppliers differs from the Japanese norm, in that apart from the few spin-offs it doesn't possess a *keiretsu* structure of tightly-knit companies like satellites around it. And it doesn't belong to a larger group (it banks with Mitsubishi, but resisted past pressures to merge with Mitsubishi's automotive operations). Moreover, Honda doesn't even run an association of its parts suppliers (it is the sole firm in the Japanese automobile industry without one). Formally speaking, Honda's relationships with its parts suppliers are more at arm's length than is the norm for Japan. Instead, and in part because it was a latecomer, Honda has tapped into the parts-making networks built up by other major companies, Toyota and Nissan especially. On the other hand Honda systematically aids its suppliers to improve their product and process innovation capacities, vital in the quest to bring new products to market as quickly as possible.

Many Westerners think that the typical geographical pattern of the automobile industry in Japan is Toyota City, the spatially concentrated manufacturing complex on the outskirts of Nagoya where nearly all Toyota factories are located in one small area. While Honda does have a small spatial concentration of facilities of its own around Sayama (including Wako and EG), its factories and other facilities are actually quite dispersed across Japan (Figure 2.1).

The parts makers that supply Honda are mostly located in the core manufacturing regions of Japan, in and around Nagoya (Toyota's location), and in and around Tokyo (Nissan's location). Honda's parts makers located close to the Sayama plant have the benefit of a cheap labour force provided by a substantial local population of ethnic Japanese who have immigrated from Brazil (though these people aren't employed by Honda itself). While some parts makers are therefore

Figure 2.1   Map of Main Honda Locations in Japan

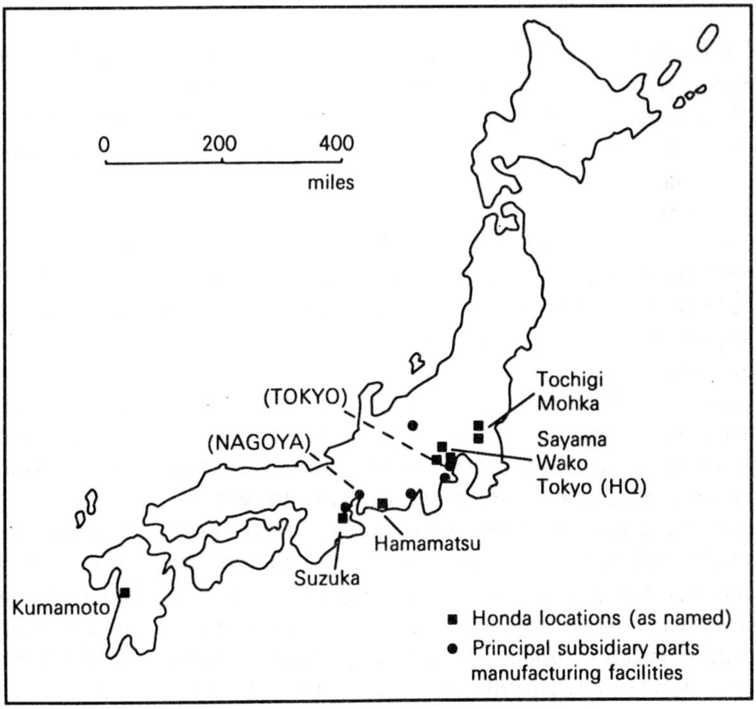

located relatively close by, in the same prefectures as the factories they supply, others are located far afield, in northern and southern Japan. Honda's purchasing patterns are as geographically scattered as its principal sites. We'll come back to why this matters below.

MANAGEMENT PHILOSOPHIES AND METHODS

We might have called this section 'management structures'. But that would have been a mistake.

In Japan, Honda is frequently seen as a 'different' firm that has adopted a rather un-Japanese style of management. This is because Honda stresses decentralized management, individualism, youth, and lack of class and status barriers. These go hand in hand in defining Honda's special style of management in Japan. But in each case the situation is more complicated than it first appears.[3]

Decentralization means continually pushing decision-making as low as it will go. Decisions are best made 'close to the ground', because they will be made better by people in the thick of the action.

Individualism means stressing that the individual comes before the group, that people should do what they want to do, should enjoy their work, and if not, should be doing something else (which they should be free to choose to do). Each person should therefore find a slot, a niche within the company, in which they perform best.

Emphasis on youth means always pushing responsibilities to younger people. The older, experienced managers and engineers can do the job of course, and perhaps quicker, but they'll tend to repeat what worked for them last time (that's why they're quicker). Younger people will not only feel more challenged but are more likely to arrive at innovative solutions.

Lack of class and status barriers means that no individual is inherently superior because of the formal position they hold, and none should be allowed to feel so. Honda runs a meritocracy, in which ability ought to determine position and promotion.

We have to place these philosophies in their Japanese context, of course. Honda operates in a society dominated by centralized control and decision-making, where the group good should come before the individual, where age should always be respected (and elders never disagreed with), and where status symbols of power assume great importance. Honda's stress on the opposite aspects is directed at its own managers, to persuade them to loosen the traditional culture-bound structures.

Is the idea to dispense with centralization, group goals, respect for age and experience, and vertical hierarchies of management? On the contrary, Honda's goal is to make these organizational features function better by counteracting the negative tendencies within each. In each case a particular advantage, in efficiency, in the ability to create innovations, in the ability to change Honda in response to external stimuli, derives from the emphasis on decentralization, individualism, youth, and lack of class barriers coexisting with their opposites.

As Honda has grown from a small producer to one of Japan's premier manufacturing firms, its leaders have been determined that it should not develop a case of 'big business disease', that affliction which slows down and seems to suck the vitality from many once vibrant small firms as they become so large that people no longer know each other personally.

The emphasis on decentralization, individualism, youth, and lack of class barriers works towards this end. And besides these philosophies, Honda has adopted all sorts of novel approaches to warding off big business disease. One of these is the 'expert system', formally established in 1968, in which production workers are recognized for their abilities and achievements without management having to move them up the administrative hierarchy. This is a parallel promotion track which motivates people, while easing competitive pressure for administrative posts (which the production employee or engineer may not really want anyway).

Another such management system is Honda's proclivity for making diagonal and horizontal links within the management hierarchy. This means that, for instance, managers from marketing departments meet and discuss problems with production coordinators in manufacturing, or that engineers visit the front-line sales staff. Each department and division ought to understand the characteristics of the others so that all aspects of the business are taken into account when decisions are made in each section of it.

Waigaya meetings are open meetings in which employees of various rank exchange ideas without regard to their position, a function also aided by the Japanese habit of after-work drinking and sharing of frank opinions that are held back in the factories. But at such encounters people also come up with ideas and problem solutions: it's not just left to the top people to make the decisions and pass on the tablets of stone for implementation lower down.

Honda's upper management organization structures have been revamped at regular intervals during its history to counter over-emphasis on one tendency or another (too much or not enough vertical structure, too much or not enough individual responsibility, and so on). Between 1973 and 1991, Honda was well-known for its collective boardroom, in which the company's top executives shared a large room and none had private offices. The idea had been to replace the retiring Mr Honda and Mr Fujisawa with a collective decision-making unit at the top, characterized by a maximum of horizontal linkages for information flow and informed decision-making. Here, then, was a group form of organization at the top of the very firm supposedly so individualist in style. But in 1991 the joint boardroom was modified by the new president Mr Kawamoto to allow more private spaces in the interests of devolution of responsibilities within the executive group. A dose of individualism was being injected.

Honda's organizational structures are therefore in constant flux. To some Western visitors the whole organization seems, well, rather disorganized. However, structure is not the point, because it is not the solution. The point is philosophy and method. These are the core, the heart, of management. Instead of adopting a certain structure as the best and sticking to it, Honda management remains fluid, with regular changes back and forth in its structure, to prevent a shift into too much individualism, not enough individualism, insufficient decentralization, not enough top leadership, and so on. This is an important topic that we'll come back to in Chapter 11, to see the same principles at work on the global scale.

Something must act as a kind of glue to keep the firm functioning through the organizational upheavals. That something is the common methodologies employees adopt in decision-making: the Honda Way, or Hondaism. This is one of the forms of intuitive knowledge that we associate with the Japanese firm (as opposed to the explicit knowledge that can be written down and passed on in a memo or instruction manual, and which glues together many Western-style bureaucratic organizations).

The company's principles express the Honda Way in its most abstract form. More concretely it is captured in apparently simple slogans, sayings and metaphors that work to communicate what are in fact complex ideas, and can actually be referred to consciously or subconsciously when an individual or group makes decisions (see Box 2.1). There is no fixed set of metaphors and slogans; they are constantly renewed with invention and creativity, and this is how new

Box 2.1 Honda's Corporate Philosophy: Metaphor for Management
Guidance

Company Principle

Maintaining an international viewpoint, we are dedicated to supplying
products of the highest efficiency yet at a reasonable price for worldwide
customer satisfaction.

Management Policy

1. Proceed always with ambition and youthfulness.
2. Respect sound theory, develop fresh ideas and make the most effective
   use of your time.
3. Enjoy your work and always brighten your working atmosphere.
4. Strive constantly for a harmonious flow of work.
5. Be ever mindful of the value of research and endeavour.

Mr Kume's Vision of Honda R&D

'Honda R&D presidents each developed their own approach while in office.
Tadashi Kume was known while he was president (1977–81) for his cryptic
expressions. He used to say that the keys to Honda R&D success were
'madness', 'an old fox', 'moon rockets' and 'the gods'. The research personnel
at Honda R&D must have an irrepressible pioneering and innovative spirit.
People who are wholly determined to reach some goal are bound to appear a
little crazy to others.

To lead a group of 'mad' engineers, a supervisor must be as shrewd as 'an
old fox'. He has to be quick to understand the moods and attitudes of the
researchers, pampering them when they face disappointment, restraining them
when they become impetuous, supporting them when they have personal
problems. In other words, he stands ready to offer timely assistance to the
individuals as and when it is needed.

When Kume was HRD president, the greatest achievement in advanced
technology was landing the first man on the moon in 1969, through the
teamwork of the NASA staff. Kume talked about 'moon rockets' to illustrate
the kind of teamwork researchers have to learn. They had to have individual
initiative (where real technological advances begin) but also to be able to work
within a team so as to bring projects to fruition.

When Kume talked about 'the gods', he was referring to the sense of justice
and impartiality that are required of the researcher as well as of the manager
and the executive . . .

Puzzling as Kume's symbols may be, they make good sense, and this shows
how thoughtful the president of Honda R&D must be, sensitive to the
psychology of the engineers and staff. He must respect individuals and their
creative endeavour, and at the same time mould them into a successful team.'

(Setsuo Mito, *The Honda Book of Management*, pp. 62, 63; reproduced with
permission of the author and The Athlone Press)

company presidents and plant managers develop their own individual styles within the overall framework, styles appropriate to the challenges they see ahead. New ideas are translated into new sayings, successful past problem solutions are disseminated and referred to; 'what Mr Honda used to say', stories of Mr Honda's own practices as a 'lone wolf' engineer who disdained formality and retired without passing the business on to his son; all these are mechanisms to express through exemplars how individuals should behave in tackling problems.[4]

This is not to suggest that philosophy and methodology are sufficient by themselves, that would be going too far. It is the interplay of core ideas with structure that counts. If the ideas are sufficiently well-developed, shared, understood, then structures of control can be kept to a minimum, people can make decisions with less fear of being contradicted later, and decisions taken at the top can quickly be translated into action further down. The constant refreshing of organization and of ideas that each new company president has brought with him sends a wave of energy down the hierarchy and renews it.

Thus the goal is flexibility within a framework that functions effectively on a daily basis. What might seem like disorganization is simply not a traditional Western way of being organized. But it works wonders. Bottom up aids top down, individualism aids the group, decentralization aids central control, youth helps age, horizontal and diagonal links help the vertical pyramid of power. This is the organization that can innovate, because individual ideas come out, where they can percolate upwards, where each person's knowledge of external conditions – and, just as crucially but too often neglected in the West, the internal workings of the firm itself – is better and so better decisions are made, and where they can be acted upon. This is the organization that can respond. This is the organization ready to be led, because it is ready to follow, and swiftly too.

None of this is to argue that Honda is a fair and just organization, or to believe that individuals are in fact always fully rewarded, or that Honda is not an intensely political organization with all the pros and cons which that entails. Neither is it the case that mistakes aren't made. But Honda has tried to develop the organizational capacity to move quickly, to take risks, to right its path when going astray, not to get caught up in the bureaucratic stalemates that afflict not only Western firms but – a point not much recognized in the West – many big Japanese firms too.

HONDA EMPLOYEES

Honda employees belong to an enterprise union which incorporates staff up to assistant managers. The union last caused real trouble to management in 1954, but this doesn't mean it is ineffectual: management had to be very careful in establishing the expert system during the 1960s so as not to upset existing socio-political expectations in the company.

Wages and salaries are divided into a basic element plus large individually calculated elements and large bonus payments that combined can equal several months of basic salary each year. Honda's workforce is young, with the average age in the early 30s and assembly-line workers averaging in their late 20s. The retirement age is 55. Honda moved on to a five-and-a-half-day work week in 1965, and a five-day week in 1972. The firm provides sports and leisure facilities around its plants, some open to the wider community.

A notable un-Japanese practice at Honda is not to work the long hours of overtime to which many Western critics attribute the success of Japanese industry. Honda's working shifts have been placed back to back (or with only an hour separating them) for several years, with no time between shifts for overtime designed to increase output. When overtime to increase output is worked, it is invariably on Saturdays, giving Honda workers regular and predictable hours. Honda also pays higher overtime wages than any other automobile producer in Japan.

Combined regular hours and overtime for Honda workers in 1990 – a year of record production and sales for Honda in Japan – stood at 1954 hours, 131 hours of which was overtime. This puts Honda on a par with the North American producers, though still 300–400 hours more than some European producers. By contrast, workers at most Japanese rivals worked around 2300 hours, including overtime of between 300 and 500 hours. None of this is to say, however, that some non-production staff do not put in very long hours.[5]

MANUFACTURING PHILOSOPHIES

In common with other automobile producers, first in Japan and now worldwide, Honda has been influenced by the manufacturing methods developed by Toyota, and known as the 'Toyota production system', or 'just-in-time manufacturing'. Toyota is held in high esteem at Honda for its manufacturing prowess (which is not true of some other Japanese competitors). But while the global spotlight has been on Toyota – so much so that Toyota is often taken to be *the* Japanese model – like other producers with their different approaches, Honda's manufacturing philosophy departs from Toyota's in significant ways.

The core concepts at Honda are precision planning and simplification. Precision planning means that manufacturing is meticulously organized in advance and production departs from the plan as little as possible. Western engineers who visit Honda plants notice that the factories are usually just about exactly on target for daily production at any point in the day, and that the number of components unused during a week because the car they were meant to go on has not been assembled due to some fault is very small indeed compared to Western practice. The idea at Honda is to simultaneously produce the correct parts and finished models according to exact preset plans with little or no divergence.

Pursuit of very high-quality parts is essential to this strategy, so that none need be discarded, or production disrupted by poor fit and finish requiring rework. In common with other Japanese firms, during the mid-1970s Honda began to actively intervene further down in its parts supply chain, demanding higher quality, providing its own engineers and managerial advice when required.

The Toyota production system has become synonymous with mixed assembly of vehicles on production lines in lots of one, with different vehicles and their derivatives apparently randomly mixed together on the assembly line. In fact the idea is to space different derivatives so as to balance the workload for workers (not too many complex derivatives at once) and to balance the supply of parts (parts for model A might be needed every three minutes, for model B every two minutes), and to be able to respond to market shifts by rejigging the mix on a computer.

Honda's Sayama and Suzuka factories also produce different models and derivatives on the same production lines. Honda, however, produces in batches, 60 at a time, of cars exactly the same (though there has more recently been a move to more varied lot sizes at the Japanese factories). For example at Sayama, several batches of different-derivative Accords may be made before the line is switched to make Preludes for several batches. Models may be switched three or four times in a day. This system much simplifies logistical planning in parts supply compared to production in lots of one, and offers similar market flexibility. But instead of mixing the cars to accommodate a fixed workforce, it is the workforce that is reorganized between batches when necessary, with workers moving about the factory to balance workloads.

At Sayama, for instance, seven types of car body can be accommodated in the factory: the basic Accord, Prelude and Legend, plus the 2-door Legend and the Accord-derived Accord Inspire, Vigor and Ascot. Some models can be made on more than one assembly line, facilitating balanced use of each line. Declining demand for one model can be counterbalanced with increased demand for others, and this is the norm, especially since the life-cycles of the different models are staggered (Accord was replaced in 1989, Legend in 1990, and Prelude in 1991).

At the same time the different vehicles are designed in the knowledge that they will be manufactured on production lines with given characteristics. For instance, a certain bolt on a Prelude will have precisely the same torque as its equivalent on an Accord, or Legend, so that the same lineside tools can be used on each model without adjustment.

Precision planning is of paramount importance at Sayama. The factory site, located in the northern suburbs of Tokyo, is the archetypal Japanese urban factory, hemmed in on all sides with no room to expand. Moreover, it has been through several bouts of reorganization to improve its productivity. Some processes now take place on three or four floors as the factory has grown upwards. Much subassembly work has been decanted out to parts makers in order to use the assembly plant only for an expanding final automobile production process. This has required upgrading the capabilities of the parts makers.

Adoption of doors-off final assembly has allowed doors to be assembled as modules too since the late 1980s. The subassembled parts are easier to install automatically or semi-automatically (for example, with mechanical arms holding the weight as the worker pushes them into place). Also to save ground space, many parts are brought to the production lines on overhead conveyors, where they arrive at the work station at the exact moment they are needed (especially for larger parts and subassemblies); here there is no need for lineside storage at all. Otherwise, lineside inventories are kept to an absolute minimum so that the cramped space can all be used for productive activities.

Urban geography plays other important roles in logistical considerations besides the implications of Sayama's fixed and cramped site. The factory receives shipments from some 300 parts makers, with over 3000 truck deliveries per day, a number swelled by small batch deliveries despatched to arrive just-in-time. But the system begins to become self-defeating as the many small deliveries designed to control inventory levels lead to traffic congestion that then disrupts the deliveries. And all the time, expansion of plant output leaves less and less space for inventory storage. As a result of low inventory levels, even snow falling on a mountain pass, preventing deliveries from parts makers located a little further afield, can halt production at Sayama until the delivery arrives.

While many parts makers are situated in the vicinity of the Sayama factory. and many others are located in nearby metropolitan Tokyo, urban traffic congestion hampers the organization of parts deliveries. One Honda solution is repackaging facilities close to the plant, where older, often women, workers, repack parts into the receptacles that will be used at the point of final assembly. Cramped and inflexible land-use conditions, together with urban traffic congestion, may have enforced certain innovations in production (like just-in-time production), but they also present considerable barriers to organizing a smooth flow of production. The better solution represented by the advantage of open spaces and controllable timing of deliveries (even over longer distances) was one lesson learned when Honda built the Kumamoto plant on the island of Kyushu.

HUMAN ROLE AND MACHINE ROLE

There is a sense in which manufacturing at Toyota is meticulously planned, whilst at Honda it is less so, or rather, it is planned differently. Whereas at Toyota the manufacturing philosophy has historically had engineers fine-tuning worker task-cycles to squeeze out all unused fractions of seconds, at Honda such precision planning is devolved to the lowest-level line supervisors and the production workers themselves. These supervisors are seen as the pivots of the whole production system, and Honda prides itself on worker autonomy in comparison to what is seen as Toyota-style regimentation.

Worker input is encouraged through suggestion schemes. Only a minority of suggestions refer to the actual production process, most being concerned with other conditions, like problems getting to work because of congestion, improvements to rest areas, and so on. Honda's quality circles are called NH circles, standing for Now, Next, New Honda. Employees organize themselves, out of hours and unpaid, and the circles are not sponsored by the firm. NH circles create very useful diagonal and horizontal links at the bottom of the organizational pyramid. They allow workers to become involved in improving the factories at no cost to management. Workers tend to organize circles to help them resolve the problems they themselves face on a daily basis, whether getting to work, facilities at work, or a particular problem that keeps arising when they try to accomplish their production tasks.

Worker input follows the Honda manufacturing philosophy of 'human-using-to-capacity'. Not to be confused with a humane system, this means seeing each person as a total resource, so that the minds as well as the bodies of production workers are utilized, and so that each person is used in their fullest capacity (as the firm judges it) towards achieving corporate goals. As part of their integration into the manufacturing process, Honda's production workers undertake routine quality-control tasks simultaneously with their other work tasks: this is a paradigm instance of human-using-to-capacity, not wasting the minds of the workers who could be looking out for results of errors made upstream in production.

The principle is that workers should not pass quality problems further on down the line, but should try to resolve them first. In final assembly operations, apart from the workforce inspecting its own work and the results of upstream work, there is only the inspection area at the end of the line to check for problems.

Workers are encouraged to learn several tasks so that they can move or be shifted at will to other work-stations. Less frequently, they can also move between work groups, and between sections or departments, to increase their abilities or simply to change scene. Supervisors have to learn all the tasks in their area so that they can step in if necessary.

What is the Honda approach to technology and its relation to the human being? Technology should not dull minds but activate them: according to the Honda philosophy, production workers should become 'machine fanatics' who marvel at their technology rather than feeling oppressed by it. With its own Sayama-based production engineering subsidiary, Honda Engineering (EG), Honda is able to control much of the design and installation of its manufacturing equipment, which ought to make it more responsive to the needs of the factory floor.

EG makes much of its automation equipment itself. This way it retains control over key manufacturing technologies. EG products are licensed to other capital equipment makers and sometimes later find themselves introduced in other Japanese car factories. During the 1970s

EG particularly concentrated on building general welding machines that not only offered higher-quality work than manual labour and fewer steps (with several robots working simultaneously at each step), but were as flexible too, able to accommodate different models with quick changeovers – a matter of minutes – between them. Another focus was to pair up dies in stamping machines, so that left and right parts could be stamped simultaneously.

When it purchases equipment (mostly Japanese, some German and Swedish), EG acts according to a motto of never installing it without some modifications to suit its use at Honda. Instead of calling in specialist capital equipment suppliers who install the machinery and then hand it over to production staff, EG thus becomes closely connected to manufacturing, which makes for a better interface between manufacturing staff and production engineers.

Mistakes have been made, however. Like other automobile producers around the world, during the early 1980s Honda's engineers became fascinated with labour-saving production technologies and the firm invested heavily in automated equipment. However, in a number of cases they did not plan well enough – the links with Honda Research and Development were missing – to permit new, unforeseen (for example, larger) models to be built on the same equipment. A lot of new equipment had to be discarded before its time.

By the mid-1980s Honda had adopted a more cautious approach to automation. The principle has been to concentrate on the most physically difficult tasks – technology adapted to humans, especially since Honda's current workforce is ageing – and those where product quality would be improved. Honda has followed the same path as most other auto makers around the world, concentrating its automation and capital investments in the early stages of manufacture – stamping, welding (90–100 per cent) and painting (50–60 per cent) – and far less in final assembly operations. At Sayama, for instance, by the mid-1980s there were still hardly any automated final assembly processes, though by the early 1990s about 15 per cent of tasks had been automated.

Suzuka is the site for most of Honda's experiments with final assembly automation. Honda built an experimental production line in the factory in the early 1980s where real vehicles were built but where automation could be tested out and fine-tuned in practice without disrupting the main production lines.

Here the engineers experimented with placing cars being assembled on separate platforms rather than being linked together by the usual chain. EG had developed a similar system at the Kumamoto motorcycle factory in the late 1970s. Confronted with the dualist opposite ideas of regimented Taylorist work and Swedish-style autonomous group work, the engineers had sought a way out. Kumamoto's 'free-flow line' dispensed with a fixed-speed moving assembly line. Each unit was separated from those ahead and behind, so that the worker sends it on when the task is completed. The system is designed to create a more humane working environment in which man possesses more control over machine compared to the traditional assembly line.

Though it is more expensive to install, there are counterbalancing advantages to such a system. When somebody has a particular problem in completing a task – perhaps a new worker who can't keep up – the whole assembly line – and all the other workers – doesn't have to be stopped while it is rectified (within certain time limits, of course).

At Suzuka too, then, Honda built a system where part-finished vehicles could stop at each work-station for differing amounts of time (appropriate to the particular process), rather than move through at a fixed pace as on a conventional assembly line. From the human point of view, the idea was to make work easier, since the platform stops at each work-station, and to allow the worker to intervene to a certain extent in the pace of his work. But again there were also other advantages which proved that more humane work need not reduce productivity. With a moving assembly line, automation has to be tailored to a strict preset time period. At Suzuka, however, not only does the platform stop still, but it can stop for slightly longer periods to conform with the needs of specific types of automation.

Once working properly on the experimental line, equipment like this could be transferred to a main production line. Suzuka's third line, opened in 1989, is the company's most advanced from a technological viewpoint. Many heavy lifting operations were automated or semi-automated: installation of spare tyres, seats, batteries, engines and suspensions simultaneously. What about the trade-off between human dignity and efficiency associated with the Taylorism/group-work discussion in the West? Honda sought humanization without impairing efficiency: indeed a form of humanization that would allow increased efficiency. With a tacht time (the period before a work cycle is repeated) of between 42 and 47 seconds, Suzuka's third assembly line is one of the world's fastest.

The original goal at Suzuka was to automate 30 per cent of final assembly operations, which was seen as feasible from a technological standpoint. But by the early 1990s automation had not advanced beyond the 18 per cent level starting point. Many work-stations and processes had been designed so that they could be automated at a later date, with the system of separate assembly platforms providing the necessary flexibility. But the high costs of further automation have meant postponement of further investments.

Beside being able to shift models between production lines within its factories, Honda has actually restructured the whole purpose of some of its factories as the company has evolved. Whereas some Western firms might have simply closed down one factory and opened up another elsewhere as their product base shifted, at Honda the principle is to keep each factory and its production workers intact and to find new products for them to make.

We might call these plants 'flexifactories'. A prime example is the Kumamoto factory. Originally set up in 1976 for CKD production of motorcycles whose parts came from central Japan and which were then exported, it later shifted its function to make the CKD kits themselves for export to plants in other countries, added agricultural machinery, and then added small car and van engine production in 1987. But the most spectacular example of a 'flexifactory' is the Suzuka factory. Opened as a motorcycle plant in 1960, by the mid-1980s Suzuka had become the highest-output motorcycle factory in the world. Automobiles were first made there in 1967, three years after Sayama. Gradually, automobile production grew in importance (reflecting the evolution of the whole company). Now, Suzuka doesn't make any motorcycles at all. In 1991 its final motorcycle production was transferred to Kumamoto, and the workers are now making automobiles.

The results of Honda's manufacturing philosophy, and its utilization of humans and machines, are clear. According to the gross productivity measure of output per employee per hour (taking into account the proportion of production undertaken in-house), Honda's productivity in Japan equals that of Toyota itself (Table 2.2).

HONDA RESEARCH AND DEVELOPMENT

Continuous research and development of new and innovative products is absolutely fundamental to Honda's corporate strategy. The company's research and development department was spun off as a separate subsidiary – Honda Research and Development Co. (HRD) – in 1962. From the start, HRD received a certain proportion of total Honda sales revenues to emphasize its formalized financial stability.

Table 2.2   Relative Gross Hourly Productivity at the Big Five Japanese
Automobile Producers, 1990 (units produced per 1000
person-hours of work)

	Index
Toyota	7.57
Honda	7.56
Mazda	6.25
Nissan	5.69
Mitsubishi	5.44

Notes: 1. The measure takes into account units produced, numbers of
employees, hours worked per year, and proportion of value
added that takes place in-house.
2. The figures must be taken as a rough guide since rates of in-house
production for some firms are estimates.
Source: 'Japanese auto industry: working hours reduction and the labor
shortage', *Asian Motor Vehicle Business Review*, 1991, pp. 2–12.

And Honda's very top people run HRD. Mr Honda was its first
president. Since his departure all Honda company presidents have
either come out of long HRD careers or have spent several years as
president of HRD before assuming the ultimate position. Indeed
Honda has always been headed by people who have spent their
careers in a combination of product research and development and
manufacturing. Institutionally, then, HRD has a very powerful
position in overall Honda operations.

By the 1990s HRD employed 7000 people. Most of them work on
the automobile development side of R&D, sited at the Tochigi proving
grounds. A smaller centre at Wako, near to the engine plant, was the
original automobile R&D centre, and now concentrates on basic
engine technology research. Other R&D centres focus on motorcycles
and power products.

The research and development effort undertaken by Honda during
the 1960s and 1970s was to be one of the prime forces in shifting the
Japanese automobile industry as a whole decisively away from its old
image of cheap copycat products to its current image of cutting-edge
high technology. Honda has always been a product-oriented company,
and within this, has kept itself particularly well-focused. The central
goal has never deviated far from Mr Honda's own: creating light-
weight, superefficient petrol engines (whether for automobiles, motor-

cycles or power products). The core function of the research effort has always been to make better and better petrol engines. Concentration on petrol engines has meant that even diesel engines have been bypassed by Honda. And Honda moved as early as 1967 to front-wheel-drive transverse-mounted engines for all its automobiles, which has since become the world standard best technology for small and medium vehicles because of its space and weight-saving characteristics.

Beyond engine technologies, a great deal of Honda research is dedicated to innovations in mechanical components, from suspensions to steering to seat belts. Here, Honda concentrates on its strengths, inventing its own mechanical systems (for example, automatic transmissions, anti-lock brakes) even as other medium-sized firms choose to buy them in from specialist parts makers. Among the notable non-engine outputs of HRD have been four-wheel steering systems (first a mechanically controlled, then an electronically controlled version, with which the Prelude has been equipped), and the unusual double-wishbone suspension system that Honda installs in its cars.

But engine technologies are definitely at the heart of Honda product innovation. The exemplary technological success at Honda was the CVCC engine, developed in the early 1970s. The CVCC was the world's first low-pollution engine not to require a catalyst to remove pollutants from the engine exhaust since its combustion process created so few in the first place. The CVCC story is repeated within the company as the paradigm of technological innovation.

- CVCC was developed in response to a call from society: environmental concerns and American and Japanese government legislation on pollution around 1970.
- Honda took the risk of concentrating its research effort: 80 per cent of all research funds went into developing a low-pollution engine for the duration of the project.
- The solution was highly innovative, elegant, simple, and it worked: with a minor and a major combustion chamber combined in one for each cylinder, the CVCC was in fact classic dualist puzzle-solving applied directly to technology, reducing nitrogen oxides, carbon monoxides and hydrocarbons all at once, whereas all previous technologies had only reduced one pollutant at the cost of increasing the others. Honda had invented a best-of-both-worlds engine.[6]
- Finally, like other Honda technologies, the CVCC was marketed to the hilt, with the Civics in which the engines were installed from 1974 carrying a large CVCC badge, allowing Honda to steal a march

on other producers who claimed the new environmental legislation was impossible to meet. CVCC technology was then licensed to the likes of Toyota, Ford and Chrysler.

A parallel approach to research innovation later led to the equally novel VTEC engine, introduced in the Civic in 1989. Here Honda attacked head-on the conventional trade-off in engine technology between performance and efficiency, to meet two apparently contradictory market demands at once. High-performance acceleration conventionally demanded either large engines or petrol-rich mixtures in the combustion chambers, which inevitably meant higher fuel consumption. The alternatives were a small engine or a petrol-thin 'lean burn' engine, which were better on the economy side but lacked acceleration. Honda's answer was a medium sized engine that alternates between a petrol-rich and petrol-thin mixture, to deliver fast performance if required, but to burn a thin mixture when not being called to produce acceleration. Here was an engine for the 1990s: fast and green.

The technical solution was to make an engine with two inlet and outlet valves per cylinder (for example, a 16-valve engine) in which the valves that let petrol into the combustion chambers can be electronically controlled to open and close according to different driving conditions. VTEC was followed by VTEC-E in 1991, promising even higher efficiency with lean-burn technology, though here Honda began to run back up against the pollution problem because the lean-burn engine emits more nitrogen oxides. Now there was a new problem to solve: how to avoid the 'trade-off' between even greater fuel efficiency and correspondingly higher emission of pollutants.

Not only do HRD researchers come up with new inventions and innovations, but the product development engineers have become very adept at getting them into production quickly. Here another of HRD's major achievements comes to the fore. Honda has led the world's automobile industry in reducing the time it takes to develop a new version of a model, reaching the unheard-of period of only two years by the late 1980s.

The Honda product machine not only spits out new models and new technologies on a regular basis, but every four years replaces each model with a new version (four years has been viewed as the minimum replacement time allowable from the point of view of the Japanese consumer, who wants the latest product but doesn't want it to become outdated soon after purchase). Thus the Honda Accord replacement cycle is 1981, 1985, 1989, 1993, while that for the Civic is 1979, 1983, 1987, 1991. Here are two comparable Western products: Ford's North American Tempo/Topaz (Mondeo) (1983, 1994) and Volkswagen's European Golf (1974, 1983, 1991).

Western engineers have frequently asked if Honda's rapid replacements can be 'real' model changeovers. In Western convention, either a model is totally changed, with all its components, or there is a 'freshening-up', which is a superficial change of trim that takes place about halfway through a model version's life. So aren't these frequent Honda changeovers just 'glorified freshenings', and so not particularly innovative?

Now here's a typical dualist approach: imposition of Western categories on to Japanese practice. And the categories don't fit reality. Let's take a closer look. There are manifold advantages to the Honda approach.

- For a start, most production equipment won't need changing because it was made flexible enough in the first place, so that is one less cost.
- The four-year model cycle permits rapid introduction of new technologies.
- At the same time, the model can quickly respond to consumer tastes, and indeed remain at the cutting edge in design. Unpopular versions won't last too long, and theoretically could be replaced before their four years were up.

Now, meeting these goals doesn't require that all components be completely changed, even if the basic body frame and skin is altered entirely. In fact, nearly everything the consumer can see usually is replaced. But some components need only minor alterations (and this helps to keep any retooling of manufacturing to a minimum).

On the other hand, Honda often introduces new technologies – frequently ones the consumer can't see but which affect performance, such as new transmissions, gear boxes and other mechanical innovations – to a model version that has already been made for a year or two. This works as an extra mid-life stimulus to demand for the model version. To complicate matters further, when a certain body style has proved successful for a model, Honda has replaced the model version, on schedule, with one that looks very similar indeed even though it is an 'all new car'. This happened with the 1989 Accord replacement.

In other words, the Western dualism of complete model change/ freshening is dispensed with, replaced by a far more iterative and flexible process of replacing a model version.

The metaphors and slogans that play such an important part in capturing and communicating management philosophy also play a key role in product development. New models and versions of automobiles are built around specific concepts that they are designed to embody, the concepts referring to the way the product is to be sold or the particular market at which it is aimed. The slogan or metaphor becomes an intermediary that represents the product's target market. The product engineers then have to 'concretize' it by embodying it in the product. Two examples are given in Box 2.2. In the first, several metaphors arc used, from the abstract to the more concrete, each involving pairs of apparently incompatible goals (dualist opposites) that must somehow be reconciled. Out of their interplay came an innovative product. In the second, the sophistication of the thought process and its translation into a real product is brought out, with the engineers creating strong guiding concepts to work around.

Important as concepts clearly are, however, until 1991 Honda had never displayed a 'concept car' at an international motor show. Concept cars are the idealized, futuristic models with which the world's major producers show off their inventiveness to the public. The trouble is, hardly any of them find their way into actual production. Honda seems to have saved its concepts for automobiles that would be made – and sold – on a large scale.

Honda's technology-product image has been enhanced, and connected to a 'sporty' image, by the company's participation in automobile racing. This brings up some intriguing insights into how Honda as a whole, led by HRD, shifts its whole strategic path in terms of product and market definition.

Automobile racing at Honda followed a long history of international motorcycle racing starting in the early 1950s. Honda began Formula 1 automobile racing as soon as it was making automobiles, in 1964. The resources devoted to racing were explained in terms of experimentation with high-speed engines, the particular technological route the firm was following to greater engine power. When Honda pulled out of F-1 in 1969 it was explained that all the necessary lessons had been learned.

But withdrawal from automobile racing also coincided with the start of the research programme that would result in the CVCC engine, as well as decisions to reduce the engine power of Honda's commercial automobiles, and a period of bad publicity in Japan over the dangers of

Box 2.2   From Concepts to Cars

The Story of the Tall Boy

In 1978, top management at Honda inaugurated the development of a new-concept car with the slogan, 'Let's gamble.' The phrase expressed senior executives' conviction that Honda's Civic and Accord models were becoming too familiar. Managers also realized that along with a new postwar generation entering the car market, a new generation of young product designers was coming of age with unconventional ideas about what made a good car.

The business decision that followed from the 'Let's gamble' slogan was to form a new-product development team of young engineers and designers (the average age was 27). Top management charged the team with two – and only two – instructions: first, to come up with a product concept fundamentally different from anything the company had ever done before; and second, to make a car that was inexpensive but not cheap.

This mission might sound vague, but in fact it provided the team an extremely clear sense of direction. For instance, in the early days of the project, some team members proposed designing a smaller and cheaper version of the Honda Civic – a safe and technologically feasible option. But the team quickly decided this approach contradicted the entire rationale of its mission. The only alternative was to invent something totally new.

Project team leader Hiroo Watanabe coined another slogan to express his sense of the team's ambitious challenge: Theory of Automobile Evolution. The phrase described an ideal. In effect, it posed the question: If the automobile were an organism, how should it evolve? As team members argued and discussed what Watanabe's slogan might possibly mean, they came up with an answer in the form of yet another slogan: 'man-maximum, machine-minimum.' This captured the team's belief that the ideal car should somehow transcend the traditional human-machine relationship. But that required challenging what Watanabe called 'the reasoning of Detroit,' which had sacrificed comfort for appearance.

The 'evolutionary' trend the team articulated eventually came to be embodied in the image of a sphere – a car simultaneously 'short' (in length) and 'tall' (in height). Such a car, they reasoned, would be lighter and cheaper, but also more comfortable and more solid than traditional cars. A sphere provided the most room for the passenger while taking up the least amount of space on the road. What's more, the shape minimized the space taken up by the engine and other mechanical systems. This gave birth to a product concept the team called 'Tall Boy', which eventually led to the Honda City, the company's distinctive urban car.

(Ikujiro Nonaka, 'The knowledge-creating company', *Harvard Business Review*, Nov.–Dec. 1991, pp. 96–104. Passage from p. 100. (The Honda City was marketed in Europe as Honda Jazz in the mid 1980s.) (Reproduced with the permission of the editors of *Harvard Business Review*)

Behind the 1989 Accord

Honda took a more mystical approach to its newest Accord. Honda wanted the car to be 'an acquired taste' that would build buyer loyalty through its life, says Takeomi Miyoshi, its product manager. As a first step toward that goal, the car's 15 product-development leaders spent a year coming up with an image to personify the ideal family sedan. Their choice: a rugby player in a suit, a metaphor for a gentleman who is strong and athletic. Then, they decided on five traits the car should exemplify.

[Then, as with the case of the City model, the abstract ideas and metaphors had to be turned into the actual physical characteristics of the car.]

The rugby player's assumed desire to be 'stress-free', for example, was translated into new ways to cut noise and vibration. The liquid-filled engine mount is one result. So are a honeycomb of sound-absorbing paper in the ceiling, a layer of soft insulation covered by foil to make the steel floor pan feel more solid and mute road noise, and triple-sealing rubber gaskets around the doors to make them close tightly.

(David Woodruff, 'A new era for auto quality: just as Detroit is catching up, the very concept is changing', *Business Week*, October 22, 1990, pp. 42–9. Passages from pp. 46–7 and p. 47 respectively.)

---

high-speed driving and supposedly shoddy vehicles that had severely cut into Honda sales. Here, then, was a clear and swift change in overall strategic direction towards emphasizing safety and the environment, with the whole company reacting on several fronts at once to change its product image.

Honda reentered Formula 1 racing in 1983, during the less ecologically minded, power-oriented social atmosphere of the 1980s (a period which also brought the CRX and NSX sports cars out of HRD). Honda won the F-1 constructors' championships six times in a row between 1986 and 1991. Yet by 1992, Honda had withdrawn again, to focus once more on ecology as a key social theme (the expense of racing was also being felt more severely in the global economic slowdown of the early 1990s). Honda's whole product image shifted again towards themes related to ecology and man–environment relations, the concrete results of which in automobile terms can be expected to emerge from HRD as the decade progresses: efforts directed at recycling old automobile parts, reducing energy consumption further, low pollution, and better safety features. Indeed the F-1 engineers, it was announced, were to be set to work designing electric battery-powered vehicles.

How is HRD organized internally to create a flow of product innovations and implement new concepts, new models, new versions of current models and new product strategies at such a rapid pace? To begin with, it is vital to distinguish between research on the one hand, and product development on the other, because these are two fundamentally different processes. And yet they have to be brought together so that they feed off and into each other.

The basic research process at HRD gives priority to the individual engineers, to the many 'lone wolves' in the style of Mr Honda himself. Researchers are able to pick their own research themes, to work on them alone or in groups. But the research effort is also given a certain direction, since managerial committees make judgements at certain points as to whether the effort should continue. Moreover, as we've just seen, HRD top management selects themes of strategic importance within which the research effort should be focused. These themes are set quite abstractly, at a broad societal level, and not just from the standpoint of technological feasibility. Establishment of broad themes therefore controls and directs the research process so that its solutions will be useful to the company, hopefully to be marketed as 'solving society's problems'.

But within these broad themes researchers are free to set up various programmes designed to meet the challenges set, and to continue to work on these in a kind of internal competition with their fellows until it becomes clear that a particular approach or technology has won the day. The CVCC engine, for instance, won an internal competition that had included looking at various possible solutions, from exhaust gas recycling to catalysis to gas turbines. The 'loser' themes are not necessarily wasted, however – the newer VTEC engine may benefit from exhaust gas recycling to clean it up.

Proper management of the research process is vital. Managers try to draw the best out of individual talents, to let them work in the ways they want to, and yet some researchers will fail, some succeed. It is crucial that the judgements over whether to proceed with or stop certain projects are seen as sufficiently just that researchers on the losing projects are willing to keep working. Leaders adopt various styles to ensure that the individual process functions effectively within group goals (see Box 2.1 on Mr Kume's ideas about HRD). HRD has to avoid 'big business disease' just like the parent company.

The individual character of the research process is reflected in the homage paid within Honda to the directors of successful projects.

There is a definite cult of individual success stories that firmly links persons to products, quite a surprising finding in light of the themes of overriding groupism and subjugation to the company that are central to the 'Japanese industrial model'. Hence it is well-advertised that Mr Kawamoto, company president in the early 1990s, was heavily involved with development of the CVCC engine and the NSX automobile. His predecessors were likewise fêted, and his likely successors are already being built up.

The product development process is organized quite differently from research. While risk, and a low success rate, are perfectly acceptable in research, in product development no failure at all can be tolerated. While working alone is acceptable in research work, in development work coordination is the key at every step. Development teams include marketing and manufacturing engineering (EG) people to ensure that the process proceeds as fast as possible with no hiccups.

This doesn't mean that the development process is as smooth as is sometimes portrayed in the Japanese Model (for example, in the 'design for manufacture' idea which implies that manufacturing staff exert considerable leverage over the development process): far from it, it can be crisis-ridden, full of arguments, of debate, of organizational politics. There are winners and losers internally. Sometimes HRD will design its products to fit current manufacturing technologies. At other times it will try to impose its will on manufacturing. At Honda in particular, research and development staff are very powerful in internal politics. The point is not that the development process is smooth, but that it takes place in a coordinated way so that differences arise and are dealt with, instead of simply not arising at all during the development process because nobody notices them, or being swept under the carpet, only to appear with disastrous results when production actually gets under way.

To sum up HRD, here we see the epitome of Honda's management philosophy and organizational approach, applied to the research and development process. A host of dualisms make their appearance – individual/group, human/technology, risk/security, performance/environment – and are cleverly dealt with in a puzzle-solving manner not by choosing between them or by playing them off, but by incorporating both elements at once so as not to lose the benefits each element can bring. Moreover, it is this same dualist puzzle-solving approach that characterizes both the social aspects of HRD organization and the technical inventions that Honda researchers come up with.

A TALE OF TWO MARKETS, JAPANESE AND AMERICAN

Honda's first cars of the 1960s were aimed principally at the Japanese market. They were little sports cars and little 4-door cars, many of which fell into the micro-car category, with small engines very popular in Japan. Yet, these early automobiles were immediately sold abroad to see what the reaction would be. And in 1970, Honda began automobile exports to the United States to test the waters in what was regarded as the world's most demanding market. Then in 1973 came the Civic, with its CVCC engine, and suddenly the whole American market was opened up with an enormous export success. Honda's annual US sales shot from 39 000 to 375 000 in the following seven years. Thus began the story of two big markets, Japan and North America, and how Honda began to devise a marketing and production strategy for both at once. And thus also began Honda's global local corporation.

With the immediate success of the Civic, Honda rapidly shifted its attention away from the Japanese market to North America. Output at Sayama and Suzuka accelerated at a rapid pace during the 1970s, from under 400 000 vehicles (automobiles and trucks) per year in 1970 to almost 1 000 000 in 1980 (Figure 2.2). Every single extra vehicle produced went overseas, with exports rising from 5.9 per cent of total output to 69 per cent between 1970 and 1980 (Figure 2.3). By the end of the decade 60 per cent of exports went to the United States alone, which was alone consuming between 40 and 50 per cent of the company's total output each year, a level maintained during the 1980s.

Meanwhile, Honda's Japanese sales and its Japanese market share were allowed to slide away, from 360 000 (8.8 per cent) in 1970 to 270 000 (5.4 per cent) in 1980 (well below Honda's US sales), even as the overall Japanese automobile market grew by over 20 per cent (Figure 2.3). Despite the popularity of its micro-cars in Japan, the company simply stopped making them in 1975. (Over 500 000 of the last micro-car, Life, had been sold in Japan in only four years, accounting for 44 per cent of total Honda sales in Japan between 1971 and 1975!). With micro-car production halted, the production lines could concentrate on the larger models demanded abroad (Accord was introduced in 1976). Honda had found an insatiable appetite for its cars in North America, and was sacrificing the home market to it.

Step by step with each model change, Honda's automobiles were designed more and more for the North American consumer. Where the Civic had pioneered, the Accord pursued. The cars became larger (see Figure 2.4), and their styling increasingly in tune with North American

Figure 2.2   Where New Sayama and Suzuka Output was Sold: Exports in the 1970s, Home Market in the 1980s

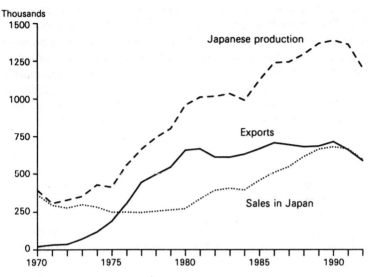

Source: Japanese Manufacturers Assocation (JAMA)

Figure 2.3   How Honda Played off Japanese Market Share Against Exports

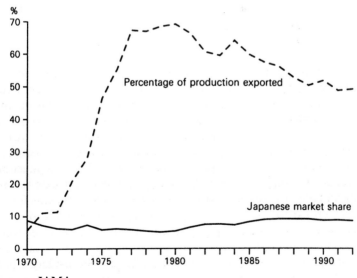

Source: JAMA

Figure 2.4   Honda Automobiles Grow (dates are new model introduction)

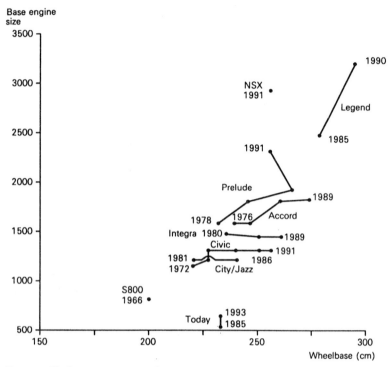

Source: Various company and press reports

tastes, a process aided by establishment of a Honda design studio in Los Angeles in 1975. In 1989, 1990 and 1991 the Honda Accord was the best selling single automobile model of any sold in the United States. By 1990 the company controlled over 6 per cent of the total vehicle market, (including vans and pick-ups, which Honda doesn't make at all). For automobiles alone, Honda captured 9.2 per cent of the market in 1990, the same proportion as Chrysler. So American did the Accord become during the 1980s that its sales in Japan became minor compared to those in the United States. By 1991 Honda sold 399 000 Accords in the United States, but only 41 000 in Japan.

And yet these figures only tell half the story. The other half introduces some rather interesting developments on the product/ marketing side that would have significant implications. In 1978 and again in 1985, Honda split its distribution network in Japan, to create three separate channels, Verno, Clio and Primo, each designed to cater to a different submarket. In 1981 an upmarket automobile based on the Accord, called Vigor, was introduced at Sayama, to be marketed in the Verno network. It was followed in 1989 by two other Accord derivatives, Accord Inspire and Ascot. While the basic Accord was now aimed at the American market, these new models were aimed at Japan (though Vigor has also been exported since 1991). The basic Accord has therefore been branched out into separate models that are basically the same car under their skins. A Civic twin called Ballade was also created, made at Suzuka between 1980 and 1987: made for the Japanese and some overseas markets, but not for North America. We will return to the great significance of this branching process later on, in Chapter 11.

Honda sales in Japan began to rise again during the 1980s. This followed first the economic recession in North America between 1979 and 1983, and then the establishment of the Honda manufacturing plants in North America to which we will soon be turning our attention. But Honda had also clearly turned back to Japan. Besides the introduction of separate distribution channels, there was the 1981 introduction of City (Tall boy, whose development story was told in Box 2.2), in a niche beneath Civic, largely for the Japanese market, followed in 1985 by Today, which marked Honda's return to micro-car production. A series of other cars were also introduced for Japan, including Beat in 1991 and Domani in 1992.

Honda's Japanese sales more than doubled between 1980 and 1990, and market share too increased rapidly (Figures 2.2 and 2.3). It was during the Japanese domestic market boom of the late 1980s that Honda built the third production line at Suzuka, largely to satisfy internal market demand. The share of Honda's Japanese output going overseas fell back to below 50 per cent for the first time in 15 years (Figure 2.3).

Notwithstanding its success in small and medium family-oriented sedan cars in North America, Honda has kept up its sporty image with the Prelude, first introduced in 1978, the CRX version of the Civic, in 1983, and the NSX ('Japanese Ferrari') in 1990. Moreover, it was Honda that led the Japanese pack up-market to begin competing against the larger American and European automobiles, with the introduction of the Legend in 1985, which subsequently became a very large and very American automobile when redesigned in 1990. Legend was marketed in the United States under a separate brand name, Acura, to be joined by Integra, NSX and Vigor. Not only had

Honda pulled the Japanese automobile producers out of their copycat image into the high-tech cutting edge (especially with the CVCC engine), but it had led them out of their small car image into the high-quality big car league too. Last but not least, this is as good a point as any to mention that after installing front-wheel-drive transverse-mounted engines in all its automobiles for years, now Honda was juggling its technologies, putting a longitudinal-mounted engine in the Legend and rear-wheel drive in the NSX!

THE UN-JAPANESE FIRM?

It should be clear by now that Honda is a special kind of company. On the one hand, it is unmistakably very Japanese, purely by dint of its location, its origins, its development history, its people. On the other hand Honda does not seem to fit the Japanese model very well: it had no help from MITI, it has no *keiretsu* and it doesn't participate in Japan Inc. Its management emphasizes decentralization, individualism, youth, lack of class structure, its production workers don't work particularly long hours, its geography diverges from the Toyota City model, it has always been oriented towards product innovation, and from the beginning it has been keenly interested in the outside, Western, world. As we said at the start of this chapter, to the Westerner Honda may look very Japanese, but to the Japanese Honda looks quite Western.

Yet to argue over how Japanese or un-Japanese Honda is would miss the point. Where Honda excels is in the combination of different characteristics. Where there is advantage in vertical pyramid, Honda retains it. Where horizontal and diagonal links can be fruitful, Honda builds these. And the same approach applies to all sorts of dualisms: individual/group, Taylorism/group work, human/technology, spatial dispersal/spatial concentration, youth/experience, product innovation/ process innovation, and so on. In each case innovative organization and ideas create less a trade-off than a retention of both elements.

It is this double side to Honda's character as a company that made it the obvious candidate to develop a global local corporation, to create new paths that Japan's more traditional companies would follow, to build not only the true Japanese multinational manufacturing enterprise, but, by exporting its Japanese side to the West too, to build a type of multinational enterprise never seen anywhere before.

Notes

1. Carl Nash, in 'Discussion'; Douglas H. Ginsburg and William J. Abernathy (eds), *Government, Technology, and the Future of the Automobile*, New York: McGraw-Hill, 1980, pp. 314–15.
2. Tetsuo Sakiya, *Honda Motor: The Men, the Management, the Machines*, Tokyo: Kodansha International, 1987 (2nd edn); Sol Sanders, *Honda, The Man and His Machines*, Boston, Mass.: Little, Brown, 1975.
3. For fuller discussion of the Honda Motor Co. in Japan and Mr Honda's role between 1950 and 1980 see Setsuo Mito, *The Honda Book of Management*, London: Kogan, Page, 1990; Sakiya, *Honda Motor: The Men, the Management, the Machines*; Sanders, *Honda, The Man and His Machines*.
4. Mito, *The Honda Book of Management*, contains many instances.
5. 'Japanese auto industry: working hours reduction and the labor shortage', *Asian Motor Vehicle Business Review*, 1991, pp. 2–12.
6. Mito, *The Honda Book of Management*, pp. 70, 109, offers a good layman's explanation of CVCC technology.

Part II

A 'Self-Reliant Motor Vehicle Company' in North America

Introduction

Japan's vehicle exports to the United States and Canada boomed during the 1970s, with its share of the big US market soaring from 4 per cent in 1970 to 23 per cent in 1980. All eyes turned to the Japanese automobile industry. Why were the Japanese so successful? What could American industry learn?

But as imports from Japan increasingly displaced automobiles manufactured by the Big Three – General Motors (GM), Ford, and Chrysler – new questions arose. North American factories whose products could no longer be sold were being closed (principally at Ford in the period around 1980), and tens of thousands of jobs were disappearing, devastating whole communities in traditional automobile-producing regions like Michigan. Simultaneously, trade deficits with Japan rose steeply, and automobile trade accounted for almost the entire gap. The issue for many Americans and Canadians became how to stop the Japanese before they did further damage to one of the central pillars of the North American economy.

By the early 1980s the Big Three were clamouring for protection. Domestic parts makers, national politicians and leaders of the United Automobile Workers' (UAW) union joined a chorus of demands for national action. The critics *knew* why the Japanese were so successful. The reason was simple: *unfair competition*. Having production bases in Japan simply gave Toyota, Nissan, Honda *et al.* too many advantages over their Western counterparts: they could exploit a cheap and servile workforce, they could transfer costs to a subservient sector of little parts maker firms, and all the while MITI looked after their interests. Factors like these explained the Japanese cost advantage. Measures to protect the automobile industry in North America were therefore fully justified.

In the short term, said the critics, Japanese imports should be strictly controlled. Then, Japanese firms should be obliged to build their own manufacturing plants in North America if they wanted to sell their products there: just like the Americans, GM and Ford, did in Europe. Investment in 'transplants' would bring jobs to compensate for the damage that exports from Japan were inflicting on the economy. It would help balance the trade deficit. But most importantly, it would eliminate all those unfair advantages due to operating from a base in

Japan. With competitive equilibrium thus restored, the Japanese advance would be stopped in its tracks.

Tensions between Japan and the United States came to a head in the early 1980s as the US economy entered recession but Japanese automobile sales continued unabated. To diffuse the political pressure, in 1981 Japan agreed to limit its exports to the United States through a 'Voluntary Restraint Agreement' (VRA). Total exports were reduced somewhat at first, to 1.76 million automobiles per year, rising in steps to 2.3 million by 1985.

Then, all of a sudden, it seemed, the second demand was also being met: the Japanese were building factories in the United States. By 1984 Honda, Nissan and Toyota were each assembling vehicles at North American factories (the latter tentatively at first, through its NUMMI joint venture with General Motors). Mazda, Mitsubishi, Subaru, Isuzu and Suzuki all followed by the late 1980s, leaving only the tiny Daihatsu without a transplant (see Table II.1). By the mid-1990s annual production capacity at the Japanese transplants will surpass 2.7 million per year. That's enough to supply nearly 20 per cent of a continental market which reaches about 15 million sales in good years.

The VRA remained in force at 2.3 million per year until 1992, when Japan unilaterally reduced it to 1.65 million. By that time exports had fallen off from their mid-1980s peaks, down to 1.7 million in 1991. That decline reflected diversion of Japanese home production to meet the booming domestic market of the late 1980s, as well as stubborn economic recession in North America. In small part it also reflected growing transplant capacity. There was, however, no dramatic fall in exports to compensate for the dramatic rise in transplant output.

Inevitably, by the turn of the 1990s, a North American market now shrinking following the end of the Reagan boom years began to experience severe problems of overcapacity. There were enough factories to build five automobiles for every four that could be sold. The long recession after 1989 turned a brewing problem into open crisis.

While some of the transplants delayed their plans to reach full capacity output, this time around it was General Motors that really bore the brunt. The world's number one automobile producer had seen its home-market share decline from 44 per cent in 1980 to 35 per cent in 1990. Meanwhile, the Japanese share rose to 30 per cent of the automobile market (25 per cent of the combined auto and light truck market). GM had spent the 1980s investing in all kinds of ultimately dubious technological projects designed to leap ahead of the

Table II.1   The Japanese Transplants in North America: Assembly Factories

Assembly plant	Location	Original Parents (Some ownership proportions have since changed)	Production start date	Announced annual capacity
Honda	Marysville, Ohio	Honda (100%)	1982	360 000
Nissan	Smyrna, Tennessee	Nissan (100%)	1983	440 000
Nummi	Fremont, California	Toyota (50%) GM (50%)	1984	350 000
Honda	Alliston, Ontario	Honda (100%)	1986	100 000
Mazda	Flat Rock, Michigan	Mazda (100%)	1987	240 000
Toyota	Georgetown, Kentucky	Toyota (100%)	1988	440 000
Toyota	Cambridge, Ontario	Toyota (100%)	1988	50 000
Diamond-Star	Bloomington, Normal, Ill.	Mitsubishi (50%) Chrysler (50%)	1988	240 000
Cami	Ingersoll, Ontario	Suzuki (50%) GM (50%)	1989	200 000
Subaru–Isuzu	Lafayette, Indiana	Fuji Heavy Indus. (51%) Isuzu (49%)	1989	120 000
Honda	E. Liberty, Ohio	Honda (100%)	1990	150 000
Nissan–Ford	Avon Lake, Ohio	Nissan (N.A.) Ford	1991	130 000
Total annual capacity				2 820 000

Source: Various press reports.

Japanese and save the company in one fell swoop: buying out high-tech companies, building 'Factories of the Future', launching the expensive Saturn project. Now it paid the price.

After resisting the inevitable for several years, by 1992 GM had been forced to announce the closure of 21 of its underutilized manufacturing plants, with 80,000 employees to lose their jobs in the early 1990s. Tens of thousands had already been dismissed as GM 'downsized' from 525 000 employees in 1985 to 400 000 in 1990. Thousands more would follow. And the secondary effects were widespread, reaching down to hundreds of domestic automotive parts makers, squeezed out of existence as their traditional markets dried up.

The result so far is that by the mid 1990s Japanese producers could be in a position to control 35–40 per cent of the North American market – if they think it wise on the political front – with half of these vehicles imported and half manufactured at transplants in the United States or Canada. Whatever happened to the 'level playing field' – manufacturing cars in North America – that was supposed to stop the Japanese advance once and for all?

3 Honda's Big Push

When we announced our plan in 1980, industry analysts and many of our competitors thought it was too great a risk. It definitely was not viewed as a competitive threat.[1]

In late 1982, at a production line in the middle of Ohio, the Honda Motor Company became the first Japanese firm to make automobiles in North America. Honda claims that it had already decided upon North American production well before protectionist demands had peaked in the 1981 VRA. Indeed when the company first announced its investment in an Ohio motorcycle plant in 1977, it was clearly testing the waters for bigger things.

But the decision to proceed with an automobile factory had been a difficult one. When the seemingly crazy idea that the medium-sized Honda should concentrate its resources on building a factory on hostile North American terrain was first mooted in the mid-1970s, internal studies confirmed that financial losses were inevitable. In the end, Honda made a classic Honda decision on whether to go ahead. The decision was 'no, but yes', which meant: take a big risk, but also take as many precautions as possible.

So it was that shortly after motorcycle production started at Marysville in late 1979, an automobile assembly plant was announced for an adjacent site. Both sites were also next to a big automotive test track that the government of Ohio had constructed during the 1970s precisely in the hope of attracting new automotive investment to the state. Production of Honda Accords (second-generation 4-door models) began in late 1982, and the first assembly line reached its full production rate of 150 000 per year in mid-1984.

Honda's investments in North America grew by leaps and bounds during the 1980s (Table 3.1). Production rose from nothing before late 1982 to over half a million per year only eight years later. Honda's production capacity in North America now exceeds the total annual production at car-makers like Volvo, Saab, Rover, BMW or Mercedes-Benz. That achievement must rank as one of history's most remarkable build-ups of industrial manufacturing capacity.

Let's take a closer look at the sheer speed of Honda's big push into North American automobile manufacturing.

Table 3.1   Honda's Big Push into North America

Year	Annual automobile output	Investments and major events
1977		Announcement of motorcycle assembly plant, Marysville, Ohio
1979		Motorcycle production begins
1980		Announcement of automobile assembly plant adjacent to motorcycle plant, to assemble Accord model
1982		Automobile production begins
1984	138 000	Major expansions announced: doubling size of automobile plant, Honda Engineering and R&D facilities to be established, Anna, Ohio engine plant to be built, automobile assembly plant to open at Alliston Ontario
1986	238 000	Announcement of further 20 per cent capacity increase for Marysville automobile assembly plant, second line at Marysville starts to make Civic model, Anna plant starts to make Civic engines, Alliston plant begins Accord production
1987	335 000	Announcement of further expansion plans: to build second US assembly plant close to first at East Liberty, Ohio, to export vehicles to Japan and elsewhere, to purchase test track site from the state of Ohio, to expand Honda Engineering and Honda R&D at Marysville, to increase Anna output to meet 85 per cent of North American engine needs. Begins production of 2-door Accord at Marysville (unique to this site)
1988	413 000	Starts exports of Marysville Accords and motorcycles to Japan. Alliston plant starts production of 3-door Civic model
1989	440 000	Production of Civics begins at East Liberty plant
1990	537 000	Production of Accord station wagon derivative begins at Marysville (not made anywhere else)
1991	550 000	Begins export of Accord station-wagons to Europe
1992	568 000	Begins production of 2-door Civic at East Liberty and Alliston (unique to North America). Now exporting to 18 countries.

ONE INVESTMENT FOLLOWS ANOTHER

The first assembly line had not quite reached full production, early in 1984, when Honda announced plans to construct a second line at the same plant. Annual capacity of the factory would be doubled to 300 000 cars per year, and the model range expanded with the addition of 4-door Civics and 3-door Accords.

Shortly before production on the second line was due to start in 1986, and after much of the new investment was in place, the original plans were revised. Output growth would be accelerated with full capacity boosted to 360 000 cars per year, a rate achieved during 1987, the original target date for reaching the 300 000 level.

Meanwhile, in 1984 the company had announced construction of a small Canadian assembly plant, at Alliston Ontario, with capacity to build 40 000 4-door Accords per year. By late 1988 this plant too had doubled in size to reach 80 000 cars per year, switching to make the 3-door Civic, a model not manufactured in Ohio. By the early 1990s that plant's annual output was exceeding 100 000 per year.

Announcement of a fourth assembly line came in 1987, with a planned 150 000 vehicle capacity. A new factory was to be sited at East Liberty, Ohio, a couple of miles from the Marysville plant. In fact the two factories are located at opposite ends of the automotive test track, which Honda purchased from the state government. East Liberty production of 4-door Civics began in late 1989, though the recession in North America led Honda to delay the expected rapid ramp-up of production to full capacity.

Construction of an engine plant at Anna, Ohio, a little village less than an hour to the west of Marysville, was announced in 1984. By 1986 the Anna plant was casting and assembling both motorcycle and Civic engines, and by 1987 had reached a production rate of 70 000 Civic engines per year. The plant also started casting aluminium wheels for the 2-door Accord variant that had replaced the 3-door version at Marysville.

Since 1987 the Anna engine plant has boomed into a massive integrated plant for production of a range of aluminium and steel mechanical components. That year saw the announcement of a major investment to allow casting and assembly of clutches, cylinder heads, and suspension systems at an iron-casting, machining and assembly unit, beginning in 1988. Finally, when plans for the East Liberty assembly plant were unveiled, a further investment was proposed for

Anna to cope with the new production targets, bringing engine and drive-train production to around 500 000 units per year by 1991.

Honda's first research and development facility in North America had been opened in Torrance (Los Angeles), California in 1975. The 'sporty' Civic CRX variant, introduced in 1983 specifically for the North American market, was partly designed in California. Honda R&D established operations at Marysville in 1985. Step by step it has been building facilities for parts and vehicle testing including durability, noise and vibration laboratories, purchasing, design and administration functions. Target employment for R&D in California and Ohio is 600 by the mid 1990s.

By 1989 Honda R&D North America was developing Honda's first station-wagon/estate variant of the Accord model ready for introduction in 1990. Like the 2-door Accord introduced in 1987, this vehicle has been manufactured only in the United States. Honda has made a great deal of the Accord station-wagon project in publicity terms, portraying it as important evidence of the company's commitment to a full design and manufacturing capability in North America.

Honda Engineering (EG) was also established at Marysville in 1985, ready to aid with model changeovers that year. Target employment for the mid-1990s is 200. Engineering capabilities have been built up steadily. The engineering staff has a mock production facility to test the stamping dies it builds (the first were for the 2-door Accord in 1987). In 1988 it installed its own assembly robot system (door-handle sub-assembly) for the first time in the Marysville factory, followed in 1989 by manufacture of all the major dies for the new version of the 3-door Civic to be built at Alliston. In 1990 the engineers made the dies for the Accord station-wagon.

THE GAMBLE PAYS OFF: AND HOW

Throughout the 1980s Honda simply couldn't make enough of its automobiles to meet North American demand. While in the 1970s growing North American demand had been met from Japanese production, in the 1980s Honda had moved very swiftly indeed to accelerate local American and Canadian output. Inventories were constantly low and very little advertising was needed to sell the vehicles. Demand began to level off in 1989, when recession first began to bite and the then current Accord version was in its last months of production. Even so, that year Honda marked a major milestone by overtaking Ford as producer of the best-selling car – the Accord – sold in the United States, a feat repeated in 1990 and 1991. (Ford just pipped Honda to the post in 1992 with a frenzied sales campaign to regain the symbolic leadership title.) Honda moved close to overtaking Chrysler as the third largest automobile vendor in the United States.

Honda's risky big push into North American production had turned out to be a gold-mine. The losses predicted at the outset didn't materialize. Indeed instead of taking three years to break even the initial Marysville plant investment took less than one, and its profits paid back its own capital costs after only two years. The later investments were covered by recycling North American profits.

Only in 1992 did Honda temporarily falter in the North American market. Accord sales began to fall off and production output was cut back. Acura marque sales too dropped back, though they remained higher than those of better known rivals like Toyota's Lexus and Nissan's Infiniti brands. East Liberty output levels were still only at two-thirds of capacity. Yet it is important not to mis-read these signs. A new Accord model was to be introduced in 1993, the Acura problem was swiftly recognized and preparations begun to tackle it (including hiring the person who had masterminded Mazda's aborted plan to introduce its own up-scale brand), and an American-designed 2-door Civic was introduced in 1992 to boost East Liberty capacity. Moreover, plans were announced to broaden Honda's range with purchase of re-badged Isuzu Rodeo leisure-utility vehicles from the troubled Subaru-Isuzu transplant in Indiana. Plans were being laid too to introduce Honda's first mini-van by 1994. Reaction to faltering, then, was swift.

Notwithstanding its own efforts to make sure the North American factories were profitable – efforts that we will be examining in further detail in the rest of Part II – Honda was given a timely financial shelter by the 1981 VRA. With Japanese imports held down, vehicle prices in North America were pushed up 'artificially' for several years. The Big Three took full advantage, raking in record profits in the mid 1980s. Japanese firms too made money hand over fist, particularly by reorienting their exports – now limited in absolute numbers – towards their new larger and more profitable cars.

Honda was able to increase not only its unit prices, providing a helpful breathing space in the crucial mid 1980s, but its sales too as its unrestricted Ohio and Ontario assembly lines started up one after the other. While the Big Three, led by GM, spent their financial windfall on expensive but questionable technologies, or diversifying their financial interests into the defence industry, or amassing war chests, Honda ploughed its profits back into North American production facilities just as fast as it could.

The American protectionist strategy that was supposed to slow down the Japanese invasion only handed Honda the resources to speed up its own market penetration, and the insurance policy to protect its gamble, all on a plate.

Honda's strategic shift towards becoming a profoundly American-oriented company, which had started with the decision to abandon mini-car production to concentrate on Civic output in the early 1970s, had now given the company a huge production base in North America. By the early 1990s Honda's profit margins in North America were still its highest in the world, with the US market contributing over half of the company's global profits.

MARYSVILLE BECOMES AN EXPORT PLATFORM

Production in North America overtook Honda's imports from Japan for the first time in 1989, as imports began to decline and local production continued to grow. The nature of the imports shifted too. While during the 1970s it was Suzuka and Sayama that churned out Civics and Accords to meet insatiable North American demand, by the end of the 1980s production of these models for North America – by far Honda's biggest sellers there – had largely been switched to Marysville, Alliston, and East Liberty (which made four-fifths of all Accords and two thirds of all Civics needed in the United States and Canada). Imports from Japan were now increasingly made up of Honda's growing series of niche-oriented models like those in its up-market Acura line (Table 3.2).

Then in 1988 came another surprise initiative, when Honda became the first Japanese company to export its North American automobiles back to Japan. The model chosen was the 2-door coupé version of the Accord, which had just entered production, made solely at Marysville and principally for the American market.

Now came the ultimate test. In the early 1970s, the key measure of a Japanese manufacturing company's ability to compete in the global market-place had become customer response in North America, and Honda's eyes were fixed on that challenge. Fifteen years later the tables had been turned. Japan's car buyers had become so used to the

Table 3.2 Imports to the United States from Japan Decline, and Honda Switches Imports to its Upmarket Acura Automobiles

Year	Acura	Honda	Total	Proportion Acura (%)
1987	109 470	312 218	421 688	26
1988	128 238	265 122	393 360	33
1989	142 061	251 569	393 630	36
1990	138 384	252 377	390 761	35
1991	143 708	177 562	321 270	44
1992	120 100	173 027	293 127	41

Source: Various press reports.

automobiles of superior quality and innovative characteristics that their own firms were selling that American cars were frequently viewed as of shoddy quality and uninspired design. How would the Japanese consumer react to Honda's 'Made in America' automobiles?

Instead of trying to conceal the Accord coupé's origins Honda made the most of them. The overall concept behind the Accord in general was already aimed squarely at the American market, and the 2-door coupé version was not a popular configuration in Japan anyway. If this was not enough to identify the car's origins, Honda hammered it home, sticking an 'import edition' label on it and selling only left-hand-drive versions in a right-hand-drive country. Nobody would be left in doubt that this was an *American* automobile, albeit one which, strangely, was made by a Japanese company with a reputation for innovative ideas.

Honda's first goal, then, was to build a niche market in Japan for its North American product. With the initial barrier of quality concerns surmounted, sales gradually increased. Honda's position in the league table of importers to Japan has improved in parallel (Table 3.3). By 1991 and 1992, when the US-built Accord station wagon (like the coupé the station wagon is also not really a Japanese type of automobile – seen until recently as too much like a commercial vehicle) was added to the coupés and took the lion's share of Honda import sales, Honda was outselling the combined total of Big Three sales in Japan. Only the Germans – VW-Audi, Mercedes, BMW, each with 30 000 to 45 000 sales in Japan – remained ahead. But then Honda had only been importing two usually unpopular derivative types of a single model which was designed for American, not Japanese, tastes in the first place.

Table 3.3   Honda's American Automobiles Begin to Sell in Japan

Year	Honda's Japanese sales of US-built automobiles	Honda in the league table of automobile importers to Japan	Honda imports as proportion of Japan imported automobile sales (%)
1987	9	25th	0.0
1988	5395	5	4.0
1989	4697	8	2.6
1990	7534	7	3.4
1991	14302	4	7.2
1992	19835	4th	10.7

Source: Various press reports.

Honda has also used its North American facilities to supply other overseas markets, including Korea, Taiwan and Israel, which have been closed to direct exports from Japan for various political reasons. Then in 1991 the company launched another innovative venture, one which completed the global circle, when it began exports from Ohio to Europe. A *Japanese* company was exporting *American* cars to *Europe*. The Accord station-wagon came first, followed in 1992 by the Accord 2-door coupé. 1992 also saw the addition of Hong Kong and Australia as destinations for North American Hondas, now being exported to 18 countries all over the world.

None of this means that exporting automobiles from North America has been easy for Honda. Japan in particular has proved a tough nut to crack. The original 1987 forecast was for overseas sales of Honda's North American products to be 50 000 in Japan and 20 000 elsewhere by 1991 (which would have accounted for 12 per cent of North American capacity). In Japan, novelty value boosted early sales beyond expectations, but it has been harder to shift the products out of the niche 'curiosity' market at which they were first aimed. The 50 000 target for Japan in 1991 was missed by a long way (see Table 3.3), as was the overall export total of 70 000 (in fact 27 000 cars were exported).

Honda's response, however, has been characteristic: in 1990, it became the first automobile producer in North America to make right-hand drive cars (on the same production lines), even though only relatively small numbers were needed (principally for Japan and the United Kingdom). In 1992 the Big Three were still gearing up to make their first right-hand-drive automobiles (General Motors' first was not expected until 1995). At Honda exports were catching up with expectations, at over 55 000. Addition of 2-door Civic exports in 1993 was set to provide a further boost, pushing the proportion of North American automobiles exported to over 10 per cent.

Honda's exports from North America have played a number of roles in overall corporate strategy. First, they have allowed increased utilization of the manufacturing capacity there, particularly as the economy entered recession after 1989. Second, they have broadened the market base (and so spread development costs) for niche products made in North America. Third, they have allowed access to otherwise closed markets, under the political umbrella provided by the United States. Fourth, they have been profitable, aided by a weak dollar and top-of-niche marketing and pricing policies. Last but by no means least, the exports have played important political roles for Honda both in the United States and in the importing countries. We return to these points in the context of the organization of the global local corporation as a whole in Chapter 11.

UNAVOIDABLE POLITICS

A decade after its automobile manufacturing began in North America, Honda was able to announce that all aspects of production – design, development, production engineering, manufacture, and sales – were now located in North America. There was even a growing programme of exports. But as we'll see, none of this was to placate the American and Canadian critics of Honda and the other Japanese producers.

Transplant investments, have spawned a series of difficult political controversies. Many transplants were given massive subsidies and aid packages by state governments anxious to attract them to their region: free infrastructures and labour-force training, tax reductions, and the like. These later provoked fierce local debate in some states, becoming central political issues in election campaigns. (Honda had received little aid in comparison with other transplants, and has not provoked this kind of controversy.)

Then the US Federal Government was criticized by domestic components manufacturers for allowing the establishment of foreign trade zones around the transplants, which permitted duty-free importation of parts and materials from Japan. More problematic still in political terms have been patterns of employee-hiring which appeared in a number of cases – including Honda's – to exclude non-whites, and the threat to the very future of the United Automobile Workers' labour union that was to follow its exclusion from worker representation at the biggest transplants, Nissan, Honda and Toyota.

We'll return to these vital questions of discrimination and labour unions at Honda in Chapter 6. But before doing so we are going to take a close look at the biggest political nightmare of them all, one in which Honda has become a central character. Simply put, the question that has dogged the company has been: are Honda's Accords and Civics really 'made in America', or are they merely assembled at 'screwdriver plants', built up from components mostly imported from Japan?

Note

1. Koichi Amemiya (President, Honda North America) 'Accord sparked Honda success as US Maker', *Automotive News*, 9 November 1992, p. 16.

4 Screwdriver Plant or Independent Automobile Producer?

Well, right now in the auto business 'produce here' is an over-statement. In the typical Ohio Honda or Tennessee Nissan the high-value parts, transmissions and most engines are produced in Japan. That means US workers miss out on jobs offering not only higher pay but greater opportunity for learning and advancement.[1]

I'm concerned that lately, emotional things have been getting a bigger spotlight than the facts themselves.[2]

By the mid 1980s, as a wave of Japanese producers followed Honda to open transplants in North America, critical eyes in the domestic automobile industry searched for new targets. They soon alighted on the components and materials used in the new Japanese-owned factories: where did they come from? Put another way, do the Japanese really make whole automobiles in North America, at functionally independent subsidiaries? Or do they simply assemble kits of parts imported from Japan at 'screwdriver plants', in which case most of the manufacturing activities that add the value – and the jobs – remain in Japan, and the Japanese producers retain the advantage of their own (exploitable) parts-maker infrastructure?

These questions have framed a stormy debate in North America, and Honda has been deeply implicated in it. The controversy threatened to spread to Europe in the early 1990s as Honda started to export its Accord station-wagons to European Community countries.

At the root of the debate over transplant 'parts sourcing' lie questions that are fundamentally economic: from Honda's viewpoint, its cost structure, its ability to transfer its Japanese-style relations with parts makers to North America have been implicated; from the critics' viewpoint, the health – even survival – of North America's own automotive parts making infrastructure, its firms, employees and communities have been in question.

Critics have attempted to push their claim of a Japanese 'screw-driver' ruse to the forefront of Japan–United States relations. By the 1992 US presidential campaign it seemed as though they had at last succeeded. If we want to properly understand where Honda sources its automobile parts for North American production we are going to have to tiptoe through a minefield of facts, viewpoints, interpretations, and even disinformation.

In the first part of this chapter we look at the parties involved in the debate and examine the claims and counterclaims they have made. This way we can get begin to grapple with the highly politicized environment in which Honda has been operating in North America. In the second part of the chapter, we look at Honda's parts sourcing in practice, and we subject the claims and counterclaims to detailed scrutiny. Then, in the third part, we ask (bearing in mind the dualist-inspired nature of the question) whether Honda in North America is really an independent subsidiary, or just a screwdriver plant, and we ask whom the continued criticism of Honda and other Japanese firms has affected most: Honda, or the critics themselves.[3]

CONTROVERSY IN THE UNITED STATES

Has the American debate over transplant parts sourcing focused on the strategic role of the automobile industry in a US national strategy towards global economic restructuring and foreign competition? Criticism that transplants were mere 'screwdriver plants' might have been expected from a broad coalition of domestic assembly companies and parts makers, local, state and national politicians and union leaders defending the national interest. On the contrary, the debate dissolved into a series of fragmented issues linked to the self-protection of particular groupings. The broad group of actors which around 1980 had been calling for limits on Japanese exports and for transplant investments melted away. It didn't reappear until the next recession, in 1991 and 1992, and the 1992 US presidential campaign. But by then it may have been too late.

The Critics' Alliance

Since the early 1980s, domestic independent automotive parts makers and their representative organizations such as the Motor and Equipment Manufacturers' Association (MEMA) and the Automobile Parts and Accessories Association (APAA) have engaged in a vociferous campaign to attack transplant parts-sourcing practices. Honda has been a frequent target, despite being the first to invest in a transplant and, all agree, having the highest local content level (proportion of each vehicle actually manufactured in North America) of all the transplants.

The domestic parts-maker firms have acted in coalition with a group of Congressional representatives from districts whose local economies rely heavily on domestic automotive parts makers, such as southern Michigan and northern Ohio. The overall approach of this critics' alliance has been to try to make a political issue of Japanese parts sourcing practices on patriotic grounds. Domestic parts makers have even threatened to raise the issue of 'national security'.[4] But at root, their chief concern was that Honda and the other transplants simply were not buying automobile parts from them for new made-in-America automobiles. We'll take a look at the specific arguments they raised in a moment, but first, let's look at what other players have done.

The Other Players

An important factor for the critics has been the lack of active backing for their alliance from other potentially interested parties during the period in the 1980s when Honda was establishing its parts sourcing strategy.

The Big Three remained on the sidelines, not surprisingly, considering their own newly acquired penchant for global sourcing, including imports of both automobile parts and whole Japanese, Mexican and Korean cars for sale under Big Three nameplates. Only occasionally did Big Three representatives join the fray to complain about the growing US trade deficit: to which, with their meagre exports and their push towards global sourcing, they were not insignificant contributors in their own right.

The Federal government in Washington has also been notable by its absence from the critics' alliance. Moreover, the state and local governments of the very same states where Big Three assembly plants and automotive parts-making factories, workers and communities are concentrated – Michigan, Ohio, Indiana, Illinois – as well as those of adjacent states – Kentucky, Tennessee – have actually tended to take the side of the Japanese. The state and local governments had vigorously sought all Japanese transplant investment, welcoming it with often generous financial aid. They have then generally refrained from criticism of transplant activities lest their state or locality should develop a reputation as being a hostile environment and therefore unattractive to further investment.

Was the critics' alliance aided by labour unions? The United Automobile Workers' union offered some, but only limited, support. While the union represents almost all production employees at Big Three factories, only a small fraction of employees at independent parts makers belong. Anyway, during the 1980s the UAW's attention was not focused on expanding union influence and membership amongst parts makers. Instead, its hands were full responding to some of the other impacts of Japanese competition: trying to hang on to jobs and conditions at the struggling Big Three firms, and attempting to retain its full coverage of assembly factory employees, which had been dealt a powerful blow by the successes of some transplants in keeping the union outside the factory gates (see Chapter 6). Despite the Japanese presence, union membership was declining rapidly, from 542 000 in 1984 to 412 000 in 1992, a fall of nearly 25 per cent.

The result is that domestic parts makers and their allies within localized territorial coalitions were more or less isolated, waging a lonely war in the political struggle for control over components and materials markets in the burgeoning Japanese segment of the North American automobile industry.

The Attack on Parts-Sourcing Practices

While strategically weak, the critics of transplant parts sourcing proved vociferous, mounting a continuous barrage of hostile commentary against Japanese automobile producers that attracted support in the media and among academic observers. Their first wish would have been to institute a national policy to defend the interests of the domestic parts industry (for example, that transplants should purchase a certain proportion of their parts from domestic, *American*, companies). The secondary goal was to spread a public perception among patriotic citizens that Hondas and other transplant cars should not be purchased because they were really still more Japanese than American, the transplants being mere screwdriver plants.

Here's what the critics said (see also Box 4.1):

1. *Transplants are just 'screwdriver plants' with low local content: a high proportion of vehicle value still originates in Japan.*

The initial criticism of transplant parts sourcing, repeated so often that it became almost a 'fact', was simply that transplants were screwdriver plants. Local content was claimed to be 50–60 per cent at most, at transplants, compared with 90–100 per cent levels at Big Three firms. Even 50 per cent local content meant that only 20 per cent of the *parts* and *materials* were bought in North America (the rest being accounted for by local assembly). Honda's Canadian assembly plant was derided by the president of the Canadian Automobile Parts Manufacturers' Association as nothing more than a 'glue factory'.

Japanese multinationals as represented by the transplants were compared unfavourably with the 'normal' behaviour of European and American firms manufacturing abroad. Early figures for predicted *foreign* sourcing of 60 per cent for Honda and 68 per cent for Nissan were compared with 30 per cent for the *European*-owned Volkswagen (VW) plant in Pennsylvania (now, ironically, closed).

A study by the United Automobile Workers' union claimed that 200 000 North American jobs would be lost as a result of transplant investments, in part because of new work practices requiring less labour, but also due to the high levels of imported parts and materials used at the transplants.

(Note from the quotations how confident the commentators were, and how they presumed that observed practices would persist into the future.)

2. *Only unsophisticated parts are sourced in North America: high-technology, high-value-added parts production and engineering remains in Japan.*

When it appeared that local content statistics were rising in the later 1980s, domestic parts makers sensed a 'window of opportunity' to gain contracts. But almost immediately they complained that the window was but partly open. Apparently only parts and materials involving low technology and simple low-cost production processes were being purchased in North America, with high-technology, high-cost parts still imported from Japan.

Box 4.1　Transplants are just Screwdriver Plants: What the Critics Said

'Wherever possible, Japanese firms source a far higher share of their cars outside the US than do, say, VW.'[1]

'What is clearly evident . . . is the limited purchase of US parts by the Japanese. While this pattern has eased somewhat, domestically produced Japanese cars still consist of barely 50 percent domestic content. Japanese auto assemblers buy a majority of their inputs from plants in Japan.'[2]

'Japanese manufacturers all claim that at least 50 percent of the value of their US-produced cars originates locally. But that's a smokescreen. The 50 percent local content counts wages paid as well as advertising expenditures, even payments to lobbyists. Meanwhile, the windshields and spark plugs and other auto parts are brought in from Japan, establishing US beachheads for Japanese parts suppliers, but threatening the parts industry here.'[3]

'These Japanese investments will not be strictly comparable to US auto investments in Europe. Virtually all of the value added in GM and Ford products in Europe is European in origin. For Japanese plants in the US, this level of domestic content is beyond reach. Japanese plants in America are for stamping and final assembly. Basic manufacturing processes such as casting, forging, machining, and powertrain component production will remain in Japan, as will high value-added operations such as engineering and research and development. Under present plans, no Japanese manufacturer will have even 50 percent domestic content. This fits the broad pattern of Japanese overseas investments.'[4]

'There's always this great promise that the US economy is going to be improved dramatically as these Japanese companies like Honda and Toyota create jobs and demands for services and supplies. They create a few jobs at tremendous expense to the state taxpayer, but they never wind up creating the demand because they have their loyalty to suppliers back home.'[5]

'The level of imported parts is sure to rise because it will be many years before Toyota, Honda and the rest stop depending heavily on foreign-made components for the vehicles they assemble here.'[6]

'The most sophisticated components and systems of automobiles are apt to be produced in Japan, even if the car is assembled in Michigan, California, or Tennessee.'[7]

'Thus far, Japanese transplants are primarily assembly operations rather than fully fledged, integrated manufacturing complexes along the model of Toyota City or Ford's classic River Rouge complex in Dearborn, Michigan. The major, higher value automotive components have continued to be supplied from Japan.'[8]

'Although the declared intention is for overseas assembly operations to use an increasing amount of locally produced components, it is usual for a proportion of the parts to continue to be sourced from Japan . . . . Parts like gearboxes and axles are likely, in many cases, to continue to be exported from Japan, rather than be sourced locally.'[9]

'[Local sourcing from domestic firms consists of] 'bulky, generic energy intensive' parts, materials and services: small stampings and moldings; seats; trim, weather stripping, and gaskets; and paint, resins, vinyl and adhesives – in short, inputs with relatively low value-to-weight ratios and relatively little process engineering content.'[10]

'Japanese auto parts firms are locating next door to new Japanese auto factories, like the Toyota plant being built in Kentucky, to monopolize supplies to those factories and, using them as a base, to dominate the US auto parts industry . . . The ties with the Big Three, plus the locked-in business from the new Japanese auto factories here, will give these Japanese partsmakers a solid US base. From this base, they can batter the remaining US competition with cutthroat prices.'[11]

Notes

1. Business consultant: Stuart Sinclair, *The World Car: The Future of the Automobile Industry*, London: Euromonitor, 1983, p. 71.
2. Academics: Amy K. Glasmeier and Richard K. McCluskey, 'US auto parts production: an analysis of the organization and location of a changing industry', *Economic Geography*, 63, 1987, pp. 142–59. Passage from p. 144.
3. Journalist: James Flanigan, 'Bush needs to show Japanese he isn't wimp on auto trade', *Columbus Dispatch*, 24 February 1989, p. 13C.
4. Academic: A. J. Dunn Jr, 'Automobiles in international trade: regime change, or persistence?' *International Organization*, 41, 1987, pp. 225–52. Passage from p. 244.
5. President of the (US) National Tooling and Machining Association, referring to the benefits of government subsidies for transplants: cited on p. 6 of Peter Gumbel and Douglas R. Sease, 'Foreign firms build more US factories, vex American rivals', *Wall Street Journal*, 24 July 1988, pp. 1, 6.
6. Academic and government consultant: Dan Luria, 'Transplants and over-capacity: can we afford a second auto supplier industry?' *Modern Michigan*, 1.2, 1989, pp. 4–9. Passage from p. 6.
7. Academics: Robert B. Reich and Eric D. Mankin, 'Joint ventures with Japan give away our future', *Harvard Business Review*, 86.2, 1986, pp. 78–86. Passage from p. 80.
8. Academic: Richard Child Hill, 'Comparing transnational production systems: the automobile industry in the USA and Japan', *International Journal of Urban and Regional Research*, 13, 1989, pp. 462–80. Passage from p. 471.
9. International business and economics magazine *The Economist*: 'Closer to the customer: a survey of the motor industry', 15 October 1988, special section.
10. Academic researchers: David Andrea, Mark Everett, and Dan Luria, 'Automobile company parts sourcing: implications for Michigan suppliers', *Auto in Michigan Newsletter*, 3.2, May 1988. Passage from p. 2.
11. Journalist: R. C. Longworth, 'Japan's script has made-in-USA cast', *Chicago Tribune*, 13 May 1987, p. 3.3.

3.   *Linkages with Japanese parts makers are transplanted too: a wave of Japanese parts makers has followed the masters to North America and they are favoured over equally qualified domestic firms.*

As the major producers were completing their transplant investments, a second wave of new factories came splashing in, as hundreds of Japanese parts makers opened their own transplants during the late 1980s (we will take a look at this phenomenon later in the chapter). Rising local content at the transplants, it was claimed, was due to purchases from these Japanese newcomers, not at all what the critics' alliance had had in mind when calling for increased purchasing in North America.

When previously the transplants had been invited, dared even, to come to North America, now the critics began to talk of a 'Japanese invasion'. One congressional representative from a traditional domestic industry stronghold complained that the Japanese 'come in and establish what amounts to colonies in the US with their suppliers'.[5] The nationalist rhetoric of one article's headline, 'Tora tora tora', with its allusions to Japanese dive-bombers in the Second World War, was clear enough.[6]

Here the UAW did step in. While a decade earlier the union had been at the forefront of those calling for Japanese transplants, by 1990 UAW president Owen Bieber was grumbling:

> When are policy makers in this country going to wake up and realize that when you already have a developed automotive infrastructure in your country, you are a little crazy if you invite foreigners to come and build a second one whose only purpose is to displace the first.[7]

The transplants built by Honda, Toyota, Nissan and the like were increasingly seen as Trojan horses; once they had been pulled inside North America's protected walls, out came dozens of highly competitive little Japanese parts-maker transplants which could never have breached the defences without guaranteed sales to assembly transplants.

It was argued that the new wave of parts-maker transplants would create severe overcapacity and fierce competition. Worse, the newcomers possessed the 'unfair' advantage of a long history of relationships with the Japanese assemblers. It was soon being claimed that '*keiretsu*' links among Japanese firms were following them from Japan, and were blocking the access of highly competent domestic parts makers to Honda *et al.* By 1990 the US Congress was requesting the Federal Trade Commission to investigate whether the Japanese *keiretsu* system was being transferred to the United States in contravention of US anti-trust laws designed to promote open competition.

4.   *Only unsophisticated parts are sourced from domestic firms: high-value-added parts are purchased from Japanese parts-maker transplants.*

A variant of the above two criticisms was that when parts *were* sourced in North America, there was a key difference between the parts purchased from parts-maker transplants and those purchased from domestic firms. The latter were only allowed to supply mundane, low-technology unsophisticated parts, whereas high-value sophisticated components were still imported from Japan or were reserved for parts-maker transplants. Electronic parts, it was claimed, were purchased almost exclusively from Japanese firms, whether in Japan or in North America.

5.   *Parts-maker transplants invade the traditional Big Three markets of domestic parts makers too.*

One of the biggest scares, however, was reserved for the late 1980s, when it dawned on many domestic parts makers that the new Japanese parts maker transplants might not stop with their traditional customers. Some of the newcomers actually intended to start off by supplying Big Three firms rather than transplants, and others – while initially supplying transplants – might soon be seeking additional Big Three markets to boost their North American production levels.

The Issue Comes to a Head

Japanese firms and organisations such as the Japan Automobile Manufacturers' Association (JAMA) and the Washington Japan Economic Institute (JEI) stoutly defended transplant practices. Local content was said to be steadily rising as production became more established. Transplants proclaimed themselves ready to buy from any parts makers prepared to (in an oft-heard phrase) 'meet our requirements in terms of quality, price and delivery'. American consumers, it was said, would suffer most under any legislation to enforce higher local content just as they had with price rises following the Voluntary Restraint Agreement on imports. Moreover, the Big Three were increasingly adopting global sourcing strategies of their own.

The state governments which had offered subsidies to transplants argued that the same packages had always been available to domestic firms. State politicians lauded their 'partnerships' with new Japanese investors. Federal government officials pointed to the benefits of investments by Japanese parts makers in rejuvenating the nation's automotive infrastructure. President Bush added his own voice:

> I welcome Japanese investment in this country. Jobs, American jobs,
> . . . people working that wouldn't have a job necessarily if there
> wasn't that investment.[8]

The critics' alliance was making a fair amount of noise during the 1980s, but not, it seemed, making much of an impression.

Then, in 1991, the tide began to turn. The US economy was in the doldrums. The recession that ended the 1980s boom couldn't be shaken off. President Bush's popularity waned, and he was facing re-election in 1992. Fine, there had been a great victory in the Gulf War. But just what was Bush doing to improve the state of the economy?

Suddenly, Japan came back into focus. There was still a huge trade deficit and Japan imported few American manufactures, especially automobiles. Japanese transplants were thriving, and yet the Big Three were making big losses. During 1991 and 1992 the Japanese automobile industry came under renewed attack from all sides, in a wave of sentiment not seen since the American recession of a decade earlier. The critics' alliance was no longer an isolated voice but one of many.

Accusation followed insinuation. Three separate federal government offices investigated whether the supposed *keiretsu* relationships between Japanese assemblers and their favoured parts makers constituted a breach of American anti-trust free-trade legislation. The tax services looked into whether transplants were manipulating internal costs (transfer pricing) to avoid taxes in the United States.

The Japanese share of the automobile market increased from 28 to 31 per cent between 1990 and 1991, in the midst of recession. The Big Three now moved into action. They brought charges of price dumping on mini-van imports against Toyota and Mazda. They picked up on an old argument that the Japanese domestic market was effectively closed to them by various restrictive practices. Chrysler President Lee Iaccoca called for overall limits on Japan's share of the US market, including transplant production. The call to 'buy American' was heard more loudly. Companies began rewarding employees who purchased American cars, and many excluded transplant output from their definition.

By early 1992 President Bush and the Big Three chairmen were visiting Japan in a grand roadshow together, being seen to 'do something' to reduce the trade gap with Japan. Under the umbrella of the general anti-Japanese sentiment, sympathetic legislators in Congress were drafting new laws to force the transplants not just to increase their local content but specifically their domestic (that is, US-owned company) content. The constant heel-snapping of the critics' alliance seemed to be paying off.

The Japanese knew they had to respond. They said they would accept American safety test results on Big Three cars rather than do their own. Toyota, Nissan and Honda would try to sell more GM, Ford and Chrysler products in Japan (though consumers didn't seem to want them). They would reduce the VRA export ceiling to the United States from 2.3 million to 1.65 million (actual projected exports anyway). They would greatly increase their purchases of parts made in North America by the mid-1990s (also planned anyway). They even raised the prices of their automobiles in order to slow down their market-share increase and offer respite to the Big Three.

How did Honda fare in the political rough and tumble? By the 1990s Honda had become even more vulnerable to American politics because of its increased dependence on the American market and its huge transplant investments. And Honda was singled out for specific attack on the parts-sourcing issue. First came a 1991 University of Michigan study. Based on detailed investigation of a 1989 Honda Accord made at Marysville, the study concluded that although the car had now reached 75 per cent local content by the official US measure that Honda used, only 16 per cent of its value came from parts made by domestic parts makers.

Then, the popular magazine *Business Week*, which had for years been praising Honda as an example of how to run a business properly, asked in a major story whether the Hondas were in fact American cars at all. But the most potent attack came in 1992. Under the Free Trade Agreement signed between the United States and Canada in 1989, any manufactured product with over 50 per cent North American content was entitled to cross the frontier without paying import tariffs. The US Customs Service decided to measure the North American content of the Honda Civics being made at Honda's Alliston factory and imported into the United States. Honda claimed their local content to be 69 per cent. The Canadian government calculated 66 per cent. Surely there would be no problem.

Wrong. The US Customs came up with only 46 per cent local content, under the 50 per cent threshold (in an earlier draft report it had managed to find only 38 per cent local content). Honda would have to pay a 2.5 per cent import duty to the US government, as if the cars came from Japan. But that was the least of the worries, because here was 'another example' of 'Japanese dishonesty'. It made front-page news.

Why the statistical discrepancy? We can't delve all the way into the minefield of how to measure local content here, but suffice it to say that common sense seems rarely to prevail. The Customs Service, strictly following very strict rules, managed to count the Civic's engine – cast, machined and assembled at Anna – as having zero per cent local content. Honda had been counting them as 100 per cent North American, also inaccurate, though probably closer to the truth.[9]

PARTS SOURCING AT THE HONDA TRANSPLANTS

In the face of the critical barrage, Honda had been working hard to create a public image of Americanization. By 1988 it was claiming 'dramatic strides toward the goal . . . of creating a truly American motor vehicle company'. The company-authorized book telling the story of its transplant operations was duly entitled *Honda: An American Success Story*.[10]

Honda vigorously denied the 'screwdriver' plant interpretation. By 1990, local content of the Accord was reported to be 73 per cent, with that of the Civic 71 per cent. The company said it was now planning how to achieve 82 to 85 per cent levels. As early as 1987 Honda had claimed to be establishing a 'self-reliant motor vehicle company' in the United States. The firm's North American executives countered the idea that Japanese multinationals were somehow different, announcing that their firm was actually building a manufacturing complex as separate from its parent corporation as Ford's in Europe.

Honda went on its own public relations offensive. The Honda Accord station-wagon was advertised as a real American product. And Honda chose to react angrily and publicly to the findings of the US Customs study, claiming it to be politically motivated and knowingly inaccurate. The Japanese and Canadian governments both stepped in to complain, the former worried about the lack of transparency in the rules, the latter seeing a blatant attack on Canada itself and its policy of attracting foreign investment based on free access to the whole North American market.

Is it really possible to measure Honda's North American content objectively? Yes it is, but the difficulty is that this would require detailed information about Honda's purchasing patterns, information that Honda is hardly likely to divulge given the charged political atmosphere and the distorted use of statistics that has already ensued. We shall now leave behind the question of local content measures, satisfying ourselves with the following statement that will shortly become clear: Honda automobiles made in North America possess a high level of local content, with a substantial number of parts made in North America, but they also rely upon a substantial number of components still imported from Japan.

So, what has been Honda's strategy for parts sourcing in North America? How has the strategy developed over time? Does Honda purchase its automobile parts from Japanese firms in Japan, Japanese parts-maker transplants, or domestic firms? Which kinds of parts are purchased from which kinds of firms? Are the patterns the same at first-tier level (when Honda itself buys parts) and second-tier level (when Honda's parts makers buy their parts)? Having answered these questions, we can then return to the criticisms of transplant parts sourcing we looked at earlier and ask: are the critics justified, or is it all a big political smokescreen?

Parts Sourcing in Two Periods: 1982–6 and Post-1986

Honda purchased certain materials and components in North America from the start of manufacturing operations at Marysville. These included low-value, bulky, generic products from several domestic firms, including sheet steel for car bodies, tyres, batteries, glass, paints and plastic. At this early stage too, an independent Japanese manufacturer of electrical auto parts, Stanley Electric, built a factory 30 miles from Marysville to furnish Honda with outside lamps and lamp assemblies. Honda itself organized, and took an 80 per cent share in, Bellemar Parts Industries, a joint-venture factory built adjacent to its assembly plant for preassembly of seats and wheels (the two minority partners were Japanese firms which supplied these parts to Honda in Japan).

Over the next few years, Honda carefully sought new parts suppliers in North America, but established relations with few. With 27 local parts makers when production started, by 1985 the figure had risen only to 40 firms. Almost all were domestic firms, supplying either bulky tyres, batteries and the like, or small plastic and metal body parts.

There have certainly been some 'success stories' among domestic firms. One domestic parts maker which gained a Honda contract early on was Capitol Plastics, an Ohio producer of plastic components. The first component it supplied was for motorcycle production, after three years of negotiations. Then in 1983, the firm was awarded a contract to furnish a single automobile part. Capitol Plastics' Honda business steadily expanded afterwards as it supplied more and more parts. But despite such cases (and Capitol has been cited time and again in media stories) during the first four years of production local content remained low, with almost all electrical and mechanical components, whole engines and drive trains imported from Japan to Los Angeles, and then trucked two thousand miles across the United States to Ohio.

After 1986, however, local sourcing increased rapidly. There were several reasons. Key among them was that Marysville production was doubled in 1985–6 leading to greater economies of scale. Between 1985 and 1987 the dollar's value against the yen halved, which greatly increased the cost of importing parts from Japan. The total number of firms which directly supply Honda with parts and materials made in North America soon increased swiftly (Table 4.1).

Local sourcing both deepened and broadened. Mechanical and electrical/electronic components had been sourced almost entirely

Table 4.1   Honda's Local Sourcing Accelerates after 1986

Year	Direct suppliers	Of which Japanese transplants (minimum)
1982	27	—
1983	—	—
1984	—	—
1985	40	—
1986	—	—
1987	60	—
1988	110	28
1989	180	—
1990	194	76
1991	240	—
1992	250	—
Mid 1990s (projected)	300	—

Sources: Press, Honda North America, author's research.

from Japan at first. But after 1986 there was a shift towards local sourcing of mechanical components, as well as expanded purchasing of low-cost low-technology parts. But what specific roles have been played by domestic and Japanese-owned firms?

Honda has steadily increased its purchasing from domestic firms. Indeed the company maintains that its first priority in sourcing for North American production has always been (1) domestic parts makers, followed by, in order, (2) joint ventures or technical licensing arrangements between domestic firms and established (that is, Japanese) Honda parts makers, (3) established parts makers that construct transplants or in-house Honda production and, finally, (4) importation of parts from Japan.

However some kinds of components have been hard to obtain from domestic parts makers, because the domestic manufacturers of many components are owned and controlled directly by Big Three firms, with their higher levels of vertical integration than in Japan. Moreover, Honda argues that in the initial years of car assembly when output volumes were relatively low, many independent domestic firms did not believe it worthwhile (and by implication, lost their chance) to meet Honda product specifications. While many domestic firms have since submitted to the 12–18 month process of seeking qualification as a Honda parts maker, less than 5 per cent of applicants have been accepted (which still does not imply a contract), since the rest 'do not meet Honda requirements'. (We'll subject Honda's relations with domestic parts makers to closer scrutiny in the next chapter.)

The apparent shortage of domestic manufacturers has led Honda to buy components from firms with no experience in manufacturing automotive parts, such as the Ohio plastics firm WEK, which had previously made tubular children's toys, and the Marysville firm K&K, which previously tested lawn seeds but now assembles loudspeakers.

What kinds of parts do domestic parts makers make for Honda? Table 4.2 confirms that Honda tends to purchase low-technology generic parts, together with basic materials, from first-tier domestic parts makers.

Transplant parts makers had only trickled into Ohio at first. A second Bellemar Parts Industries plant started production in 1985, making an assortment of steel components such as exhaust systems, seat frames and brake lines. Honda had also persuaded four smaller Japanese parts makers to form the joint-venture firm KTH, which constructed a plant to manufacture various stamped and welded steel components. The Japanese window manufacturer Asahi Glass

Table 4.2   What Kinds of Parts Honda Buys from Domestic Parts Makers:
First Tier

aluminium ingots	robot repair
batteries	sheet steel
batteries	sheet steel
carpeting, flooring and mats	sheet steel
jacks	speaker assembly
paint	specialty steel bars
paint	specialty steel bars
parts carts	specialty steel bars
plastic products	stamped parts
plastic products	stamped parts
plastic products	stamped parts
plastic products	stamped/welded parts
plastic resins	tooling components
rivets	trim

Sources: Honda, press sources.

established two plants, AP Technoglass to make windows, and
Belletech to finish (add trim to) them. Finally, by 1986 Honda had
begun to buy parts – seat belts, steel wheels, steering wheels – from
newly arriving parts-maker transplants which also began to supply
Nissan's new Tennessee factory.

But after 1986 the pace of parts-maker transplant investment
accelerated rapidly. As the decade ended and the flow came to an
end, there were over 76 Japanese parts-maker transplants in North
America making parts for Honda.[11] While Honda continued to aid
some of them through minority financial support, the vast majority of
the new investments resulted from more independent decisions to
maintain their market links to Honda, and to try to overcome the
doubling of dollar costs caused by the dollar's dramatic decline in value
during the mid 1980s by shifting production into the dollar zone.
Meanwhile, the parts-maker transplants already established were
adding new production lines, doubling or tripling their production
capacities to meet Honda's burgeoning output.

What kinds of parts does Honda buy from parts-maker transplants?
A sample is shown in Table 4.3. In stark contrast to the parts supplied
by domestic first-tier firms (Table 4.2) transplant parts makers make a
whole range of parts, including the most complex high-value
manufactured components, but also in fact many low-technology,
low-cost parts too.

Table 4.3   What Kinds of Parts Honda Buys from Parts-Maker Transplants:
First Tier

accelerator cable	interior parts
aluminium die castings	machine tools
arm bushing/joint assemblies	plastic compounds
assembled seats	plastic injection-moulded parts
assembled seats	plastic interior decorative parts
assembled wheels	plastic moulding, interior door panels
automatic speed-control devices	plastic parts
automobile keys	plastic parts for windscreen washers
bearings	power steering systems
belts and hoses	power window motors
body-part stampings and welds	pressed metal parts, engine
brake assembly	mountings, bolts and brackets
brake components	prototype parts for new models
brake lines	radiators
brake-line tubing	radios and cassette players
catalytic converters	rubber engine mounts
chassis and suspension components	rubber weather stripping
chemically treated replacement parts	seat belts
coil suspension springs	sheet steel
condensers, evaporators, tube	sheet steel
assemblies for air-conditioners	shock-absorbers
condensers, evaporators and heat	sound-control products
exchangers for air-conditioners	stabilizer bars
crankshaft forgings	stamped and welded parts
door locks	stamped parts
door sashes	steel moulds for plastic injection
engine ducts and rubber mouldings	moulding
engine valves	steering-wheels
exhaust systems	suspension-control arms
fitted windows	thermostatic expansion valves for
floor mats	air-conditioners
front-lamp assemblies	transmission controls
fuel injectors	V-belts
gaskets	wheel hubs
generators and alternators	windscreen wipers
heat exchangers	windscreen wiper motors
hose and tube assemblies	wire springs for transmissions
indoor panels and sun visors	wiring harnesses
instrument clusters for dashboards	wiring harnesses
interior fabric panels, door and roof	wiring harnesses
panels	

Source: Author's research.

Who Supplies the Parts Makers?

Comprehensive information on the significant second-tier level – who supplies the parts makers – is hard to obtain, and perhaps for this reason this important issue has been passed over in the political debates. Fortunately we are in a position to plug this gap, at least for the case that matters most, second-tier suppliers to the parts-maker transplants.[12]

The data at second-tier level (Table 4.4) confirm and magnify the conclusion just drawn from first-tier analysis. There is a striking divergence in the kinds of components and materials supplied to Honda's transplant parts makers between domestic sources and Japanese – transplant or imported – sources. Again it is the Japanese firms which manufacture the complex high-technology automobile components (as well as some low-tech parts), whereas domestic firms have been brought in to make generic materials like metals, plastics, chemicals, fabrics, foam and cardboard. Moreover, parts-maker transplants occupy some pivotal second-tier positions making important subcomponents (Table 4.5).

Honda Parts-Maker Transplants: Springboards for Big Three Sales?

Many of Honda's parts-maker transplants don't supply Honda exclusively. Are they moving into Big Three markets too? The answer is yes. When questioned about this as early as 1988, 25 per cent were already supplying a Big Three firm, and more than half of these also had another Big Three firm in their sights. A further 22 per cent intended to sell to a domestic producer in future. Thus a total of 47 per cent had already established or intended to establish sales links to the Big Three.

SCREWDRIVER, INDEPENDENT, OR . . . ?

Are the Honda factories screwdriver plants or are they the core of an independent manufacturing structure? Or is this a false (dualist) question that we will never satisfactorily answer because neither is correct? We return to the criticisms of transplant parts sourcing reviewed earlier and respond to each for the case of Honda.

Source to Table 4.4:   Author's research.

Table 4.4   What Kinds of Parts Honda's Parts-Maker Transplants Purchase from Different Sources

From Japan

aluminium wheels	oil-less bearings
all at start	plastic components
all components at start	plastics and vinyl
bolts	precision machine parts
components	rubber parts
components	seat belts
door components	steel
electrical components	tubing
finished parts	tubing
metal components	washers

From transplants in North America

aluminium wheels	plastic pellets
automotive belts	seat covers
chrome plating for moulds	seat covers
electric motors	steel
electrical components	seat frames
electrical components	steel wheels
fabric	tyres
plastic components	windows

From domestic firms in North America

aluminium ingots	padding-barrier
aluminium ingot	paint
aluminium ingot	plastics
asphalt	plastic buttons
box	plastic materials
box	oil
cardboard	plastic pellets
carpets	plastic pellets
castings	plastic suspenders
castings	polymers
catalyst for catalytic converter	processed steel
chemicals	rubber
chemicals	rubber material
chemicals	sheet metal
chemicals	sintered iron
chemicals	sintered iron
cloth goods	springs
cloth goods	steel
cloth goods	steel plate
cord welt	steel tubes
fabric	thread
foam	treated fabric
foam	tyres
foam pads	tyres
glass	urethane chemicals
hardboard	vinyl
insert/facing material	vinyl
material/piece goods	windlace
moquette	wire

Table 4.5   Parts-Maker Transplants Occupy Pivotal Second-Tier Places Too

Second-tier part made by transplant	First-tier part made by transplant in which it is used
rear-window brake light	rear-window plastic insert
electrical part	instrument panel
plastic part	interior plastic part
seat cover	seat
seat cover	seat
window	window plus surrounding trim
seat frame	seat
steel wheel	wheel plus tyre
plastic resin	plastic part
plastic colour compound	plastic part
seat part	seat
seat part	seat
chrome plating for dies	stamped metal parts

Source: Author's research.

1.   *Transplants are 'screwdriver plants' with low local content:*

This was correct for Honda during the early 1980s but has not been true since 1986. Honda built up its North American sourcing very gingerly to begin with. However, after 1986, with assembly operations at Marysville an assured success, with the components and materials supply situation in North America fully explored, with production expanded to allow increased economies of scale, and with increased pressure on import costs due to the doubled value of the yen, expansion of North American purchasing into the high-value, especially mechanical, parts followed rapidly.

The critics who implied that low local content was more or less permanent were incorrect in Honda's case.

2.   *Only unsophisticated parts are sourced in North America:*

This was correct for Honda during the early 1980s but since 1987 it has been less and less true. When production started at Marysville, local sourcing did consist largely of unsophisticated parts – materials and generic components – or very bulky items. But with increased local content the nature of parts sourced in North America has changed. Local sourcing has progressed over time from (i) generics (for example, tyres and batteries), materials (for example, sheet steel, glass) and bulky parts (for example, seats), to (ii) Honda-specific small metal stampings (for body parts) and interior and exterior trim (for example, moulded plastic, interior panels, rubber parts), and to (iii) major and minor mechanicals (for example, engines, shock absorbers, brakes) and electricals (for example, instrument clusters, motors for windscreen wipers, heaters, wiring).

To continue to claim that only unsophisticated low-value parts are sourced in North America would be incorrect in the Honda case. On the other hand, if the local content of Honda's automobiles is approximately 75 per cent, then one-quarter of each automobile's value is still imported, ample room to keep making many of the key sophisticated parts, particularly electronic components, in Japan.

3.   *Linkages with Japanese parts makers transplanted too:*

This is correct for Honda. Dozens of Japanese parts makers located in North America help raise Honda's local content. These firms often supply the same part to Honda in Japan. Particularly during the early years, Honda invited Japanese firms to establish parts-maker transplants and aided them in setting up operations. A handful of these were firms of which Honda owns all or part. During the later and larger wave of transplant investments, decisions were made more independently.

But what role did favouritism and *keiretsu* links play? Honda is an intriguing case for the critics who claim *keiretsu* collusion, because it neither belongs to, nor controls, a *keiretsu*. Moreover, it is the only Japanese auto maker that doesn't even have its own parts makers' association. In fact, there are plenty of commercial and economic reasons to explain the wave of parts-maker transplant investments, reasons related to the availability and capability of domestic North American parts makers, to the interests of the Japanese parts makers, and to the nature of interfirm relations in the Japanese system of producing automobiles. We will take a closer look at these reasons in the next chapter.

4.   *Only unsophisticated parts sourced from domestic firms:*

This is correct for the Honda case. There is a clear division between the kinds of parts sourced from parts-maker transplants and those sourced from domestic firms. Domestic firms supply generic parts, small stampings and materials. parts-maker transplants furnish a whole range of parts: from non-sophisticated but specific-to-Honda parts such as interior and exterior trim to more complex parts like seats and major metal stamped and welded parts (for example, exhaust systems) and highly sophisticated mechanical and electrical components. Significantly, the same pattern is visible at second-tier level.

5. *Parts-maker transplants invade Big Three markets too:*

This is correct. Honda parts-maker transplants represent an important competitive threat to domestic parts makers which have heretofore relied upon Big Three markets.

We return to the question of whether Honda runs screwdriver plants or an independent company in North America. As we have seen, it might have been reasonable to call Honda's Marysville factory a screwdriver plant during the first few years of production. But this was hardly surprising given the firm's concentration on getting the assembly plant functioning and exploring the unfamiliar manufacturing environment.

There is no evidence that Honda expected to maintain mere screwdriver operations indefinitely. If it did, then it soon changed its mind. Moreover the pattern of parts purchasing analysed above clearly refutes claims that Honda's transplants are 'screwdriver plants' now. Indeed a broadly based and deeply rooted parts-making infrastructure was in place only six to seven years after automobile assembly began, which with hindsight must appear a remarkable feat.

Does this mean that Honda in North America is becoming an independent company – along the lines of Ford or General Motors operations in Europe – as implied by describing the operations as 'self-reliant'? Honda makes much of having located activities falling under all the categories involved in automobile-making – design, development, engineering, manufacturing, parts sourcing, sales – in North America. The company seems to want to paint a picture of having reached, or being about to reach, Step 3 on the multinational ladder.

But is it really Honda's goal to run North American operations quite independently of Japan or Europe, as Ford and GM have historically done in Europe? We saw in the last chapter how the North American operations quickly became integrated into global marketing, with exports to Japan, Europe, and other parts of the world. As far as parts purchasing is concerned, nobody has yet talked of 100 per cent local content, and there is no reason to expect it. The global local corporation plans its parts sourcing on a global scale. This doesn't mean that all its parts deliveries criss-cross the world, as in global sourcing. But neither does it mean that each local manufacturing structure buys all its parts locally. Honda seeks the best of both worlds for its North American operations, sourcing locally when that is advantageous, sourcing in Japan when that option is best. The solution to the dualist puzzle: independent *and* screwdriver.

Let's pause for a moment to think about how Honda itself describes its North American operations. It doesn't talk of 'independence', it talks of 'self-reliance'. The difference is easy to pass over. It is our conventional understanding of the multinational enterprise that leads to the question: 'screwdriver or independent?'. 'Self-reliant' looks like independent but it isn't. Independence implies being separate, but self-reliance doesn't. It means being able to do things for yourself. Similar, but not the same.

The Japanese don't choose their words lightly. They sometimes struggle to find the right word, to the point of inventing new words that combine two or more existing ones. But perhaps sometimes we treat them as if they were less careful than they are.

Who Has Been Most Affected by the Parts-Sourcing Debate: Honda or the Critics?

What effect has the political debate over parts sourcing had? In the first place, little effect upon Honda. In the second place, perhaps a perverse effect on the critics themselves.

First, there is no evidence that Honda has embarked upon unsound parts-sourcing strategies in order to placate critics. Despite the attacks, the critics' alliance had little political muscle throughout the 1980s when Honda was building up its local sourcing. Not until 1991–2 was the issue picked up as one of a number of questions about Japanese competition, all related to the American recession, forthcoming elections and so on. And we should not forget that the transplants now have friends in significant places, including politicians representing most of the states where transplants are located and where they provide economic stability and employment. Thus Honda felt able to react openly and strongly to the US Customs study criticizing its Canadian-built automobiles.

In the second place, certainly some of the criticisms were correct for Honda at a certain period, and some of them remain so. But many analysts have succumbed – perhaps too willingly in their desire to place their Japanese competitors under political pressure – to the temptation of assuming that a momentary picture represents the future.

If the critics have been astute and politically devious, they actually knew the real situation, but wanted to play on a potent public issue when they asked: but are they *really* American automobiles? In some cases this does seem to have been the case. On the other hand, what is worrying is that the critical attack on the local content issue follows a well-worn path: it is yet another misleading interpretation of the Japanese firm and the reasons for its success that avoids the real issues, and not in Japan now, but right on its competitors' home-ground. Honda builds half a million automobiles in North America every year and purchases most of the parts for their manufacture from factories located there and employing Americans and Canadians. But too many people have clung to the notion that the Japanese are somehow still cheating, unfair, that they run screwdriver plants, that they have their secretive *keiretsu*, and so on.

Aren't there some hard truths still not being faced? Surely an honest appraisal of what Honda is doing in North America is needed if we are to respond coherently. Waging the competitive battle in the political arena is a risky business in the first place. Worse, it too easily leads to self-delusion and an inability to face up to the real challenges posed by companies like Honda becoming multinational manufacturers.

Notes

1. James Flanigan, 'Contract talks open window on US priorities', *Columbus Dispatch*, 2 September 1990, p. 2G. (Flanigan's column is reprinted in newspapers across the United States.)
2. Honda President Tadashi Kume, cited in Paul Ingrassia, 'Ford's Petersen, on eve of retirement, is 'uneasy' with Japan's role in US', *Wall Street Journal*, 28 February 1990, p. B6.
3. A brief glossary may prove useful. 'Domestic' refers to North American-owned firms operating in North America. 'Assembly transplants' are Japanese-owned and run automobile assembly plants in North America. 'Parts-maker transplants' are Japanese-owned and run plants manufacturing automotive components and materials in North America. 'Local' refers to any production that takes place in North America. 'Local content' figures refer to the proportion of a vehicle's value constructed in a given area: in this case, North America.
4. Peter Gumbel and Douglas R. Sease, 'Foreign firms build more US factories, vex American rivals', *Wall Street Journal*, 24 July 1988, pp. 1, 6;

Drew Winter, 'Japanese come to town', *Ward's Auto World*, April 1986, pp. 35–40.

5. In Gumbel and Sease, 'Foreign firms build more US factories, vex American rivals', p. 6.
6. Joseph M. Callahan, 'Tora, tora, tora: 232 Japanese supplier plants are gunning for your business', *Automotive Industries*, February 1989, pp. 89–112.
7. Cited in Scott Pendleton, 'Honda leads the transplants', *Christian Science Monitor*, 30 January 1990, p. 8.
8. Cited in Roger Lowe, 'Foreign-owned plants termed good for US', *Columbus Dispatch*, 4 April 1990, p. 1A.
9. Local content can in fact be accurately measured (though consent of the manufacturer would be needed) but nobody agrees on the rules. Strict definitions of what is local count only the cost of parts bought, not including for example, capital equipment costs. Looser definitions count expenses like advertising in the local market. In between there are myriad questions that allow different interpretations. For instance, does a part purchased for $100 in North America but which includes $30 of subcomponents from Japan count as $100 or $70? Common sense says the latter, but in practice the former may be reported because at 70 per cent local content it is considered sufficiently 'American'. Various branches of the US government use different rules for different purposes. The companies invariably advertise their score according to the definition that shows them in the best light. In Europe the situation is as bad if not worse, with transplants continuing to utilize very lax measures of local content allowed them by the United Kingdom government which is 'protecting' the several transplants located on its territory from criticisms elsewhere in Europe.
10. Robert L. Shook, *Honda: An American Success Story*, New York: Prentice Hall, 1988.
11. These are parts makers individually confirmed by the author. There are doubtless more of them, but 76 represents a reasonably good sample for our study.
12. A detailed questionnaire survey sent to parts-maker transplants in 1988 allows the compilation of a substantial body of evidence on second-tier suppliers to Honda's first-tier parts-maker transplants. Parts-maker transplants were requested to identify up to five of their major suppliers. This information is available for 30 of Honda's transplant parts makers, a large enough sample to allow clear patterns to emerge. The questionnaire survey was undertaken at Ohio State University by the author, James Curry, Martin Kenney, and Sandi Kulkowski-Walden.

5   Honda's Just-in-Time Region

Competition in the North American market is going to become very tough in the early 1990s. The firms which succeed will be the ones with the best supplier network.[1]

The dualist analysis we have become used to in the West paints a sharp contrast between the Japanese system by which automobile parts are manufactured and parts makers relate to assembly companies on the one hand, and the prevailing Western system, on the other. As a result, many doubted that this element of Japanese management techniques, which all agreed was quite fundamental to their success, could work effectively outside Japan. In this chapter we'll see how Honda has tackled this problem, by studying how its network of parts makers in North America is organized and how the firms involved in it interact with each other.

In Chapter 1 we looked at several pairs of opposite ideas that are said to portray the distinction between Western and Japanese parts-supplying relationships. These included: in-house production/outsourcing, dual sourcing/single sourcing, conflict/cooperation, short-term/long-term, spatial dispersal/spatial concentration, and market relationships/vertical integration. The 'Japanese model' of relations between an automobile assembler and a parts maker consists of either one from each pair – outsourcing, single sourcing, close cooperation, long term relationships, spatial concentration – or a variant of one of the opposites – the 'quasi-integration' of the *keiretsu* with its multiple-tiered pyramid of parts makers.

In transferring this system abroad, several difficulties were foreseen. Most frequently mentioned were the loss of ability to exploit a hierarchy of little, often family-run firms where wages were low, and loss of the spatially concentrated 'Toyota City' type of production complex that permits just-in-time deliveries of components to assembly lines. Moreover, if Japanese assembly firms attempted to make purchases from Western parts makers, it was suggested, the legacy of a whole history of running interfirm relations according to the Western model – with its opposite culture, practices, mindsets, organization – might sabotage the transfer process.

How would Honda function in such an unfamiliar environment? Would it have to modify – perhaps weaken or undermine – its particular style of relations with parts makers when it localized its parts sourcing in North America?

In this chapter we'll see how the organizational frameworks and the practices of Honda's North American network of parts makers are closely related to the pattern of parts sourcing that emerged in the previous chapter. The explanation behind those controversial patterns will come into focus. We'll also see how problematic the dualist approach can be in sensibly discussing parts-supplying relationships, with Honda adopting neither the Japanese nor the Western model but pursuing the best of both worlds.

By the end of the chapter it will be clear to what extraordinary lengths Honda has gone to ensure successful functioning of its network of parts makers in North America. The surprise is that some of the modifications that have been made, far from undermining it, may be making it work better than in Japan.

The chapter proceeds as follows. First, with the aid of case studies, we examine the organizational frameworks that characterize interfirm relations. Second, we look at the spatial framework that creates what we will call Honda's 'just-in-time region'. Third, we examine the practices that make the network function effectively on a daily basis. Our focus here is purely on the relationships between physically separate firms and factories. We'll look at what goes on inside them in Chapters 6 and 7.

ORGANIZATIONAL FRAMEWORKS

There are seven distinctive organizational features to examine:

1. Tiering arrangements
2. Outsourcing and in-house production
3. Complex interfirm divisions of labour
4. Single and dual sourcing
5. How parts makers reduce their dependence
6. Joint ventures
7. Formal ties

The boxed case studies show some real examples that we will refer to as we proceed.

1. Tiering Arrangements

The vertical tiering of parts makers is rather 'shallow' in comparison to the Japanese model. For the most part, the pyramid is only two to three tiers deep beneath Honda, at which point it has already reached down into manufacturers of basic materials. On the other hand, the establishment of a detailed division of labour among parts maker transplants has resulted in creation of more tiers than normal in North America.

A prominent example of the latter is seat manufacture. In Western firms this is traditionally undertaken within the final automobile assembly plant (this is now changing rapidly due to mimicry of Japan). By contrast, Honda's network of parts makers has separate firms that respectively sew materials and assemble seats, and which are inserted as new tiers between the fabric manufacturers and the assembly plants (see Cases 1 and 2).

The overall tiering pattern is symbolically represented in Figure 5.1. As we saw in the last chapter, the transplant parts makers mostly manufacture specific automobile components at first-tier (and sometimes second-tier) levels. Basic materials and simple parts are

Figure 5.1   Idealized Parts-Sourcing Hierarchy

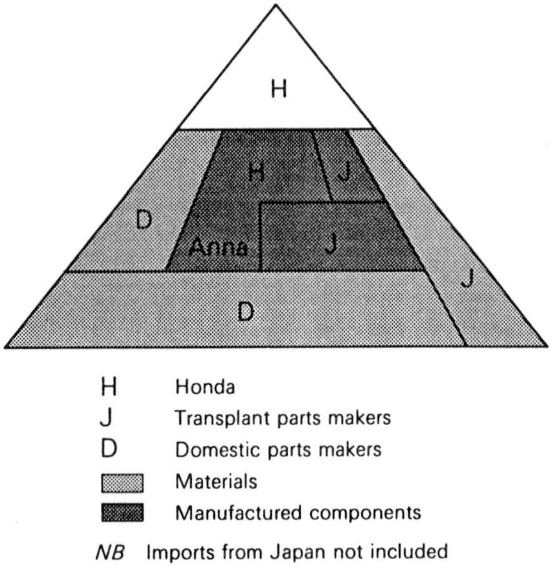

H	Honda
J	Transplant parts makers
D	Domestic parts makers
	Materials
	Manufactured components

NB Imports from Japan not included

Box 5.1   Case Studies of Interfirm Links

Case 1: Windscreen Manufacture

This case illustrates multiple tiering and one type of joint venture. During early production years at Marysville, Honda had purchased windscreens from the domestic firm Pittsburgh Plate Glass (PPG), which also made the glass sheet. PPG proved unable to resolve persistent quality problems, and Honda asked the major Japanese glass producer Asahi Glass to establish transplant operations, which opened in Ohio in 1986. Now a second-tier factory at Bellefontaine, near Marysville, occupies the pivotal place in the parts-maker chain, making the windscreens from sheet glass. A separate, first-tier transplant located in the same town adds trim to the windscreens to prepare them for final assembly at Honda.

PPG was allowed to become a 20 per cent joint-venture partner in the second-tier plant, with the stated aim of teaching it new manufacturing methods. PPG still supplied raw glass, although it was later reported that Asahi was considering establishing its own glass production transplant because quality problems at PPG could not be resolved. Asahi has subsequently used its Bellefontaine factories to supply other Japanese assembly firms located in North America, and also to supply windscreens to another Japanese firm located in Japan, which installs them in vehicles which are then exported back to the United States.

Case 2: The Crankshaft Production Chain

This case illustrates multiple tiers, an extensive division of labour, and an intricate spatial pattern. The crankshaft production chain begins in the traditional steel town of Warren, Ohio, passes through a new transplant parts-maker, moves on to a domestic firm in a traditional industrial area, and then back to the transplant before continuing on to Honda's Anna mechanical components plant and finishing in Honda Accord engines taken to Marysville (see the table below). Worth noting is the presence of Japanese ownership far upstream in the parts-maker chain, in steel-making other than sheet steel production.

Making Crankshafts Involves Multiple Tiers of Firms
and Several Journeys Within Ohio

Firm	Ownership (% Japanese)	Process	Location
Copperweld Steel	64	making steel bar	Warren
TFO Tech	100	forging crankshaft	Jeffersonville
Metallurgical Services Inc.	0	heat treatment	Dayton
TFO Tech	100	further treatment	Jeffersonville
Honda	100	machining, assembly into engine	Anna
Honda	100	assembly of engine into Honda Accord	Marysville

Sources: Press reports.

Case 3: A Joint-Venture Transplant

This case reveals a complex woven pattern of interfirm relations instead of
the crisp linear tiering structure of the 'Japanese model'. This joint-
venture transplant makes several different plastic parts for Honda.

The Japanese parts-maker involved was initially reluctant to construct a
transplant factory. Less than one year after production had started in
1987, however, it had become embedded in a complex web of interfirm
linkages (see below). Not only is it linked to its major customer, Honda,
and to its domestic suppliers of raw materials, but it has developed a
nexus of relations with other Japanese parts-maker transplants so that the
factory simultaneously occupies diverse niches at both first- and second-
tier level. Moreover, a domestic firm that also supplies Honda with plastic
parts, and which is a potential competitor, successfully pressed to become
involved as a minority partner.

Linkages Developed by a New Joint-Venture Transplant

With Honda:

1. Japanese firm enticed to construct transplant by Honda financial and
   organizational aid. Honda owns 35 per cent of transplant; Japanese
   partner, which is manager, owns 55 per cent.
2. Transplant supplies Honda with three different painted plastic parts.
3. Vice-president seconded from Honda to ensure that 'Honda Way' is
   followed.
4. Honda Engineering approval required for all new subcomponents
   sourced in North America, down to nuts and screws.

With domestic firms:

1. Domestic firm (90 miles away) that supplied Honda and domestic
   assemblers with other plastic parts asked to, and became, 10 per cent
   joint-venture partner in transplant and sought further technical
   collaboration.
2. Bulk raw materials purchased from giant domestic firms and also
   from small domestic firms.

With other parts-maker transplants:

1. Complex part used in subassembly purchased from transplant A (60
   miles away) which also supplies Honda and other parts-maker
   transplants directly.
2. Subcomponent purchased from transplant B (80 miles away) for use
   in component for Honda.
3. Manufactures subcomponent used by transplant C (120 miles away)
   that supplies component directly to Honda.
4. Waste materials processed for reuse by transplant D (25 miles away)
   which also supplies Honda directly.

With Japan:

1. One year after production started nearly all the dozens of very small non-plastic parts required were still imported from Japan; sometimes they had to be flown in at short notice to the regional airport.
2. Engineers to repair some machinery fly in from Japan, causing significant delays and hence difficulties for transplant management.

Case 4: A Web of Relations Around Seat Manufacture

Seat manufacture is the longest established of parts-maker transplant activities. The figure overleaf reveals a sample of the wide array of relationships in which Bellemar Parts (Marysville plant), Honda's major seat manufacturer, is embedded. This diagram includes only part of Bellemar's relationships, revealed in discussions with six of the parts-maker transplants involved.

Since Bellemar itself manufactures more than one component, it is linked to parts manufacturers outside seating, in interior trim, wheels, and brake tubes. The general pattern follows the pyramid in Figure 5.1. Some of the firms are also linked with each other financially.

Case 5: Flexifactories: Reorganizing the Interfirm Division of Labour

Several transplant parts makers manufacture multiple products in the same factory (see other cases). This complicated organizational framework was encouraged by Honda during the early years of production, when Honda output stood at only 150 000 cars per year, and when Nissan was the only other transplant producer in the eastern United States.

The interfirm division of labour deepened over the course of the 1980s to be appropriate to a 600 000 vehicle per year output rather than one of 150 000. As a result, Honda's earliest parts-maker transplants have undergone significant evolutions in the products they manufacture (see the table on p. 120).

This capacity to evolve new divisions of labour indicates an important dimension of flexibility. Here we see 'flexifactories' changing their products like Honda's own Suzuka factory in Japan. As far as parts-makers are concerned, the principle is that the factories and the employees are retained, but they change their roles to make different components as needs evolve.

This process also resembles the 'spinning off' of separate companies which characterizes accounts of the growth of the Japanese automobile industry in the 1950s and 1960s. Note too the shifting pattern of financial holdings as activities change, and the rapidity of organizational restructuring, occurring only 2–7 years after initial production had commenced.

118

Bellemar's Links in North America

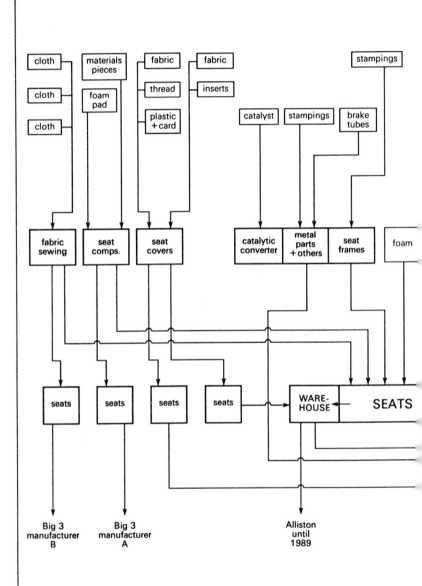

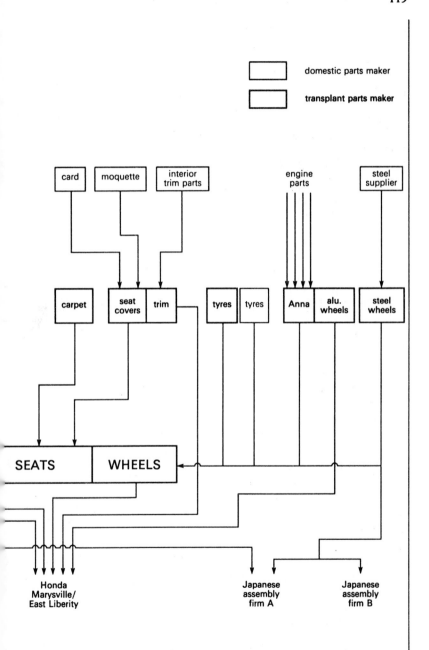

Case 5: (continued)

Deepening of the Interfirm Division of Labour at
Early-Established Parts-Maker Transplants

1987	Shift of brake-line production out of Bellemar Parts Russells Point factory to new specialist Japanese–US joint venture Hisan (Findlay, Ohio, 40 miles away).
1989	Shift of sourcing for Alliston seats from Bellemar Parts Marysville, which had built third production line for this purpose, to new Bellemar factory in Canada: line at Marysville then switches to supply newly opened East Liberty assembly plant.
1989	Shift of some stamping and welding production (together with capital equipment) out of KTH (St Paris Ohio), four-way Japanese joint-venture transplant established in 1985, to Jefferson Industries (Jefferson, Ohio, 45 miles away), 3-way joint venture established by two of the KTH partners and Honda (30 per cent) in 1989.
1989	Honda subsidiary Yutaka Giken, major producer of metal stampings in Japan, builds new stamping facility for torque converters and oil pans adjacent to Bellemar Parts Russells Point factory. Yutaka Giken takes 10 per cent share of Bellemar Parts, Honda increases its share from 80 to 87 per cent, other Japanese partners reduced from 10 to 1.5 per cent each.
1989	Sankei Giken, one of the Bellemar Parts owners reduced from 10 to 1.5 per cent, opens Blanchester FCM in southwest Ohio, to make power steering systems for Honda. Tokyo Seat, the other Bellemar partner reduced from 10 to 1.5 per cent, has meanwhile built several of its own factories in North America, making seats and seat parts for Honda and for other assemblers.

purchased from the existing industrial infrastructure that serves North American manufacturing industry in general.

As we might have concluded from the data we have already examined, Honda has almost entirely bypassed the traditional North American automotive parts industry, and set up its own. Thus Honda, which is also the only transplant producer operating in North America not to have some kind of joint production relationship with a Big Three firm, has established a separate supportive base to supply it with automobile parts. We'll look at Honda's relationships with domestic firms later in the chapter, but for now, suffice it to say that the worries of the domestic firms about being largely cut out of the market were well-founded.

2. Outsourcing and In-House Production

The conventional dualism has it that Japanese producers create far less of the total value added in each vehicle than their Western counterparts because they outsource a larger proportion of their production to parts makers.

At Honda, however, the pattern is mixed. While some processes normally undertaken by the Western automobile producer are indeed outsourced to parts makers, other processes that some Western producers outsource are carried out in-house at Honda (Table 5.1). The conventional dualism doesn't fit Honda's decision to keep certain activities in-house, which derives principally from its focus on key mechanical technologies.

Table 5.1   Vertical Disintegration, Vertical Integration

(A)   Processes outsourced at Honda in North America that are done in-house at some Western producers

> bending brake-tubes into form
> fixing plastic stripping to windows
> seat assembly
> seat sewing
> pressing small stampings
> making steel wheels
> wheel/tyre assembly

(B)   Processes done in-house at Honda in North America that are outsourced at some Western producers

> plastic moulding of bumpers
> casting of engine blocks and cylinder heads
> casting and manufacture of transmissions
> brake manufacture
> casting and machining of suspension components
> casting aluminium wheels (in late 1980s)

Moreover, there is evidence that Honda's practices differ across the world. For instance, in Japan, major body panels are bought in from parts makers. In North America they are made in-house. As we will see, in Europe they are purchased from another assembly company, Rover.

3.   Complex Interfirm Divisions of Labour

Whilst the automobile industry in Japan is commonly described as a structure of distinct tiers, Honda's North American network involves many complex arrangements in which firms occupy more than one tier simultaneously, because they make more than one part. In fact, the threads of interfirm relations weave complex patterns, which are illustrated in all the boxed case studies.

4. Single or Dual Sourcing?

Several parts makers are involved in relationships where they simultaneously collaborate and compete with each other. In Case 3, Honda encouraged establishment of the transplant parts maker even though it already purchased similar parts from a domestic firm. At the same time the domestic firm became a joint-venture partner in its own potential competitor.

Case 4 contains a further instance of collaboration between competitors. In 1988, Honda provided its main seat maker Bellemar with a potential competitor when it began to purchase seats from a second transplant seat maker, Setex, majority-owned by a different Japanese seating firm from the one involved at Bellemar. Setex initially provided special types of seats for more expensive models. Yet the semi-competitive relationship between the two seating transplants has been nuanced by Honda's requirement that Setex deliver its seats directly to the small warehouse within Bellemar's factory where Bellemar places its own seats in sequence for final assembly at Honda. This gives the two firms involved a point of contact and enforces a certain level of collaboration between them. American managers at both plants are quite aware of their peculiar relationship, both collaborative and competitive.

What is the relationship between this framework and the single sourcing/dual sourcing dualism? Each part is purchased only from one firm, so there is no duplication of research and capital equipment effort: the advantages of single sourcing. Yet Honda purchases from separate firms making very similar parts and they know well of the other's existence. Some of the advantages of dual sourcing are therefore also apparent: prices can be compared, and Honda might vary the amount of purchasing from each firm. But, whereas in conventional dual sourcing, parts makers compete 'blind' by tendering offers, in the Honda case the competitors can identify each other, and because they collaborate they know each other's capabilities.

Single sourcing or dual sourcing? The best of both in one system.

5. How Parts Makers Reduce Their Dependence

Many transplant parts makers also sell components and materials to assembly firms besides Honda. In this way they broaden their markets and reduce their dependence. In the last chapter we saw that many are selling or trying to sell to the Big Three. Honda's network of parts makers is also partly shared in common with firms like Toyota, Nissan and Mazda (Table 5.2 and Case 4). Compared to the conventional *keiretsu* model of firms tied together to the exclusion of other relationships, these multiple linkages have clear advantages for the parts makers: permitting economies of scale and reducing dependence on a particular purchaser.

Table 5.2   Several Honda Parts-Maker Transplants Also Sell to Other Transplants – Sample

Transplant assembler	Honda parts makers that sell to it
Nissan	14
Mazda	13
Toyota	11
Diamond Star	5
Subaru–Isuzu	4
CAMI	1
NUMMI	1

Source: Author's research.

On the other hand, a number of transplant parts makers are more or less exclusively tied to Honda. It helps to divide Honda's parts maker transplants into three broad categories. Category A is those firms that can be considered 'exclusive' Honda parts makers (90 per cent or more of output sold to Honda). Category B is firms supplying two or more assemblers (89 per cent to 11 per cent of output to Honda). Category C is firms that are only minor parts suppliers to Honda (10 per cent or less of output). Of our sample group of 76 parts-maker transplants, 32 are in category A, 29 in B, and 15 in C.[2]

6.   Joint Ventures

Joint ventures account for fully 45 per cent of Honda's transplant parts makers. Twenty-eight per cent are part-owned by domestic firms (as in Cases 1 and 3). The other seventeen per cent are joint ventures between Japanese firms.

Joint-venture ownership patterns evolved significantly over the course of the 1980s. Early on, there were several joint ventures involving only Japanese firms, but these became less common over time. Honda's low early outputs encouraged factory-sharing by parts maker transplants to pool overheads. By the late 1980s, with the quadrupling of production levels, this was no longer necessary, and new interfirm divisions of labour developed (see Case 5).

Towards the end of the decade there was a shift towards 50/50 or majority domestic joint ventures between major independent domestic parts makers and Japanese firms. The products have often been specific mechanical components: thus domestic firms like Dana Corporation, ACCO Controls and TRW built new plants with Japanese partners to produce gaskets, transmission control cables and engine valves respectively.

Why this shift towards incorporating domestic firms producing higher-value automotive components via joint ventures? Possible explanations include political sensitivity on Honda's part, adoption of new manufacturing techniques by domestic firms, or agreement that Japanese partners will manage the new plants. These factors may each have played a role.

A different set of Japanese–domestic joint ventures involves domestic firms that had been supplying Honda since early production days – often providing the vital basic materials and generic parts (glass, steel, tyres). Honda had never been satisfied with the performance of some of these domestic firms, and subsequently pressed them into cooperation with Japanese parts makers, usually in order to improve product quality (Case 1).

A significant example involves Inland Steel, one of Honda's three original domestic sheet steel makers. Inland received considerable technical aid from the Japanese steel manufacturer Nippon Steel during the mid-1980s, to improve the quality of steel supplied to Honda, before announcing construction of a new sheet steel plant as a joint venture with Nippon Steel, soon followed by announcement of a second and a third new joint-venture steel plant. Total new investment in the three plants was to be $900 million, making enough steel to build 2.5 million vehicles, about a fifth of North America's total annual production.

Several other Japanese firms have invested in North America's basic steel and rubber industries to supply Honda, though usually by buying into existing plants. Dunlop, one of Honda's three tyre makers, was purchased by Sumitomo Rubber in 1986. In 1988 Kawasaki Steel entered a joint venture by buying 70 per cent of Armco, a Honda sheet steel maker.

These large-scale investments by Japanese steel and tyre companies mean that a substantial part of the basic industrial infrastructure of North America is now also under Japanese control. This is a significant modification to the parts-sourcing pattern we described earlier in which basic materials tend to be bought from domestic firms.

7. Formal Ties

As we have noted already, Honda is an intriguing case among Japanese companies because it eschews some of Japan's characteristic formal inter-firm ties. This does not mean that formal ties are unimportant, however. Financial links between firms play a prominent role.

We have seen the significant number of joint-venture arrangements. Indeed Honda has itself invested in several of its own parts maker transplants: firms like Bellemar are essentially Honda subsidiaries, resembling the spin-off firms Honda has created in Japan to supply crucial components (see Case 5), and there are other transplant parts makers in which Honda holds a minority share (see Case 3).

Which is the correct model: vertical integration or market relationships? Or is it quasi-integration? In fact there is no one characteristic model. There is a wide range of types of formal ties between parts maker transplants and Honda, ranging from the spinoff controlled by Honda, to the minority ownership, to no formal relationship at all.

As we saw above, Honda keeps production of many key mechanical components in-house. And when it does outsource, it retains tight formal control – through partial ownership – over makers of many highly visible parts like seats, dashboards, exterior trim. In yet other cases there is a quite distant, more or less market, relationship.

Whatever their form, however, these ties are clearly meant to last.

SPATIAL FRAMEWORK

Spatial frameworks and industrial location aren't the usual subjects of books on management. Perhaps that is because they do not really appear so significant to the Western firm. But in the Japanese model Toyota City's spatial concentration is often referred to, and it does seems to play a role in just-in-time inter-firm relations.

What is the spatial framework of Honda's network of parts makers in North America? Is it modelled after Toyota City? What role does it play in overall manufacturing operations?

1. Regional Location

Where are Honda and its transplant parts makers located? Honda
selected a site in a rural part of Western Ohio, and most of Honda's
parts-maker transplants chose sites within a one-hundred-mile radius
of Honda. Ohio is one of the United States' major industrial areas,
located at the geographical centre of the traditional 'manufacturing
belt' that stretches from New England to Illinois (Figure 5.2).

Figure 5.2   Honda's Factories and its Transplant Parts Makers in Relation
to the North American Manufacturing Belt

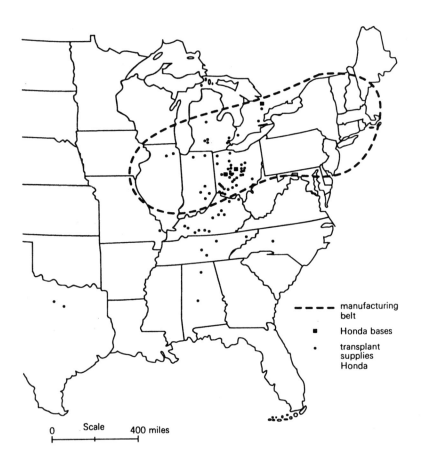

This geographical core of Honda-related transplants has important 'tails' outside Western Ohio, stretching northeast and south, and also has 'outliers' in other manufacturing belt states like Michigan and Illinois. The northeastern tail includes the Canadian assembly plant at Alliston. The more significant southern tail includes a series of transplant parts makers located along the interstate highways that run south from Ohio towards the new factories built by Toyota and Nissan (as well as General Motors' new Saturn subsidiary) in Kentucky and Tennessee.

Like Honda, other Japanese transplants have their own group of transplant parts makers located around them (Figure 5.3). As we saw above, Honda shares part of its parts maker base with these firms. This accounts for the extent of the southern tail: several of these factories belong principally to the Toyota or Nissan transplant parts maker networks. Others belong to the group of Japanese firms – and the Big Three – as a whole.

Are the parts maker transplants located closest to Honda also more dependent on Honda? Recall the ABC categorization described earlier. Transplant parts makers most tightly tied to Honda do tend to be located closest to Honda's assembly plants, whereas the ones less dependent on Honda tend to be located further away (Table 5.3). So parts maker location is closely related to the location of the major purchaser.

Table 5.3   Relationship between Location and Dependence on Honda

Category	Number of transplants(N)	Located in Ohio or Ontario(O)	% (O/N)
A	32	25	78
B	29	10	34
C	15	3	20

Note: Categories   A: 90% or more of output to Honda
B: 11–89% of output to Honda
C: 10% or less of output to Honda

In fact the clusters of Japanese assembly plants and transplant parts makers are neatly separated into different states, Honda in Ohio, Toyota in Kentucky, Nissan in Tennessee, Diamond Star in Illinois, and so on (in Canada, the province of Ontario is too large and the clusters too small to create this effect). In contrast to the traditional

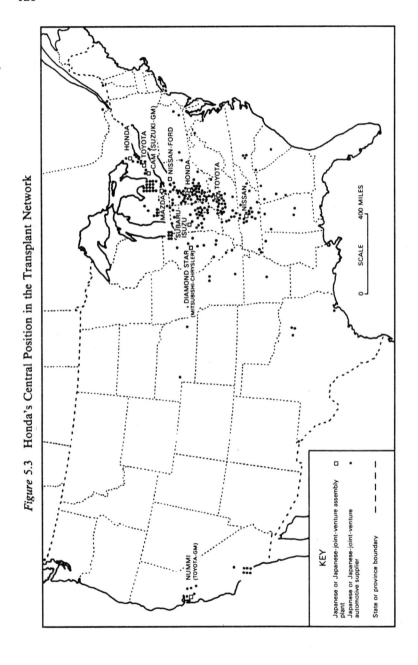

Figure 5.3   Honda's Central Position in the Transplant Network

geography of the US automobile industry, in which the spatial frameworks of the different firms overlapped, as far as Japanese firms are concerned the fortunes of Ohio are tied to one firm, Honda, and its parts maker cluster.

In this way Honda inevitably secures a heightened degree of influence over its social environment (for example labour market), political environment (for example support of politicians) and physical infrastructures (for example new roads). But is this pattern of one transplant cluster per state a purely political Japanese gambit? Probably not; it also reflects a combination of two important economic considerations: clustering is to facilitate implementation of just-in-time deliveries and other interfirm practices (see below), and separation into different states reflects the ideas of Japanese corporate planners who wanted enough room to create labour pools for each firm in each cluster without overlap (we will return to this point in the next chapter).

2. Internal Spatial Framework

Honda's cluster of parts makers is located in the heart of the North American manufacturing belt. However, a closer – local-scale – look reveals that it is slightly 'off-centre', situated largely in rural gaps between the major industrial centres. We can see this best by zooming in on Western Ohio (Figure 5.4).

The Honda assembly plants, together with the engineering and research and development centres, are sited 30 miles northwest of the state capital, Columbus (metropolitan area population around 1 million). Most transplant parts makers have located in rural areas adjacent to small towns stretching south and west, outside the major cities. The urban exceptions are nearly all cases in which a Japanese firm purchased an existing domestic manufacturer.

At this local scale we can look right inside the spatial framework. Transplant parts makers have dispersed themselves throughout rural Western and southern Ohio, but still within a radius of 100 miles (under two hours) of Marysville. At the same time, they selected locations to the south and west of Marysville, rather than evenly dispersed around Honda. This skewed pattern, in which the cluster of factories is set off to one side of its functional centre, means that transplant parts makers are located within a short distance of each other as well as of Honda. (If parts makers were spread uniformly

Figure 5.4   Core of the Just-in-Time Region

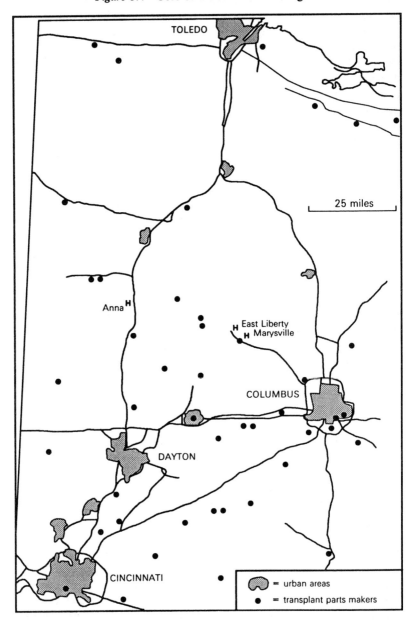

within a 150 kilometre radius around Honda they would still be within two hours of Honda but some would be four hours from each other.)

There are several advantages to this particular spatial framework. At base, the pattern permits just-in-time deliveries of parts, as we'll see shortly. This is all the more important to the extent that a vertical division of labour has developed and lots of semi-finished parts move between factories (see Cases 1 and 2). In this context, the framework plays a useful role in permitting the restructuring of interfirm divisions of labour, since the factories are all relatively close to each other in the first place (Case 5).

3. Rooting in the Existing Industrial Infrastructure

So far we've been examining the transplant elements of the network of parts makers. Where are the domestic firms located? The Western Ohio region that Honda selected is geographically central to the manufacturing belt. The domestic parts makers are nearly all located within the manufacturing belt, though on average further away from Honda than the transplants parts makers (Figure 5.5).

Through their own investments Honda and its transplant parts makers could establish a brand new spatial framework. But with domestic parts makers they have been constrained by the existing industrial geography. Within the manufacturing belt Honda and the transplant parts makers have found suppliers of metal and plastic materials and of semi-finished metal and plastic parts. Outside the manufacturing belt, the legacy of the spatial dispersal associated with previous industrial geographic restructuring out of the manufacturing belt (often to escape from labour unions) is evident, in the supply of textiles from seven of eight firms located in North Carolina, and the supply of tyres from three of the firms located in the deeper southern states. The result of sinking roots into this already dispersed pattern is that, in contrast to most links with transplant parts makers, several of Honda's supply lines from domestic firms stretch over long distances.

Honda has created a functional region of transplant parts makers, concentrated largely in Western Ohio, which is centrally located for access to the North American manufacturing belt. Because this spatial framework has been specifically created to permit particular types of interfirm practices to work efficiently, we will call it *Honda's just-in-time region*. This is a quite novel phenomenon for the West.

132

Figure 5.5 Domestic Parts Makers Supplying Honda or Supplying
Transplant Parts Makers

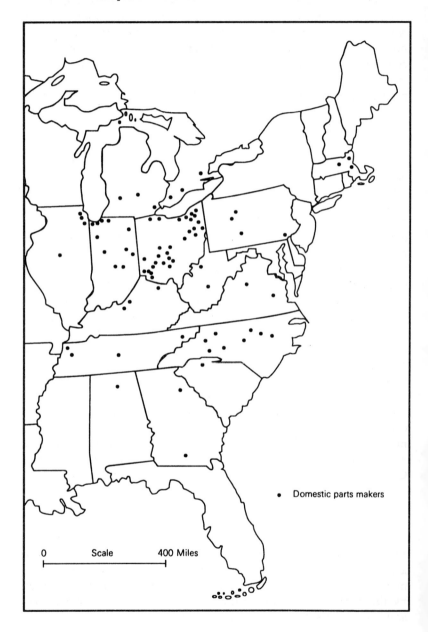

Now we can return to the usual way in which we in the West have interpreted the Western/Japanese difference as far as spatial frameworks are concerned. Has Honda, free to start from scratch in North America, built a clone of Toyota City for itself? The answer is, yes and no. Yes in the sense that, as the maps make plain, geographical concentration clearly is a significant aspect of the just-in-time region's spatial framework. Yes in the sense of a concentration within a political jurisdiction that is reminiscent – albeit in less acute form – of Toyota's domination over Toyota City.

Yet the just-in-time region does not resemble Toyota City at the local scale, where the factories are spread so far apart that to any European or Japanese, for instance, they look positively well dispersed. So as well as being spatially concentrated (at the regional scale), the just-in-time region also follows the Western tendency of spatial dispersal (at the local scale). In a pattern that may now be getting familiar, what we see once again is that striving for the best of both worlds: sufficient spatial concentration to permit just-in-time and other interfirm practices requiring proximity, but also sufficient spatial dispersal to allow the factories to have separate labour pools (see Chapter 6), permitted by an efficient American system of interstate highways, four-lane roads and lightly travelled but well-built and well-maintained rural roads.

While the conventional argument holds that Japanese-style interfirm relations should be harder to operate outside Japan, in the Honda case the reverse may be true. For Honda, which doesn't have its own Toyota City-style production complex in Japan, and whose spatial organization is under constant pressure from cramped sites, high land prices, dispersed factories, and poor transport infrastructures, the just-in-time region in North America is more efficient, less disrupted, less expensive, more easily reorganized if necessary, and indeed avoids the problems of spatial overconcentration that are now making life difficult at plants like Sayama and are forcing a rethink at Toyota City itself.

INTERFIRM PRACTICES

We are now ready to look at how the factories in the just-in-time region are related to each other in daily practice, during the actual manufacture of Honda Accords and Civics, practice which is governed by the organizational and spatial frameworks examined above. We address the following features in turn:

1. Just-in-time between factories
2. Quality control
3. Reducing prices of parts
4. Moving personnel between factories
5. Integration of R&D
6. Honda Engineering's role
7. Intervening inside partner firms
8. Dealing with domestic parts makers

1.   Just-in-Time Between Factories

Just-in-time delivery is the norm at first-tier level. Ninety-two per cent of transplant parts makers say they deliver just-in-time to Honda.[3] Just-in-time is not, however, a single uniform system. Frequency of deliveries varies greatly, from every half-hour or every two hours for bulky components like seats, wheels, fuel tanks, or windows, to every day or every two and a half days for small metal stampings, small trim items and paint concentrates.

In some cases parts makers operate a full system of simultaneous sequential just-in-time manufacturing. Here, parts are manufactured by the parts maker in the same sequence they will be installed in automobiles and at the same time as those automobiles are being made; on the assembly line this is only possible for parts that will be installed towards the end of assembly and where there is therefore sufficient lead time – after cars are placed in their final sequence for assembly – to manufacture and deliver the parts. This system accounts for many of the cases of frequent small-batch deliveries.

But such a complex system is only necessary for parts that vary according to colour or to model version. This is why seat manufacture is often quoted as a good example of just-in-time manufacturing. Indeed Bellemar Parts, the primary seat manufacturer, manufactures and delivers seats within three hours of receiving its orders from Honda.

Two hours is the outer limit in travel distance for firms that deliver frequently. Transplant parts makers located in southern states have adopted what they call a 'modified just-in-time system' due to their distance from Honda; one, located in the south primarily to serve other transplants, utilizes a warehouse in Ohio as an intermediary location. Another firm delivers larger lots less frequently to save on transportation costs.

Just-in-time deliveries are less common at second-tier level. Only 47 per cent of Honda's transplant parts makers report that their own major supplier delivers parts and materials just-in-time.[4] Is this difference due to the larger number of domestic firms involved at second-tier level? Not entirely: while many of the major second-tier parts makers are domestic firms, the proportion of these that deliver just-in-time, 44 per cent, is not significantly below the average.

That delivery frequency at second-tier level is consistently lower than at first-tier is due to the nature of the manufacturing processes as much as to some inability to deliver just-in-time. One factory that supplies Honda eight times per day receives its own main deliveries two times per day. Another factory that supplies Honda every few minutes receives two parts one or two times per day and eight times per day respectively.

Is the system used significantly different from that in Japan? Box 5.2 shows the kinds of modifications made at second-tier level. Here, it does appear that dealing with domestic parts makers can cause problems.

Indeed there is much supporting evidence that the transplant parts makers have had some difficulty persuading domestic firms to deliver just-in-time. One transplant parts maker finds that very large domestic firms like Dupont simply refuse to deliver small amounts of raw materials at regular intervals according to schedules dictated by the transplant, to the great frustration of Japanese staff. On the other hand, a small domestic firm from Northern Ohio that manufactures similar raw materials was eager to accept just-in-time schedules to win new orders from this transplant. Japanese staff prefer to contract with such firms because of what one American manager calls their 'fixation' with keeping a zero inventory level.

Another parts maker transplant keeps a six-to-eight day stock of its domestically supplied raw materials on hand, because the lead time for new orders is three days and there are frequent quality problems with the materials sent.

Besides difficulties related to domestic parts makers, the spatial framework has also caused modifications at second-tier level. It is here that problems arise due to distance. Whereas much of the first tier of parts makers was purpose-built from transplant investments during the 1980s, the second tier relies upon existing and more widely scattered domestic firms.

What kinds of modifications have been made? Typically, there are longer lead times, due both to longer distances and to the slowness of

Box 5.2   Honda's Transplant Parts Makers have Modified Just-in-Time
Systems with their Second-Tier Parts Makers

'Kanban used in Japan, computerized JIT in USA.'

'We cannot always count on this system working because America is much larger and many companies don't practice it'.

'Minimums increased – to allow for full exposure (i.e. larger inventories to ensure all needed parts available).'

'American raw material suppliers are undependable on promised delivery dates.'

'Same as Japan except lead times for US made parts are longer.'

'Until we can source more components in US, we have to maintain a larger than necessary inventory.'

'Can't practice JIT because US suppliers are too unreliable on delivery.'

'We use JIT for some vendors and some parts. We currently utilize a large portion of imported parts and JIT is not possible in that area.'

'Adjusted to compensate for longer lead times required by American suppliers.'

'Modified due to distance. Longer lead times.'

'Some inventories must be maintained due to distance of delivery of products and delivery of suppliers.'

Source: Mail questionnaire

---

domestic parts makers in responding to orders, and larger inventories, either to guard against the risk of late deliveries or because parts delivered from distant domestic parts makers are sent in less frequent, larger lots in order to keep transport costs down. For parts still sent from Japan the same complications arise. Moreover, there is a tendency to keep larger stocks of parts from Japan, both to meet unexpected changes in Honda requirements and as insurance against potential quality problems. (Despite the legendary high quality of Japanese parts, problems do arise. In one case a batch of parts manufactured months previously and sent from Japan turned out to be too small to fit where required, causing great difficulties for the workers installing them at a transplant parts maker.)

2. Quality Control

We will discuss quality-control methods within the factories in Chapter 7 when we look at manufacturing systems. What is of interest here is how quality control works at an interfirm level.

For Honda's manufacturing system to work properly it needs perfect quality of parts supplied: not only an absence of defective parts, but also shipments of the correct quantities. One way to deal with this would be for quality-control inspectors to test all incoming parts. But at Honda it is simply made the responsibility of the parts maker to assure quality. This puts great pressure on the parts makers.

Quality-control staff in charge of incoming parts at Honda have other tasks. At Anna, for instance, it is the quality engineering group that is responsible for parts quality. But rather than inspecting parts when they are received, the group spends its energies on working with parts makers to analyse their production systems and quality-control methods. And the quality engineering group for Anna is based in the Anna factory itself, not at Marysville, so that it physically observes the parts and the processes in which they are used on a daily basis, and so that production staff only need take a short walk to discuss any issues to do with incoming parts.

But it is not as if nobody at Honda inspects the incoming parts. We'll see just who has this task in Chapter 7. And problems are certainly discovered.

When they do occur (ranging from mix-ups of different parts to too few or too many shipped and to actually defective parts), Honda engineers telephone the responsible firm immediately. 'One little thing and we hear about it', according to one transplant parts maker manager. According to another, 'Honda may understand a scratch, but mis-assembly or paint problems are a big deal'. A third parts maker transplant engineer reports that after each incident, there is 'no finger pointing, no excuses either', and Honda requires – for every single defect – a full explanation and a plan to prevent recurrence, prepared and signed by managers and filed within a week. Honda sends its own personnel to parts makers to resolve persistent problems. In turn, every transplant parts maker immediately contacts its own suppliers if it finds any defective parts deliveries.

By the late 1980s the overall parts rejection rate at Honda's Marysville plant was reported as 0.07 per cent (7 in 10 000). One parts maker transplant had only 0.01 per cent of its parts rejected by Honda, which in its case translated into about one per month, although on a new production line a 'high' 4 parts per month was being returned by Honda. Honda rejected 0.03 per cent of parts from another firm, while at a third, which was experiencing considerable quality problems with its major domestic parts maker, the reject rate from Honda sometimes reached 0.1 per cent.

3. Reducing Prices of Parts

Most contracts between Honda and its parts makers in North America follow the Japanese model of expecting price reductions over the life of contracts. In turn, Honda's parts maker transplants have instituted the same practice at second-tier level.

Honda justifies this on the basis of 'learning curves': as manufacture of a part continues, the firm should become more adept and make less mistakes, and therefore be able to reduce costs. Domestic parts makers are not spared this demand, sometimes voicing complaints that profit margins are kept lower than they should be by Honda pressure.

4. Moving Personnel Between Factories

The regionally concentrated spatial framework of the just-in-time region lets Honda and the parts makers shift personnel back and forth between factories with relative ease. Several kinds of personnel movements take place.

First, there are long-term reassignments which, because of proximity between plants, do not require employees to move house. When Honda opened the Anna mechanical components plant, west of Marysville, in 1985, it could draw on an experienced cadre of managers and production associates already employed at Marysville for permanent reassignment to Anna without many of them having to move house. Then, with the 1989 opening of the East Liberty plant only a few miles from Marysville, the backbone of the new workforce, including many managers and engineers and the core production workers, could simply be transferred from the Marysville plant. These reassignments of experienced personnel sharply accelerated the pace at which the new plants could be started up.

A second form of personnel movement is the temporary reassignment. This often involves Honda engineers who are sent to other Honda plants or to parts makers to help with the introduction of a new product or new process. Alternatively, if a parts maker is experiencing particular quality problems, it may find Honda engineers from

Marysville commuting every day to its plant until the problem is resolved.

Finally there is the regular meeting. Here the spatial framework of the just-in-time region plays a vital role, because it allows all sorts of meetings between people working at different plants to take place with minimal inconvenience. Meetings variously involve Honda, first-tier and second-tier parts makers. At one transplant parts maker, for instance, the preproduction phase was characterized by meetings at least once a week with Honda engineers to discuss product quality, meetings which sometimes included second-tier parts makers. Similarly, personnel managers from the Western Ohio transplant parts makers have held regular meetings to compare notes on policies and problems.

5. Integrating R&D

The transfer of research and development activities from Japan to North America on an integrated basis poses a number of questions for Honda, which as we saw in Chapter 2 is a product-oriented firm in which the R&D subsidiary plays a prominent role.

A basic difficulty is the sheer wealth of experience built up in Japan and the long period that will be necessary to create an equally good structure for complex R&D work in North America even with the transfer of a core Japanese staff. But an equally significant problem concerns the role of Honda's transplant parts makers. Many of their parent firms are medium and small enterprises, which may be able to support an R&D staff in Japan, but for whom a full R&D facility in North America is difficult to contemplate financially.

If R&D is to be maintained as an integrated activity involving parts makers, how can it be transferred to North America? Potentially, Honda faces the unhappy prospect of having its Marysville R&D staff collaborating with parts maker R&D offices in Japan for design of parts that will then be manufactured only a matter of miles from Marysville. In which case perhaps all R&D should remain in Japan. But where would that leave the 'self-reliant company' in North America?

In the late 1980s Japanese staff at Honda's transplant parts makers were talking openly about the possibility of adding R&D functions to their activities, but several American staff noted pointedly that nothing had happened yet. By the early 1990s, however, progress seemed to have got under way. We will see part of the solution Honda found to the dilemma of where to locate R&D in the global local corporation when we discuss the R&D process for Honda's new 'global local cars' in Chapter 11. What has happened in North America is that in 1991 Honda announced that it planned to involve 35–40 of its North American parts makers to a substantial degree in R&D activities destined for the next (1993) Accord model. Responsibility for the design and development of the Accord range seems to be steadily following the shift we noted earlier of its manufacture from Japan to North America.

Decentralization of R&D activities to parts makers is characteristic of the Japanese model. But in North America Honda itself may play a more active role. In 1990 a new transplant opened a 70-employee machine shop in suburban Columbus, Ohio, close to Marysville, specifically to build parts for full-scale prototypes of new Honda cars developed by Honda R&D in Marysville. This operation is set to become part of a coordinating structure for R&D activities involving parts makers, in which Honda's R&D facilities at Marysville provide a collective pool of resources that they can share.

The critics' alliance, of course, will be waiting to see whether the parts makers drawn into the R&D process are transplants or domestic companies.

6. Honda Engineering's Role

Honda Engineering is responsible for the design and manufacture of much of Honda's capital equipment. The EG branch at Marysville has also developed purchasing arrangements with several transplant and domestic makers of capital equipment, including makers of flexible manufacturing systems, of moulds for plastic injection moulding machines, of chrome plating of steel stamping dies, and manufacturers and repairers of robot welding-heads.

Honda is well-located for access to US engineering companies: many of the best are clustered in the southwest quadrant of Ohio around Cincinnati and Dayton, traditional midwestern engineering cities and within short drives of Marysville. This region is at the geographical heart of the corridor of Japanese transplant investments, and several Japanese capital equipment manufacturers have taken advantage of this fact and of the skilled engineering workforce available to establish bases to service transplants (new factories or purchases of existing firms).

7. Intervening Inside Partner Firms

When production is organized on a just-in-time basis, difficulties experienced at one factory can rapidly infect the whole manufacturing network, potentially halting production at many plants simultaneously. This, together with the importance attached to quality, explains much of the extraordinary interest that Honda and its parts makers maintain in each other's 'internal' affairs.

Whereas in the conventional Western industrial model, assemblers and parts makers treat each other's factories as private, at Honda, related firms learn as much as they can about relevant parts of operations at their partners. Parts-maker engineers and production workers alike visit Honda to learn about the downstream process in which 'their part' is used. More importantly, Honda and its transplant parts makers directly intervene in the 'internal' activities of their upstream parts makers.

Interventions are quite focused. For quality-control systems, Honda inspections and advice are the norm. Manufacturing techniques are also the subject of intervention. By contrast, labour recruiting and training are left to the parts makers unless they ask for help.

It shouldn't be thought that transplant parts makers are a privileged group exempted from this kind of activity. Transplant managers and engineers frequently feel themselves under great pressure from Honda. When a new product line for Honda was being introduced at one transplant parts maker, Honda engineers 'practically lived here', according to an American manager. With production successfully under way, however, Honda 'backed off'. The high level of Honda intervention underscores how crucial it sees the parts maker role to be.

Honda's transplant parts makers behave no differently with their second-tier (usually domestic) parts makers. Most intervention comes in quality control, somewhat less in production, and little at all in labour recruiting and training. According to American staff, Japanese engineers at transplant parts makers are extremely demanding of potential second-tier parts makers, appraising all aspects of each firm's operations. Honda engineers sometimes participate themselves in inspection visits to second-tier parts makers. Indeed Honda Engineering approval is required for second-tier parts purchasing by first-tier firms, even of the most mundane parts.

The activities of Honda's purchasing department at Marysville thus penetrate deep into the chain of parts makers. To ensure that its parts are made of high quality materials, Honda actually selects and places orders for steel, aluminium and plastic resins on behalf of its first-tier parts makers. This keeps prices lower and allows Honda to vet and approve all the materials that will end up in its automobiles.

Even as many responsibilities are devolved to parts makers in line with the Japanese model, then, Honda maintains centralized control over key aspects of the whole just-in-time region. Decentralization and centralization together? Another example of dualist puzzle-solving.

8. Dealing with Domestic Parts Makers

We have already alluded to some of the difficulties that Honda and parts maker transplants have experienced in implementing just-in-time relations with domestic firms. Let's take a closer look at how Honda deals with them. The evolution of this relationship plays a major role in explaining the Honda parts-sourcing strategy we examined in Chapter 4, with lessons learned during the early 1980s influencing later decisions over whether Honda would source its components and materials from Japan, from domestic firms, or from transplant parts makers. Moreover, the experience of domestic parts makers is central not only to the ability of Japanese manufacturers to transplant themselves overseas, but also to the much wider diffusion and penetration of Japanese management techniques deep into the basic industrial infrastructure of the West.

Prior to starting production at Marysville in 1982, Honda gave a carefully selected set of domestic firms advance plans for the manufacturing of the Accord. We can safely presume that the selection was meant to indicate to these firms that they stood a good chance of winning Honda contracts. But perhaps they didn't all understand that message. Whereas in Japan parts makers are expected to maintain secrecy even when they deal with several assemblers at once, some of the domestic parts makers circulated Honda's plans, leading to their publication in the American automotive press. Honda viewed this as a betrayal of confidence, concluding not only that it could not trust domestic parts makers but that they in turn were not ready to trust automobile manufacturers to protect their interests.

This inauspicious start was aggravated when many of the domestic parts makers that were contracted simply did not take seriously enough Honda's requests for particular levels of product quality and tight delivery scheduling, tending to treat them with a flexibility that Honda did not expect. The problem, according to a Japanese Honda manager who has been in the United States from the start of production, was that domestic firms claimed to understand 'total quality control' and just-in-time techniques, but in reality couldn't fulfil their promises.

American managers at transplant parts makers concur: domestic parts makers only had a superficial understanding of just-in-time and other Japanese techniques. According to one, neither have they been able to adapt fast enough to handle rapid changes in what is demanded of them. Less than a third of the original group of domestic firms selected were still supplying Honda by the late 1980s, the rest discarded because of problems related to quality, delivery or confidentiality.

After suffering these early setbacks, Honda developed a fresh approach to dealing with domestic firms, which has guided it since the mid-1980s. Rather than adapting itself to the typical North American organizational framework, and then expecting the domestic firms to learn Japanese-style practices, Honda sought exclusive long-term relations with its domestic parts makers where possible, and became prepared to invest a determined organizational effort if necessary to bring them up to required standards.

Adherence to exclusive long-term relations (where parts makers are preferred not to also supply other automobile assemblers) has constrained Honda's ability to widen its network of domestic parts makers. There was already a dearth of independent parts makers (that is, not vertically integrated into Big Three firms) in North America. And to gain truly exclusive relations Honda has had to pursue contacts with firms previously outside the automobile industry, such as the children's toy maker now making tubular plastic parts, or the lawn-seed testing firm that now assembles radio-cassette loudspeakers, or the aluminium casting firm whose other customers are all outside the automobile industry.

It is in this fashion that, as we noted earlier, to the consternation of the traditional domestic parts industry, Honda has effectively developed a parallel automobile industry rather than rooting itself in the existing parts-making base. One of the significant implications of this parallel industry is that it severs potential channels of innovation diffusion into the domestic automobile industry. To all intents and purposes, except for transplant parts maker sales to the Big Three, only at the level of basic materials does Honda share the parts-making infrastructure of the domestic industry.

Domestic parts makers have found it particularly difficult to gain contracts with Honda because of the changes they are put through compared to their traditional methods of manufacturing, quality control, and delivery scheduling. Honda has refrained from simply drawing up contracts with a given parts maker to supply parts and then leaving the parts maker to fend for itself in typical traditional North American fashion: trying this at the start did not work out.

Honda has therefore frequently been obliged to offer the services of its engineers to aid domestic parts makers with basic restructuring of their manufacturing processes. The alternative is to risk costly disruptions to tightly planned production schedules in the assembly plants as the new parts maker brings itself on line and up to speed. Many domestic firms have found their whole internal structures – from production techniques to organizational frameworks – gutted and rebuilt: they have either done it themselves or Honda has done it for them. On other occasions Honda's Japanese parts makers have been drafted in to aid new domestic parts makers, and the latter have been obliged to buy new capital equipment from Japan.

The American Vice-President for Purchasing at Marysville previously worked for the major domestic parts maker TRW as worldwide purchasing director. He was 'flabbergasted' by Honda's quality requirements:

> We expect basically zero defects. Our goal is to have four hours of inventory. They think we're quoting from textbooks ... It is with great difficulty in almost every instance that we localize parts with an American source.[5]

Did Honda's problems ease off as time progressed? Not at all, because by the late 1980s and early 1990s the kinds of parts it was trying to source in North America had changed. The 'big, easy parts' had been dealt with, and the issue now was to find local manufacturers of the small, complex components still sourced from Japan. It was just at this stage that Honda began (as we noted earlier) to enter into arrangements with joint ventures being set up by some of the larger independent domestic parts makers, firms like TRW, DANA, Johnson Controls, in alliance with major Japanese firms.

Two lessons emerge consistently from Honda's efforts to purchase parts from domestic parts makers, whether they are success stories or failures. The first is the gulf that existed between American and Japanese managers on correct practices of business management, production organization, and relations with the partner firm. The second is the high degree of Honda pressure to alter the internal operations of domestic parts makers – either active intervention or simply telling the firms to come back with 'something really new to offer' – the goal being to enforce acceptance of particular Honda practices and to not water them down.

THE JUST-IN-TIME REGION: A KEY RESOURCE

If in the early days Honda experimented, and tried to form relationships, with domestic parts makers according to traditional North American rules, by the mid-1980s it believed that only firms with a long history of Japanese management techniques, or those exceptional companies able to learn rapidly, would suffice. The alternative would be to abandon the manufacturing techniques that worked so well in Japan. And that would mean succumbing to competing on the level playing-field, just as the Big Three hoped.

Most domestic parts makers had neither the history nor the ability to change quickly. In contrast, transplant parts makers brought considerable advantages with them, including not only their previous R&D investment in the product itself, but their familiarity with (and ability to meet) just-in-time quality and delivery targets, and their profound knowledge of all Honda's particular ways of doing things and idiosyncrasies. Many transplant parts makers could be switched quickly into direct supply shortly after their establishment, without the slow and painful learning process that many domestic parts makers have endured.

What about the transplant parts makers themselves? With the political accent tilted towards collusion and *keiretsu*, it's easy to forget that most of them have parents in Japan which are fiercely competitive firms in their own right. Despite the risks entailed in building North American factories, many Japanese parts makers risked more if they didn't establish transplants. The dollar's 1985–6 collapse was already eating up profits and making North American prices for Japanese parts look expensive. If Honda searched for cheaper parts elsewhere in North America, not only would the Marysville market be lost, but Honda might establish a relationship with a domestic firm that could challenge the traditional Japanese parts maker not only in global aftermarkets but in Japan too.

At the same time the risks faced by the Japanese parts makers which chose to establish transplants were curtailed by three factors. First, there was direct aid: from state and local governments, which looked after much of the external environment, from Honda itself for site search, advice and development engineering, and from other parts maker transplants. Second, the influx of other Japanese assembly transplants and the willingness of Big Three firms to enter into contracts with transplant parts makers significantly broadened markets and increased economies of scale. Third, the shifting currency values of the mid 1980s created a window during which low-cost production in North America was not immediately essential because it was still cheaper than importing from Japan: an insurance policy – thanks to the US government and its monetary and foreign exchange policy – just like the one Honda had benefited from a couple of years before.

We have seen in this chapter how the wave of transplant parts makers has been fundamental to Honda's successful transfer of Japanese management techniques to North America. At the same time, a novel spatial framework has been created, based on regional concentration and local dispersal in a network form, which allows the supply of parts from factory to factory to function potentially more smoothly than in Japan.

Honda insisted upon a full transfer of Japan-developed interfirm practices, simply refusing to transform them to meet existing local conditions. Difficult as this was, it helped to ensure that the competitive advantages built up in Japan were maintained intact as parts making for Marysville and the other factories was steadily shifted from Japan to North America.

Notes

1. Honda engineer assigned to parts maker transplant in Ohio (author's interview, 1988).
2. Data in this chapter refer to the sample of 76 parts maker transplants, or, where indicated, to a smaller sample for which there is more detailed information.
3. Based on a sample of 24 parts maker transplants whose major customer is Honda.
4. Sample size 32.
5. Cited in Norm Alster, 'US electronics in Japanese cars? not with *that* quality', *Electronic Business*, 1 August 1988, pp. 78–82.

6 Mobilizing Human Resources

Can the peculiar 'Japaneseness' of [Japanese industry's] success be transferred onto the international scene? There is little doubt that Honda, perhaps even more than some other Japanese companies, may have problems. Can one imagine a white-suited, Honda-style manufacturing operation set up in Peoria? Perhaps.[1]

Honda may even discover an America that has not yet been discovered by Americans.[2]

Honda and the transplant parts makers have mobilized an army of people to make the just-in-time region work. Some came in from Japan. The vast majority were hired locally. The Japanese had years of experience building automobiles the Honda Way, but in few cases did they have much real idea of American or Canadian life and culture, let alone how best to work with a Western workforce. The North Americans knew about their own life-styles, their own motivations, but with few exceptions had no idea how to build automobiles. None knew how to build them the Honda Way.

The question of human-resource mobilization had been fundamental to concern over whether Japanese management techniques would work outside Japan. The main fear was that Western workers would reject Japanese-style work-place behaviours and thereby undermine the manufacturing methods. Western racism and cultural clashes might well lead to rejection of Japanese ideas without even attempting to understand them properly.

Dualist analyses fuelled the fire, labelling all things Japanese as different from 'the way we do it'. The Japanese worker was said to accept employment conditions that no Western worker or labour union would put up with: subordination of personal goals to the firm, long hours of work, unforeseen overtime. Images of the Japanese worker as a robot, as an ant, the phrase 'they live to work, we work to live', all testify to the predominant Western view. Moreover, no Western automobile industry had a tradition of unions organized at enterprise level that cooperated with management rather than 'standing up for the worker'.

In this chapter we take a close look at how Honda mobilizes its human resources in North America. What kind of people would it look for? Could Honda find the right people? How would it try to mould them? What terms of employment would workers be offered? Would Japanese firms mimic American habits or bring Japanese behaviours? Or would they invent some kind of hybrid? What about the labour union question? What roles would American managers and engineers play? And – one question that seems to have been largely ignored – would Japanese staff be able to operate well in the West?

Just why Honda has gone about mobilizing human resources the way it has – the goal of getting people to build automobiles the Honda Way – remains an implicit theme in this chapter. In the next chapter we will study what people do when they come to work, and so how the very particular way the human resources are mobilized dovetails with the very particular way the automobiles are made.

THE RIGHT PEOPLE, THE RIGHT PLACE

The American media have indulged in an image of Honda's factories surrounded by cornfields, of a workforce composed of young people more used to farm labour than to factory work. How accurate is this portrayal?

The right place has indeed been an important factor. When a firm chooses a site, it also chooses the area from which it will select most of its workforce. As we saw in Chapter 5, Honda chose a location at the heart of the North American manufacturing belt. Yet it didn't go for one of the big cities – Chicago, St Louis, Toledo, Cleveland, Cincinnati, Detroit itself – where there is a ready-made labour pool of people who know how to make automobiles and what it takes to work in a car factory.

State and local political leaders from the cities did try to attract the transplants by playing on the experienced workers available in the urban areas. But Honda selected a rural area of Western Ohio with no automobile industry at all, and most of the transplant parts makers followed suit. They had decided that workers who knew how to make cars the American way would be worse for their purposes than workers with no idea how to make them at all. And the places they chose are too far from the cities for commuting. Like the domestic parts makers (see Chapter 4), domestic automobile workers were to be largely cut out of Honda's North American production.

Did Honda therefore want to start with a blank page on which to write its own script? Was the goal to harvest a fresh young workforce 'off the farms'? Was Honda looking for people who would be fundamentally opposed to labour unions? The situation was in fact more complex, more subtle, than this. The common image results from a dualist approach. If the workers haven't made automobiles then they have no experience, if they aren't from a big city they must be rural, if they aren't union members they must be against unions.

In fact there's no such thing as a blank page. And Western Ohio has quite definite characteristics. It is home to a population of mostly white Americans of German descent. And they have particular cultural attributes. Despite the 'melting pot' ideology of America, there are important contrasts between this region and Southeast Ohio, for instance, with its Appalachian population of Scots–Irish descent, and Ohio's cities like Akron, Youngstown, Cleveland, Toledo, Cincinnati, with their mixtures of both these groups, black Americans, eastern Europeans and southern Europeans. Whereas Appalachia appears untidy, ramshackle – it *looks* disorganized – Western Ohio is neat, with fences and houses painted and in good order, gardens tidy and attractive, and *looks* well organized. And Honda selected a quiet and settled region, unremarkable, different from the big cities: free from political and economic conflict and turmoil, from poverty, from histories of mass emigrations and immigrations with their shattered and fragmented communities. Yet this quiet and settled region suffered from a slow leakage of young people unable to find a place, a niche, a job even, in otherwise self-contained communities.

In Western Ohio, religious sentiment is strong, and 'small c' conservatism reigns. Foreigners are (were) a novelty, but welcomed with naïve and open arms as they often are in rural middle America. This is not an anti-labour union environment – particularly when compared to many of the southern states – but it is an area where family and community come first. Honda's transplant parts makers uniformly rate the work ethic in the region very highly. People are organized, self-disciplined, and have a good sense of responsibility to others.

Honda chose exactly the same kind of place at Alliston, described by a Canadian journalist as 'a self-contained, close-knit and thriving community, the hub of a wealthy farming area with a small, but sound, industrial base', as a place where 'the idea of pitching in to help your neighbor holds sway'.[3]

Are Honda's workers straight off the farm? Some are, but Western Ohio is also home to a series of small towns – Marysville, Bellefontaine, Urbana, Greenville, St Mary's, Troy – where home-grown and branch plant industries are commonplace. Indeed for Honda and the transplant parts makers, the network of small industrial towns is more important than the farms as a recruiting ground (Figure 6.1).

Some transplant parts makers chose small industrial town locations to guard against local rejection, reasoning that industry would not be a novelty. Moreover, local people would be accustomed to working indoors, to factory life. The great majority of production workers at the transplant parts makers have worked in factories before (Figure 6.2). Locations in small towns with self-sufficient community bases also made it easier to persuade Japanese and American management, engineers, and skilled (for example, maintenance) workers to move to the area.

What is behind the dispersed spatial pattern of transplant parts makers we saw in Chapter 5? We have to start from Honda itself. Honda's actual location was determined by the existing automotive test track a few miles outside Marysville. With this site fixed, Honda drew first a 20 then a 30-mile radius to define its local labour market (Figure 6.1).

Early transplant parts makers located within the 30 mile hiring radius, close enough to permit frequent contacts with Honda. But these sites caused a number of problems. Why? Because the parts makers didn't want to pay their workers as much as Honda. And yet employees at the transplant parts makers know full well that their factory is part of Honda's just-in-time region: some of the factories are part-owned by Honda. This naturally invites comparison of their pay and conditions with their Honda counterparts.

The early transplant parts makers turned out to be located too close to Honda. Their managers had difficulties justifying lower wages than Honda's. At the Bellemar Parts seating factory for instance, the management has had problems convincing workers that their company, 87 per cent Honda-owned, only supplying Honda, and located actually within sight of the assembly plant, is a separate company that can legitimately pay lower wages. A 'Honda effect' has therefore boosted wage rates within the 30-mile radius (Table 6.1). Pay at the close-in factories is 'out of sight', according to managers at transplants located further afield.

151

Figure 6.1 Where Honda's Marysville Employees Live

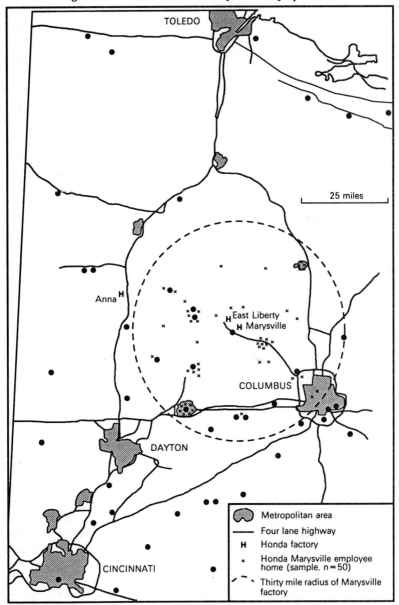

Source: Author's research, employee newsletters.

152

Figure 6.2   Characteristics of Production Associates at Honda's Transplant Parts Makers

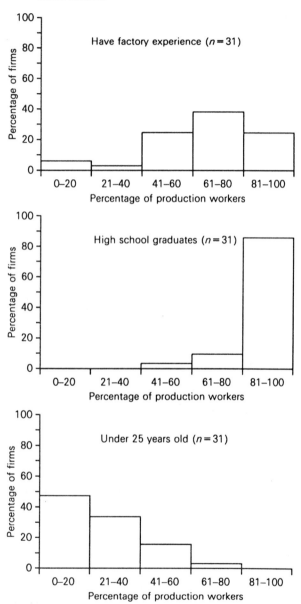

Source: Mail questionnaire.

Table 6.1 Honda's Wage Shadow: Parts-Maker Transplant Wages are
Highest Close to Honda

	Distance (miles)	Wage index
Honda	0	100
Firm A	1	77
Firm B	15	71
Firm C	25	78
Firm D	48	47
Firm E	52	50
Firm F	58	57

Source: Author's research.

The later arrivals among transplant parts makers learned their lesson
and avoided Honda's hiring area as far as possible. They dispersed
themselves into Western and Southwestern Ohio (still within a two-
hour radius), and they also separated themselves out, minimizing
labour market overlaps.

The small-town locations of the dispersed transplant parts makers
are ideal places to recruit. There are existing communities that can be
tapped into without straining physical or social infrastructures, local
labour markets can be separated, comparisons with Honda wages can
be minimized, and Honda won't have creamed off the best workers.

Other solutions had to be found for the factories caught within
Honda's hiring area. First, Honda simply won't hire anyone who has
previously worked for a parts maker, so there is no leakage of workers
from parts makers (or threats to leave) followed by wage increases
designed to counteract the tendency. Second, Honda keeps many
thousands of job applications on its files. Those who can't wait for
Honda employment, or who are not accepted, often end up at the
transplant parts makers. Whereas in a traditional American industrial
area people might shift from one automobile parts maker to another,
anyone who wants to stay employed in Honda's just-in-time region
ends up locked into the firm they started with, for there is no external
job market within it; this certainly recalls one aspect of Japan's lifetime
employment system.

While the typical transplant parts maker sought a site in a small rural
town, variations on the theme indicate considerable resourcefulness.
Some opted for sites in Ohio's capital city, Columbus. This metropolitan area, of approaching one million inhabitants, is dominated by its
university, government offices and financial institutions, and has little

in common culturally or politically with industrial cities elsewhere in Ohio. Factory shells in Columbus purchased from a recently closed slipper manufacturer provided ideal cheap investments for two transplants. In one case the slipper factory's personnel manager was hired. Given the transplant's products, headliners (that is, interiors for roofs) and seat covers, this was a quick and reliable means to then select a workforce well-suited to the manufacturing processes to be introduced.

Another interesting hiring strategy comes from a Western Ohio transplant parts maker which hired a manager from a big unionized American manufacturer in a neighbouring town that had recently closed down and moved production to Mexico. This manager too could select workers he knew personally. The policy of hiring from a formerly unionized firm was at first contested at meetings with other transplant personnel managers, but was defended in terms of the workers knowing what working in a factory was like and having just suffered a bad experience with a unionized working environment.

These examples show the importance of personal networks. The personnel manager of one transplant parts maker had never worked in industry before, but he was recommended by a local lawyer 'with Honda connections'. Honda itself has hired American managers it first came across in other capacities, selecting people according to their personalities rather than advertising and interviewing people with a paper curriculum vitae.

On the other hand, there is one personal network Honda won't touch: it will not hire the spouses of people who are already employees. The argument is that wealth created at Honda should be spread around the community. There may also be other advantages: a pool of spouses is left for transplant parts makers to recruit from, and all the disputes we can imagine taking place over 'why my husband/wife wasn't hired but so and so's was' simply don't arise.

JOB CREATION, JOB LOSS, JOB SHIFT

Employment at Honda increased rapidly during the 1980s in line with capital investment, until there were 10 000 employees in Ohio by the early 1990s (Table 6.2), and a further 1900 at Alliston.

Compared to Honda, transplant parts makers are very small, ranging from only three or four dozen employees to 800, with a median size of 150. But while each factory is small, there are many of

Table 6.2   Honda Employment in Ohio Grows Rapidly during the 1980s

Year (Jan)	Employment	% increase
1980	98	
1981	356	263
1982	482	35
1983	917	90
1984	1 985	116
1985	2 452	23
1986	3 053	25
1987	4 377	43
1988	5 336	22
1989	6 965	30
1990	8 800	26
1991	10 000	14

Source: Various company and press reports.

them, and their total impact on job creation is significant. If we estimate the minimum employment at transplant parts makers that is actually due to Honda – from their own estimates of employment and from the same information used in Chapter 5 to develop the 'ABC' categorization of Honda suppliers – we come up with 10 276 jobs as a minimum at the transplant parts makers.

But how many jobs have been lost in the domestic automobile industry as Honda output has replaced Big Three sales? We can't know the exact answer, but the net result must be a considerable fall in employment. While many of the gains are in Ohio, so are many of the losses. Ohio has long been a major centre of automobile production, concentrated in the major cities of Cleveland, Cincinnati, Toledo and Youngstown, around the northern and western edges of the state. The problems faced by the Big Three and the domestic parts makers have severely affected Ohio's automobile industry employment base.

Honda's investments have been trumpeted by Ohio newspapers as proclaiming the end of manufacturing decline in the state, providing a new 'engine of growth' for Ohio. But the overall picture tells another story. The main effect in employment terms has been to shift employment within the state, away from traditional industrial regions around the edges, towards the greenfield small-town sites of Honda's just-in-time region.

For many displaced workers in the cities, the future holds no prospect so far as the automobile industry is concerned. Honda and its transplant parts makers certainly weren't interested in them.

WHAT MAKES A GOOD HONDA WORKER?

Actual recruitment methods varied considerably. Some factories tapped into local networks. Others launched grand competitions with widespread advertising, which thousands of people entered, and then went to considerable effort and expense to meticulously sort records and interview people, scientifically selecting only the best. Still others, including Honda itself, made use of Ohio's state government schemes for preliminary screenings and assessments (often part of a location enticement package). But what is it that makes a good Honda worker?

The managers of some Japanese transplants in North America and in Europe have made much of the fact that they want to hire workers with an independent mind, who will think, rather than just accept dull physical routines. This all becomes wrapped up in the idea that working for a Japanese transplant offers a humane environment, where workers are treated as human beings, quite different from the alienating drudgery of traditional Western factory work.

But is it a (dualist) exaggeration to stress the mental side of factory work over its physical side. The ideal Honda worker certainly possesses a mind that is free enough to accept a new value system. But it seems that he or she should not be so free-spirited (or imbued with the philosophy of another system) as to challenge the new. Thus the ideal Honda worker has ambition, but not too much ambition, and is willing to make a positive input, but is also ready to accept given boundaries (see Box 6.1). We'll be taking a closer look at how the mental work/ physical work dualism plays out at Honda in North America in the next chapter, where we'll see that these characteristics fit snugly with the nature of work at Honda.

The importance Honda attaches to a job candidate's high-school record is revealing. Employees must almost always have graduated from high school (see also Figure 6.2). Attendance records are carefully scrutinized. Is this because Honda values academic achievement and wants to hire people capable of applying that intelligence at work? In part, yes. But mostly, records of high-school graduation and good attendance are used to measure the perseverance and self-discipline of candidates: a predictive measure of whether they will come to work every day. In the American education system, high-school graduation is as much an indicator that the student has not 'dropped out' early but has stayed at school until 18 years old as it is a record of academic achievement. What Honda wants is discipline: low employee turnover and low absenteeism.

What about youth? Are Honda's factories full of 18-year-olds running about at breakneck speed, wearing themselves out before they are 30? In fact the workforce is young, especially in comparison to Big Three factories. But it is a different kind of youth – average age early 30s, as in Japan – quite likely to be married and have children (see also Figure 6.2). Physically fit, yes, but also possessing a certain maturity and mental self-discipline.

At the same time, having hired few older workers, neither Honda nor the transplant parts makers stand to pay out much in the way of retirement benefits over the next twenty years or so, which significantly improves their cost structures.

TEACHING THE HONDA WAY

But for Honda it is not just a question of choosing the right people. Honda actively seeks to mould them into the kinds of people it wants. That process takes place principally after they are hired, but Honda is also investing in its future local labour pool, in the schools.

To look briefly at the second activity first: Honda has ensured that most of the local taxes it pays goes straight into funding local schools. Around Marysville and Anna that means that some school districts have more than doubled their incomes. By strategically locating the East Liberty plant on one particular plot of land, Honda has also ensured that a further school district from which it recruits also gets a share of the new income. Besides these financial resources, there are also Honda programmes in the schools for increasing cultural awareness, for sending teachers to Japan, and so on.

After workers are hired, however, their mental preparation primarily means learning the Honda Way. This raises all sorts of questions. If there is a special Honda approach to work, to puzzle-solving, to innovation, if there is a Honda Way, is it not intimately bound up with Japanese culture, with Japanese ways of thinking, with Japanese metaphors and ways of understanding? Could Americans be taught? Would they understand? Would the Japanese be able to teach it to them, or even make explicit what they themselves often accept only implicitly? In short, how are specific ideas about production and manufacturing organization diffused across cultures?

The task of working out how to teach the Honda Way to Americans was taken up by Soichiro Irimajiri, president of manufacturing operations in the United States between 1984 and 1988. There were

A 'Self-Reliant Company' in North America

Box 6.1   The Ideal Honda Production Worker

Stable, 'Good Attitude', Not Overly Ambitious in Life

'Honda didn't want a highly mobile, city-style workforce that changes jobs at the drop of a hat. What it did want was people willing to work hard and who had, or were going to put down, roots. At Honda, it's a matter of attitude. If you don't have the right one, you don't get on the payroll.'[1]

Willing to Change to Meet the Company's Goals

'We are looking for people who are open minded, who understand the world of business in this economy, and who are flexible enough to know that all organizations and industries have to be open to change if they are to survive in today's world of free enterprise.'[2]

'To succeed at Honda, you have to be willing to learn, to be flexible and willing to change rapidly.'[3]

Not Too Much of an Individualist

'Honda likes to hire a "T" person rather than an "I" person. The "T" person is one who has the capability or potential for doing and thinking both vertically and horizontally, has no one specialty, but can do several totally different things. The "T" person has good common sense, and quick responses. The "I" person, by contrast, can do and think only vertically.'[4]

Hasn't Too Many Ideas of Their Own

'Honda seems to be interested in certain types of workers, which aren't necessarily those that other firms want. They don't seem to want those who score highest on mental aptitude tests. Maybe they don't want bored workers.'[5]

Definitely Not the Wrong Kinds of Ideas

'In order to build a work force that understood [its] values, Honda chose to hire people who were not already accustomed to working another way. For its assembly line jobs, hiring was restricted to high school graduates, preferably with no automobile manufacturing experience.'[6]

'We hired non-experienced workers because we thought that if we hired experienced workers they might have some bad habits. We thought it better to train them fresh'.[7]

Notes

1. Bob English, 'Orientation', *Canadian Business*, March 1988, pp. 58–72. Passage from p. 70.
2. Al Kinzer, then Marysville Manager of Personnel and Associate Relations, 1982, cited in Susan Porter, 'Into the cornfields of Union County comes The Honda Way', *Columbus Monthly*, November 1982, pp. 72–81. Passage from p. 81.
3. Al Kinzer, cited in Peter Behr, 'Honda is rolling success off its Ohio assembly line', *Washington Post*, 3 May 1987.
4. Roger Lambert, Corporate Communications Manager, cited in Yoshiaki Iwao, 'Honda in the US – working for the perfect circle', *JAMA Forum*, 9.1, November 1990, pp. 13–17. Passage from p. 14.
5. State of Ohio employee working with programme to preselect Honda recruits: author interview, 1988.
6. Iwao, 'Honda in the US – working for the perfect circle', p. 14.
7. Tetsuo Chino, President of Honda North America, cited in George Melloan, 'Honda's cash goes a long way in the USA', *Wall Street Journal*, 13 October 1987.

round-table discussions at which Japanese managers and engineers tried to explain what key phrases, sayings, slogans, meant to them in concrete terms. The Americans in turn tried to come up with slogans, metaphors, parables, that would perform the equivalent function for American workers, and they in fact managed to successfully arrive at a – now top secret – document that managers use in training the American workforce.

There are videos too, with American staff explaining what 'proceed always with youthfulness and ambition' and other Japanese slogans mean to them in practice. In training exercises, workers and managers are asked to come up with their own interpretations as a way to get them to understand the principles through meaningful examples: what does 'proceed always with youthfulness and ambition' mean to a local corn farmer, for instance?

Making it all quite explicit, whether written or on film, has seemed the best way to diffuse the principles that Honda wants its American workers, engineers and managers to adopt. This is a vital aspect of the Americanization of Honda. Hence spreading the Honda Way has meant setting it out in a form that has never been necessary in Japan. But isn't it just another set of rules? No, the Honda Way in North America is a set of principles to guide action, more abstract than rules. On the other hand they are still principles that can be referred to in solving concrete disputes.

The seriousness with which induction into the Honda Way has been taken is reflected in the opening of an Associate Development Center (ADC) in 1988. This building, located at the Marysville site, houses all sorts of training facilities, from meeting rooms to resource centres to videos to be borrowed, and it has a permanent staff to provide support for quality circles. Courses are run on leadership, communications, project management, administration, and how to appraise employees.

So important does Honda consider its particular ideas to be that it keeps its knowledge and its training programmes almost entirely in-house. A full-fledged Technical Development Program (TDP) was launched in 1989 with pilot courses expanded to all production departments by 1991. The goal is 'technical self-reliance' by 1995. TDP courses teach workers how to understand technology beyond their on-the-job experience. Production departments use ADC facilities to run their own specialist training programmes: how to treat the new type of steel used in the 1990 Accord, for instance. At any given time, some factory departments may be concentrating on courses for maintenance workers, others on team-leader training, still others on the implications of new processes and materials.

JAPANESE-STYLE TERMS OF EMPLOYMENT: ADOPT, ADAPT, OR . . . ?

What is it like to work in a Japanese-owned factory? Do you have to do exercises before work? Are you offered lifetime employment? Do you sing company songs and join the company union? These are the images that captured the Western public imagination, attracting fascination, curiosity, and no small measure of hostility.

Traditional terms of employment (how employees are classified, how their pay is determined, how they negotiate these with managers) in the American automobile industry terrified Japanese executives. Categorizations and classifications of employees closely tied to tasks performed, and above all the governing role that the United Automobile Workers seemed to play in allocating workers to specific work tasks, appeared totally incompatible with their own manufacturing methods, which demanded a flexibility of task assignments, under managerial control, that the American system was specifically designed to curtail.

Imposing Japanese-style terms of employment would be risky, but the traditional American system was a non-starter. What would Honda do? What kind of system would mesh in with Western culture and yet also allow Japanese management techniques to flourish?

Single Status

Terms of employment for Honda workers in North America are based squarely on the concept of 'single status'. 'Single status' means the absence of visible distinctions among employees related to their position in the company: from factory floor up to company president. The 'class symbols' of rank, hierarchy, status and position that permeate both Japan and the West are dispensed with.

Let's take a closer look. Production workers are called 'associates'. All employees share the same facilities: the same canteens and the same food, the same car parks with no reserved spaces. All employees wear the same uniforms, and they address each other by their forenames, which are clearly marked on uniforms to facilitate direct, personal communication. Managers work in open-plan offices, often with glass walls so it is easy to see if a sought-after person is there. They promote 'open-door' (in fact there literally are no doors) communications with employees: the latter should be able to speak directly to managers without regard to position.

All employees share the same private health insurance plans, and have the same number of vacation days. Moreover, all production workers receive the same basic wages as each other, with no complex system of wage gradation based upon position, task, skill or seniority.

But wait a minute, say the critics, isn't single status just superficial symbolism that workers will soon recognize for what it is: a masquerade of democracy? If there were real equality, how could managers exert authority: how could they manage? Wouldn't the workers be able just to say 'no' to their orders?

That's right. Class and authority structures do still exist at Honda. But this doesn't make single status just window-dressing. Seeing single status as the opposite of class structure is a dualistic approach (in which, it must be said, some transplant managers have indulged, wanting to emphasize how democratic their system is). But, paradoxically to some, single status and authority structure go hand in hand.

Far from being hampered by single status, authority works better because of it. This is because status symbols automatically become barriers between people. Not only are they not necessary for authority to function, but they can have profoundly counteractive effects. Lots of people in their work places have experienced petty 'empire building', wars over who has which office, which car, which privileges, the secrecy of closed-door meetings, the inept manager protected by position and symbol. Is that a good atmosphere for information flow, for trust, for understanding?

With single status, people are equal and yet they are not equal. Dualist puzzle-solving. Managers get paid different salaries, engineers too. Everyone has a boss. Single status strips off all *symbols* of authority so that the hierarchy of management – which, be in no doubt, still exists – functions in a pure sense, based mainly on the knowledge of the subordinate that a superior has power. Single status clears the path for authority channels. Naked management. Barriers to communication are removed for good managers, and so are shelters for poor managers.

Single status is a double edged sword in Honda's hands. The first blade cuts away barriers to communication both downwards and – as we shall see in the next chapter – upwards too. The second blade builds on this by clearing away many of the causes of resentment, mistrust, hostility, and the continual reminder of belonging to different status and class groups.

So is this Japanization? Not at all. For the Japanese managers this can all seem very novel indeed. Single status is rooted in Western liberal traditions, with their notions of all people being fundamentally equal. This is an ideological strain that runs deep in Western democracy, and Honda has tapped right into it. Funnily enough, for the most part American and European automobile producers never have. This may be how Honda is discovering an America previously undiscovered by Americans.

Money Rewards

There is another way Honda has leapt right into American culture and ideology. This is the great stress placed on giving monetary rewards to workers. Are new recruits told about the need for group loyalty, about the overriding needs of the company, Japanese-style? To some extent, of course they are. Thus Honda has attempted to bond its American workers with the notion, much used in Japan during the 1960s and 1970s, that it is an underdog, an outsider in the automobile industry.

But more stress is laid on what employees will get for themselves by working for Honda: bluntly, how much money they will earn, how they will be able to get that big auto, that fishing cabin in Michigan, that holiday in Hawaii, that motor home, that they have always wanted. Honda positively encourages new workers to plan how they're going to spend their new income.

Let's take a closer look at how Honda uses monetary rewards. The starting point is that all production workers are paid the same basic wage, no matter what they do or where they work, rather than a wage based on seniority or individual characteristics (in Japanese style). But on top of this come two types of mechanism for increasing payments. The first type leads to regular wage increases for all employees. The second type allows employees to earn more money individually by sticking closely to the rules.

General wage increases are frequent. During the first 18 months of employment, wages start below the basic wage (87 per cent in 1987, 80 per cent in 1991), and rise six times at three-month intervals until the basic wage is reached. This lag is legitimated in terms of a learning process, but it is also a monetary carrot to help new employees through any 'hump' period. Apart from this there is no pay for seniority.

Moreover, since manufacturing began at the Marysville motorcycle plant, the basic wage has increased by small amounts at regular six-month intervals (rather than every three years, the norm in North America's automobile industry). New benefits have also been added at regular intervals. During the 1980s, these pay rises led to an increasing differential over average US production worker wages (Table 6.3).

Table 6.3   Index of Basic Wages at Honda

Year	Index (average US wage for manufacturing workers = 100)
1980	109
1981	109
1982	110
1983	112
1984	116
1985	123
1986	127
1987	129
1988	131
1989	133
1990	135

Source: Company reports, author's calculations.

Honda also pays a year-end bonus. In early years this was paid as a percentage of regular earnings, 2 per cent in 1984, 2.25 per cent in 1985, for instance. In 1986, however, a new bonus scheme was introduced, dependent in part upon Honda's worldwide profitability. So bonuses have varied: 1986, $2688; 1987, $1541; 1988, $1824; 1989, $1602; 1990, $1712, 1991, $1600. At these levels, bonuses amount to about 5 per cent of annual earnings.

On top of these payments, Honda then rewards workers on an individual basis for adhering to its rules. The key here is the attendance bonus.

Honda requires full attendance of its workers, which means every day bar the two weeks' annual holiday and public holidays. Those who fall below 98 per cent are officially counselled to find out 'what the problem is'. They may have to enlist in a programme to improve their attendance. If this fails they are simply fired, having 'dismissed themselves'. To take the sting out of this draconian policy, workers have an allowance of 5 days per year when they can phone the factory to say they won't be coming in.

But full attendance is also rewarded financially. The attendance bonus is paid at regular short intervals, every four weeks, then counting starts again. It is higher for those with over one year's continuous attendance. In 1987 the attendance bonus made up 2.8 per cent of money earnings for those receiving the full sum, rising to 6 per cent in 1991. Workers know that if they miss a day's work they will be about $150 short at the end of the month. That means this cost can be weighed when decisions are taken at home over whether to go to work or stay to look after the children or recover from feeling unwell.

The total variable element that can be added to the basic wage has therefore been increased since the mid-1980s to over 10 per cent of take-home pay.

Rather than an individualized wages system Japanese-style, then, at Honda in North America there is a basic floor of equal wages, an emphasis on rising monetary rewards for all, and monetary rewards awarded on an equal basis to individuals who stick to the rules. Each element is perfectly in tune with American cultural values, and it gets the people to come to work every day, motivated by what they will get out of the job financially.

Here we have been discussing Honda itself. How do wages at transplant parts makers compare? Is there a gulf between wages at Honda and those at parts makers, as the Japanese model suggests? The short answer is yes, there is. The slightly longer answer is that wages and conditions at the transplant parts makers are no different from the norm in North America.

Wages at transplant parts makers fall far short of those at Honda: the median wage at the parts makers is 59 per cent of Honda's. Without exception transplant parts maker wages are below average US manufacturing wages (Figure 6.3). The need for the spatial separation of labour markets that we examined earlier now becomes crystal-clear.

Figure 6.3   Hourly Wage Rates, Honda and its Transplant Parts Makers Compared (1988 figures)

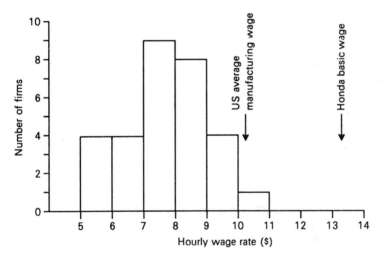

Source: Mail questionnaire.

The Promise of Lifetime Employment?

When Honda workers are first hired they are told what they can expect from Honda in terms of job security. The highly competitive nature of the automobile market is explained. Workers can expect to be employed at Honda for the long term, but it all depends on them: they must come regularly to work and build a high-quality product that provides customer satisfaction. Spouses and children are invited to the factory with the newly hired employee, to hear the same speeches, so that no one is left in any doubt as to what is demanded. There are no explicit promises of life-time employment.

Managers at transplant parts makers agree that an implicit, but not explicit, promise of long-term employment has much to recommend it. But they don't want to lose any management prerogatives over hiring and firing, and they remain guarded about how loyal American workers can be to their firm (Table 6.4). Note that they also come out against Japanese-style individualized wages.

In practice, several of the transplant suppliers, and Honda itself, hire *temporary* workers from employment agencies to meet short-term demands. At cost to those temporary workers who would prefer permanent employment, this protects the security of the permanent employees and at the same time creates a pool of workers who can be tested in action for possible transfer to permanent status.

Table 6.4   Should a Japanese-Style Long-Term Employment and Compensation System be Adopted in the United States?

Opinion	Honda transplant parts makers (%)
Strongly agree	9
Agree if modified	50
No opinion	16
Disagree	22
Strongly disagree	4
	(n = 32)

What Honda transplant parts-maker managers think

- 'Although there are many merits, some of the cultural differences/background/expectations of Americans would make adoption of the Japanese system impracticable.'
- 'As I understand the system, I feel the cultural differences would curtail its adoption.'
- 'US worker still needs a small hammer over his head [potential termination].'
- 'Practice of compensation linked to age and family size and sex would not work here.'
- 'I feel some of the traditional American incentives need to be used.'
- 'Management philosophies do not agree in this area of business.'
- 'The Japanese compensation system would not fit well into the US [hourly] style of pay.'
- 'It would require the same loyalty commitment from all production associates.'

Source: Mail questionnaire.

Life-time employment, then, is in no sense a right that workers have won. They may end up working at Honda or a transplant parts maker for many years to come, but that depends on the continued competitiveness of Honda, and managers remain firmly in control over whether particular individuals stay or go. The question of lay-offs during prolonged recessionary periods or production cutbacks has not really arisen yet (because sales have remained high, and as we will see in Chapter 7, production has been reorganized to keep up output levels).

ADOPTING SOME BAD AMERICAN HABITS

We've seen how Honda has Americanized its workers' terms of employment by tailoring them to American culture and ideology. But there is a dark side to this.

Soon after automobile production started, job applicants who had not been hired were accusing Honda of discrimination against women, ethnic minorities, and older workers. The Federal Government's Equal Employment Opportunities Commission (EEOC) launched an investigation in 1984.

In 1987 Honda awarded back-pay to 85 workers, hired in 1986 but rejected for employment when they had originally applied, and who had claimed that Honda at first rejected them for being over 40 years old. To settle the EEOC investigation, in 1988 Honda agreed to hire all the 370 unsuccessful black and women job applicants who had complained of discrimination and to award them back-pay dating to their initial job application. The EEOC appears to have reached conclusions damaging to Honda's image, but we don't know the extent of the problem because as part of its settlement Honda insisted that no information concerning the grounds for the suit be made public.

Honda also agreed to implement a positive programme to counteract its past practices. The self-imposed 30-mile hiring radius had neatly cut out the black neighbourhoods of Columbus, the nearest city, whilst allowing Honda managers to live in the wealthier suburbs of Colombus closer to Marysville: this radius was now expanded. Honda also agreed to make special efforts to recruit black workers and to inform its managers about anti-discrimination laws covering race, age and sex. The EEOC would monitor Honda for five years to assure compliance.

Let's take our own look at Honda's women workers. Honda actually employs about the same proportion of women (1/3) as American

Table 6.5   The Position of Women at Honda

	% women
New hires	
1986[1]	28
1991[2]	28
Women on the final assembly line [3]	
New associates hired (n = 125)	48
Associates in VIP contest* Top 100 (n = 19)	5
Winners of safety slogan contest (n = 19)	16
Associates promoted (n = 11)	18
Team leaders (n = 42)	14

Note: * VIP contest: Honda's annual contest for employee suggestions (see Chapter 7).
Sources: 1. Newsletter for Honda employees 1991 (n = 158).
2. Newsletter for Honda employees 1991 (n = 85).
3. Internal company newsletter for associates in auto assembly department 1988.

manufacturing industry in general. On the other hand, women participate less in activities that might lead to promotion, and are less likely to have been promoted than men (Table 6.5).

But this doesn't imply that Honda discriminates against women. Even when working outside the home, women in Western Ohio tend to remain less 'career'-oriented. They often view advancement at work as less important than do men, and so they are less interested in extra participation and advancement. The men, imbued with the idea of achievement at work, push themselves forward.

How do the transplant parts makers rate as employers of women, racial minorities, and older people? Proportions of women production workers vary greatly (Figure 6.4). At some, most employees are women. Does this mean that management is engaged in what Americans call 'positive discrimination', to counteract past negative trends? Far from it. Variation in employment of women is linked closely to the nature of the manufacturing process and to wage levels.

Women are mostly employed to do 'women's work' – intricate and patient handwork – sewing textiles, making wiring harnesses. The pay

Figure 6.4   Production Workers at Transplant Parts Makers: Variable
Proportions of Women, Few Ethnic Minorities or Older People

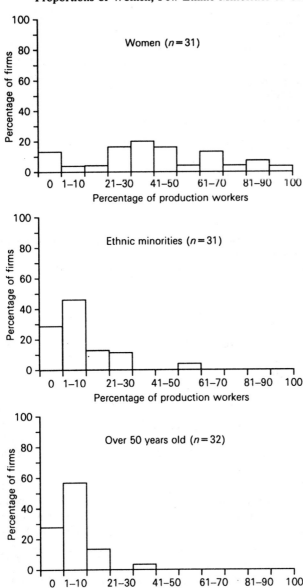

Source: Mail questionnaire.

is usually poor. The strong tendency is for firms with the highest proportions of women to have the lowest pay and to be located in the conservative southern states, outside the manufacturing belt. Conversely, there is a low proportion of women in the heavy industry factories: metals, chemicals, machines. Here wages are higher and locations are mostly in the manufacturing belt. These patterns reveal how the transplant parts makers have slotted right into conventional American practices (Table 6.6).

With the regular flow of overt racist comments about black Americans coming from Japanese politicians over recent years, race is an issue that bubbles below the surface at the transplants. As we have

Table 6.6   Transplant Parts Makers Adopt American Practices on 'Women's Work' and Pay

Proportion of women (%)	Product made	Hourly wage (1988)	State
Top employers of women production workers			
95	Seat belts	$7.25	Michigan
90	Seat covers	$5.50	Kentucky
90	Seat sewing	$5.50	Missouri
80	Wiring harnesses	$5.00	Kentucky
70	Seating	$5.50	Tennessee
70	Rubber weather strips	$7.25	Indiana
65	Small stampings	N.A.	Ohio
63	Seat sewing	$6.75	Ohio
60	Seating	$6.15	Ohio
		Mean $6.11	
Bottom employers of women production workers			
25	Mechanical control arms	$7.00	Michigan
25	Generators/alternators	$7.00	Ohio
25	Shelving and boards	$8.50	Illinois
11	Suspension springs*	$9.25	Kentucky
0	Steel wheels	$8.50	Kentucky
0	Colour chemicals	$7.50	Ohio
0	Machine tools*	$10.00	Ohio
0	Moulds for machines	$6.50	Ohio
0	Mechanical bearings	$7.50	Michigan
		Mean $7.97	

Note: * Existing firm purchased by Japanese supplier
Source: Mail questionnaire.

seen, it has already appeared at Honda in complaints over discrimination in hiring.

In 1988 two American scholars published an article which linked the location choices of Japanese automobile transplants to racial discrimination.[4] Many transplants appeared to have purposely selected areas with very small black populations. Instead of openly and illegally discriminating against black Americans, it seemed that the transplants had adopted a subtle ploy of site selection to make their preferences on the race of their employees simple and legal.

The location pattern of Honda's just-in-time region fits this pattern closely. Non-whites account for 16 per cent of the total United States population. Large swathes of rural southern states have high black populations, but in the north, like Ohio, which is 12 per cent non-white, almost all blacks live in the cities. By contrast, the core of Honda's just-in-time region is located in the rural north, where there are very few non-whites. Not surprisingly, by 1988 only 2.8 per cent of Honda's workforce was non-white. The numbers at transplant parts makers were no better (see Figure 6.4).

Does this amount to overt racism? Yes and no: racism, quite probably, but not racism alone. As we observed earlier, Japanese firms have been very particular about whom they have hired. In this regard Western Ohio provided a number of positive coincidences: stable communities with little competition from other employers, conservative communities, not union strongholds, and, yes perhaps, home mostly to white Americans.

Finally, regarding age, while it is true that most workers are not in their teens or early twenties, there is also a strong tendency not to hire older workers. Few transplant parts makers employ workers aged over 50 (Figure 6.4). What will Honda do as its workers become older? Will it be able to decant workers to parts makers Japanese-style? Will they have earned enough money to want to take early retirements? The question of an aging workforce of essentially lifelong Honda employees is one to watch for in the future. But we have plenty of time yet to speculate on what Honda will do.

KEEPING THE UNION AT BAY

Fear of American labour unions was uppermost in the minds of Japanese executives as they contemplated overseas manufacturing in the early 1980s. Though its strength had been weakened by recession during the 1970s, the United Automobile Workers still represented all production workers at the Big Three firms in the United States and at Volkswagen's Pennsylvania plant. The Canadian Automobile Workers' (CAW) union, which split from the UAW in 1985, covered all Big Three production workers in Canada.

The issue at the core of North American unionism, especially at plant level, was the defence of workers from the whims of capricious managers and capricious management systems, by drawing up regulations governing who could do what job, and who could be moved from one job to another. This focus seemed to the Japanese to be completely incompatible with their manufacturing methods. So it was that Honda management embarked on an audacious strategy to create the first non-union automobile assembly plant in the United States since the 1930s.

Nobody doubted that the UAW would try to gain the support of Honda workers. Under US law, unions ask the Federal Government to oversee a secret ballot among workers, who choose whether they want to be represented by a union. The key question would be whether 51 per cent of Honda employees wanted to be represented by the UAW like their Big Three counterparts. If so, Honda management would be facing up to the United Automobile Workers' union across the negotiating table.

Honda's site selection near Marysville stood the firm in good stead for the test ahead. While not in real anti-union country, most of Honda's workers still had little experience with labour unions, except for those who had recently lost their jobs when local unionized manufacturers had closed down. Yet Honda was not resisting unionized construction workers for its building projects (though it insisted on no-stoppage guarantees).

The company and the union analysed early sparring incidents for portents of what promised to be a mighty battle over union recognition at Honda. Even before production started, in 1982 some employees came to work wearing UAW caps, only for Honda to ban the caps as contravening company uniform regulations. The union denounced Honda, and the Federal Government's National Labor Relations Board ruled that Honda had to allow the caps and was not to resist union-organizing efforts.

The UAW waited until late 1985 to launch a full campaign, setting up an office in Marysville and getting union sympathizers at the factory to lobby their co-workers. In local media advertisements, the union denounced what it saw as the inhuman nature of production work at Honda, levelling charges of unwarranted production line speed-up, of gruelling work rates, and of managers moving people from job to job seemingly at whim.

But suddenly, in 1986, the union campaign fizzled out. UAW organizers twice cancelled scheduled elections. Since 1986 the union has maintained only a minimal presence and has made no further efforts to organize the workforce.

How did Honda succeed? Through propitious circumstances, with a positive strategy, and because of the UAW's lack of a well thought-out strategy.

- As fast as the UAW could gain supporters, Honda hired fresh new workers. The constant addition of new faces, feeling fortunate to have landed such a job and prepared to 'give Honda a chance', undercut union organizing efforts.
- Production was expanding all the time. Attention was directed towards getting the second Marysville assembly line up and running, and at launching production at Anna. There was constant upheaval on the factory floor with little time for lasting relationships among co-workers. Moreover, many of those already employed stood a good chance of promotion.
- As it recruited, Honda management pointed to mass redundancies that had taken place only a couple of years before at several Big Three factories, workplaces where there was a union present. The connection was clear. Managers described the UAW as a 'third party', as an outsider. And since 1986 management has perpetuated an obsessive anti-union ideology within the Honda plants.
- Other employers in central Ohio, including well-known anti-union business leaders in Columbus, funded an anti-union 'Associates Alliance'. This group of workers campaigned, with Honda approval – though Honda denied actually supporting it – against union representation.
- Honda launched a positive strategy to win its workers away from the union. It was during 1985 and 1986 that wages rose rapidly (Table 6.3), to settle just below rates at UAW factories. The benefit package was expanded at this time to resemble the one UAW members at the Big Three received (including a pension plan supposedly better, though few at Honda would be taking advantage of it before the year 2010). Indeed high wages at Honda (compared

to transplant parts makers) are due in no small part to Honda's anti-union strategy.

- All these specific factors helped to set back the UAW's organizing effort in 1986. But equally important is the role of Honda's terms of employment, designed to minimize the kind of dissatisfaction and unrest that would push workers into wanting union representation. The money is vital. But single status is the key. Opportunities for self-expression and communication when problems do occur relieve the kinds of pressures that build up in the conventional Western management hierarchy. There are fewer shelters protecting incompetent managers whom workers don't respect. (Beyond this, there seems to be a commitment on the part of management to make the manufacturing process function properly, including a role for workers themselves in this, that is not always apparent in the West, and which builds up a certain respect for the system itself: see Chapter 7.)

In such a context, management efforts to paint the UAW as a 'third party' coming in from outside may ring true with employees because they express the important truth that Honda management attempts to maintain direct relations with its thousands of production workers.

Moreover, while Honda was ready for the UAW, the UAW was not ready for Honda. The union adopted a traditional strategy of focusing on complaints that work was too hard and too fast, pointing to instances of management caprice, and playing on employee fears that automation would lead to mass redundancies: all the kinds of problems that might have emerged at a Big Three plant without a union to protect workers. The trouble was that while some of these practices may exist at Honda, they're not endemic. The union campaign simply didn't ring a loud enough bell.

The UAW simply had not fully analysed Honda's management structures and strategies and then designed its approach accordingly. Honda wasn't playing by the old rules, but union organizers didn't adapt. Instead they became increasingly frustrated. According to one:

They had no pride. If something was wrong, and we said it was wrong, they right away went out and corrected it.[5]

What was happening at the transplant parts makers while Honda and the UAW fought it out? Nothing at all. American labour unions have always been much less influential at automotive parts makers. In the Honda just-in-time region they seem set for extinction. Transplant parts makers have followed Honda's example and assiduously avoided union representation. Finding a non-union environment was an important factor in their location decisions, and most report no 'trouble' with unions.

As for union representation of workers in negotiations with management, this only takes place at one transplant parts maker, which is an existing capital-equipment supplier purchased by a Japanese firm. Steel workers are unionized at the steel factories. But otherwise there simply is no labour union involvement at all in Honda's just-in-time region.

In all large organizations, even the best-run, there are multiple sources of tensions than can lead to disputes, and Honda is no exception. Workers may be injured on the job and find themselves sidelined into menial tasks whereas they had previously been keenly and actively involved in factory life. Experienced workers may find themselves working under team leaders they consider incapable. Workers may be reluctant to accede to management requests to change from one shift to another to balance the workforce. And there is sexual harassment. In short, there are lots of avenues for resentment to build up.

In the absence of an independent representative organization for the workforce, how are the inevitable disputes and other problems dealt with? On the one hand, there is a management team specializing in labour relations questions, whose job it is to resolve disputes that have come into the open. On the other hand, there is the Associate Review Panel. Established in 1988, the panel reviews cases in which management wants to dismiss workers: for poor attendance, for instance. The majority of members are production workers. Are they therefore more sympathetic to workers? Apparently not. In fact the Associate Review Panel can be harsher than management, telling workers who come before it that they knew what the rules were, and that all (including panel members themselves) have to obey them, like it or not. Another clever Honda labour relations strategy.

MANAGERS AND ENGINEERS, JAPANESE AND AMERICAN

So far we've focused on production workers. But who are Honda's managers and engineers? Are they Japanese or Americans? Is the

Japanese contingent a skeleton staff brought in to supervise and to communicate with Japan, or is it a mass transplanting of people and know-how? Can Honda utilize American managers with no practical experience of Japanese management techniques? Can Japanese managers be effectively integrated with a North American workforce? What roles do Japanese staff play, what roles the Americans and Canadians? Are the Japanese in fact any good at managing in a foreign country?

Honda's basic strategy has been to transplant a large group of Japanese managers and engineers to North America. Numbers have varied between about 300 and 380. Many Japanese staff are semi-permanent, which in practice means about three years' service before returning to Japan (although some have elected to stay permanently). Others are 'JTs', Japanese temporaries who wear JT badges and are brought in for specific projects – introduction of new products or new technologies – or to gain initial experience abroad without a full household move.

The potential wider political issue presented by the presence of large numbers of Japanese managers at Honda has not really come to the surface, eclipsed by the question of local content (see Chapter 4). In the open controversy over local content Honda's spokespersons are usually Americans. However, Japanese managers too give regular interviews, hold press conferences, and make after-dinner speeches locally. There is no pretence that Honda is somehow not a Japanese-owned firm.

The Japanese staff has definitely not been brought in to 'show Americans what to do', then to retire gracefully back to Japan. They are there to ensure that the Honda Way is transplanted lock, stock and barrel. That is a long process. Many American managers have shadow Japanese managers who follow their every move.

Japanese staff retain most control over manufacturing technology and production organization. They already knew how to make automobiles the Honda Way, and they are therefore concentrated in functions related to engineering, manufacturing, quality control and relations with supplier firms. Americans are given responsibilities for overall plant management, for front-line dealings with production workers, and especially for issues to do with employment conditions.

This division explains the peculiar fact that many of Honda's top American managers had never worked in industry, let alone automobile manufacturing, prior to joining Honda in the early 1980s. The Marysville plant manager and the Vice-President for Corporate Planning, later Anna plant manager, were previously local lawyers. Now though, it is an internal labour market that provides candidates for promotion: virtually all promotions are made from within the firm rather than hiring from outside.

Production workers report directly to American managers, who in turn have Japanese staff parallel to them, occupying different functions. This pattern is shown in Table 6.7, where general management is vested in Americans, but the top technical engineers remain Japanese. The management structure at the Marysville motorcycle plant is also shown, for comparison. Here Americans do occupy top engineering posts, which may indicate the future for the automobile plants, though the top posts in the smaller motorcycle factory are all lower down the management hierarchy than at the automobile plants.

Moving to the United States was a formidable task for Honda's Japanese managers and their families, albeit one made easier by the large numbers involved. Most of Honda's Japanese staff don't live in Marysville, but in the well-off Columbus suburb of Dublin: families live in large modern ranch-style houses on big lots, single men stay in apartment blocks. Schools present the biggest problem, but having a Japanese colony in Dublin has led to a special local sensitivity to the needs of incoming Japanese students, about 300 of whom attend Dublin schools. Saturday schools in Japanese, at Columbus and Dayton, are paid for by parents and run by the Japanese Ministry of Education.

At the transplant parts makers, managers are mostly white American men. There are very few women or ethnic minorities (Figure 6.5). Japanese managers stay for periods of three to four years. But their situation is more difficult than at Honda. The downside of spatial dispersal into small towns is that there may be only a handful of Japanese families in each area and isolation is felt more intensely. Local voluntary groups have often 'godfathered' new Japanese families, and small local colleges have set up courses to help them adjust, all part of the welcome mat for new investments.

The same division of roles we saw at Honda – whereby American managers are responsible for general management functions and for relations with production workers, whereas Japanese staff take charge of the technical aspects of production – is mirrored at transplant parts makers. American managers expect a gradual shift over time, with replacement of Japanese technical staff by Americans they are currently training, and there is already some evidence of this at the longest-established parts makers.

There is plenty of friction between American managers and their Japanese counterparts. Being paired up with a Japanese shadow means both being responsible for the same job, sharing the same desk. Some

Table 6.7   Japanese and American Staff Play Different Roles in Honda's
Management

1. *The basic hierarchy at Honda*

Production	Technical
P1: Manager	T1: Senior staff engineer
P2: Assistant manager	T2: Staff engineer
P3: Production coordinator	T3: Engineering coordinator
	Engineering
Team leader	Staff {
	Production
Production Associate	

2. *Who occupies what position* (A = American, J = Japanese)

Anna engine plant:

Die casting		T3 A
Engine machining	P2 A	T1 J
Engine assembly		T1 J
Quality assurance		T1 J

Marysville auto plant:

Plastic injection and body parts stamping	P1 A	T1 J
	P2 A	
Welding	P1 A	T1 J
	P2 A	
	P2 A	
	P2 A	
Paint	P1 A	T1 J
	P2 A	T1 A
	P2 A	
Material service	P1 A	T1 J
	P2 A	
Assembly	P1 A	T1 J
	P1 A	
	P2 A	
	P2 A	
	P2 A	
Quality assurance	P1 A	T1 J
	P2 A	T1 J
	P2 A	

Marysville motorcycle plant:

Welding	P3 A	T3 A
Paint	P3 A	T2 A
Material service	P3 A	
Assembly	P3 A	T3 A
	P3 A	
Quality assurance	P3 A	T2 A

Source: Derived from information packets for new employees, late 1980s.

Figure 6.5   Managers at Transplant Parts Makers are Mostly White
American Men

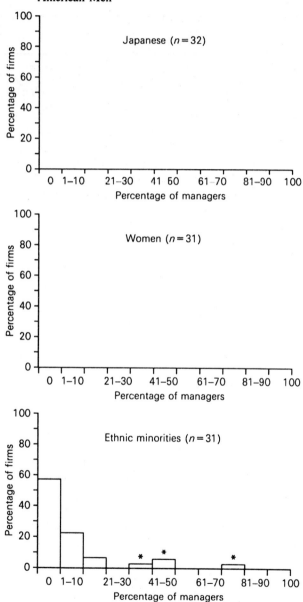

* Examination of individual cases shows that these refer to Japanese managers.
Source: Mail questionnaire.

of the Japanese have simply failed to adopt appropriate American behaviours, like going home when the work-day is over (this is aggravated because some have no family with them). American managers feel pressured to stay at work too for long hours or risk losing their control over the job they share with often highly competitive colleagues.

The Americans tend to view the Japanese as interfering, as not letting them do their job. The Japanese tend not to trust the Americans to do the job 'properly', and some cannot seem to help seeing the North American factories – and their employees – as children to be patronized.

At transplant parts makers, a common complaint is that Japanese staff make all important decisions behind closed doors. Or that in open meetings they start to talk in Japanese. American managers see such secretive procedures as quite unnecessary and as sometimes leading to wrong decisions (frequently to do with the needs of production workers) which the involvement of an American manager could have avoided.

For some Japanese managers, an open-door single status operation is hard to get accustomed to. Some, out of their depth and unable to make the conceptual leaps necessary to work in a foreign culture – a core theme of this book – return time and again to 'we don't do it like this in Japan' in order to reject novel suggestions put forward by American managers. In one case American managers wanted to accede to employee requests that a pond on the factory site be stocked with fish so that workers could fish in it. Japanese managers simply refused, creating friction and resentment around a trivial issue which took far too long to resolve.[6]

In 1992 two of Honda's top American managers announced that they were leaving Honda to work for BMW. The German company had launched its own plans to build an American transplant. One of those who left was the first American Honda hired at Marysville, hence a person with a wealth of experience. We do not know whether their leaving reflects any dissatisfaction with Honda, but it certainly reveals a loosening up of one aspect of the Japanese 'job-for-life' concept, and the functioning of a more open labour market *for the American managers at least.*

Honda's human resources strategy in North America has been carefully developed from the start. Choice of location, employee selection, terms of employment, adoption of American habits good and bad, determination to keep the union at bay and the intermeshing of Japanese and American managers all attest to this.

When Japanese and Westerners first contemplated international diffusion of Japanese manufacturing techniques, they focused on Japanization of the West as the precondition. What we have seen here, however, says that something more complex is going on. In fact the theme that has emerged has been the Americanization of Honda.

It's not that Honda has simply adopted conventional American human resources strategies to help it sink roots in North America, nor that it has just turned over its management to local citizens. Honda has done neither of these. Instead, the company has searched for, chosen, modified and adapted, American people, elements of American culture, American lifestyles: further instances of dualist puzzle-solving.

In some cases, American habits have been borrowed with little alteration (and not always for the best). But in other cases there is an attempt to focus clearly on American culture and ideology, and to build out of them a human resources strategy that will let Japanese management techniques grow and prosper. The Japanese staff certainly didn't do this alone. Many American managers were deeply involved in designing these schemes to fit with Japanese requirements.

The result is that, contrary to some expectations, it is not necessarily the American employees who pose the biggest obstacle to the introduction of Japanese management techniques. Japanese staff can have considerable difficulties operating abroad. In fact the Westerners may be more adaptable than the Japanese. Sure, they have a different type of adapting to do, but perhaps there is something more basic too.

This leads us to speculate that there may be distinct advantages for a firm like Honda, available in the West, that it cannot get in Japan itself. North America or Europe as a better environment for manufacturing than Japan? That would be a turn-up for the books. What does it imply for the future competitiveness of Western firms? Will the Japanese let the Americans translate their adaptability into power, position and authority? We return to these questions later in the book.

Notes

1. Sol Sanders, *Honda: The Man and his Machines*, Boston, Mass.: Little, Brown, 1975 pp. 194–5. The reference to Peoria is to a small town in Illinois frequently used to symbolize an average, ordinary, middle America: a town rather like Marysville.

2. Setsuo Mito, *The Honda Book of Management*, London: Kogan Page, 1990 p. 102.
3. Bob English, 'Orientation', *Canadian Business*, March 1988, pp. 58–72.
4. Robert E. Cole and Donald R. Deskins Jr, 'Racial factors in site location and employment patterns of Japanese auto firms in America', *California Management Review*, 31.1, 1988, pp. 9–22.
5. In David Gelsanliter, *Jump Start: Japan Comes to the Heartland*, New York: Farrar-Straus-Giroux, 1990, p. 106.
6. Case described in Thomas F. O'Boyle, 'Under Japanese bosses, Americans find work better and worse', *Wall Street Journal*, 27 November 1991, pp. A1, A5.

7 People, Machines, and Making Automobiles

That plant is already where we'd eventually like to be.[1]

We want to have the ability to protect jobs and respond to the market by being able to flex production as we introduce new models.[2]

In this chapter we get to the heart of Honda's North American operations, how automobiles are made. We focus on how Honda puts its human resources to work, and on how manufacturing functions from a technological and organizational viewpoint.

The key questions are: Does Honda mostly want the physical capabilities of its North American workforce, or does it want their mental capacities too? Can American workers in fact make cars the Honda Way? And has Honda watered down its Japanese technology and organization to make them work in North America?

Underlying these issues is the idea of *mass production* as a way for society to make things. It is normal to think of mass production as a lumbering juggernaut, consuming great resources to churn out hundreds and thousands of identical articles. In this view the technology and organization of mass production are fundamentally inflexible. Change only takes place every few years, with big investments and a new product installed all at once. Otherwise it is a case of churning out the same product, day in, day out, in a regimented way: 'getting metal out of the door'. And if demand falls for product X made at factory A, then factory A may simply stop working, because it is so specialized that X is the only product it can make.

It has become increasingly common recently to jettison the idea of mass production in its entirety and propose alternative ways for society to make things. If mass production doesn't work too well any more because it has lost its old productivity drive and its markets have lost their old stability, the dualist approach steers us towards rejecting the old in favour of its opposite. So we are presented with a series of new theories based on dualisms, like mass production/lean production, mass production/flexible specialization, mass production/beyond mass production. Proponents of these new theories invariably cite the example of Japanese industry to support their argument that mass production is dead and buried.

So is it true that Honda is not a mass production company? If it is not, how would we characterize its manufacturing system? If it is still doing mass production, then why is it so successful when the era of mass production is supposedly over? We might as well say it now: Honda is a mass production company, and the answer to the last question is that it is possible to simultaneously obtain stable and efficient mass production on a day-to-day basis, and to modify it at short notice to increase its productivity and product quality and to respond to market stimuli.

Such a system is the result of dualist puzzle solving, it's a 'best of both worlds' idea. It is called *flexible mass production*, and Japan isn't the only place where you can do it.

UNREMARKABLE FACTORIES

Let's begin in a down-to-earth way by noting six unremarkable similarities between Honda's North American factories and typical Big Three factories.

1. Honda's four automobile assembly lines employ thousands of workers to churn out hundreds of thousands of cars per year. There are two basic models, with a limited number of derivatives and very few optional extras.
2. The products are basically similar to automobiles everywhere in appearance, materials, technologies.
3. Daily production is planned well in advance and schedules are adhered to as strictly as possible.
4. Production workers spend nearly all their time doing the same tasks as at any automobile factory: loading or unloading machines or containers, attaching components together or to the automobile by hand or with tools. The tasks are divided up in such a way that a worker repeats the same task or group of little tasks about 60 times per hour on the assembly lines. Expert engineers and trained maintenance staff design, install and repair the automatic and semi-automatic machinery used.

5. Body parts are stamped by big presses and then welded together mostly by robots, and painting also utilizes high levels of automation. In final assembly, the automobiles are brought to the workers one after the other, and while there is creeping automation, the work is mostly still done by hand.
6. Organization and authority frameworks are basically hierarchical and top-down: the big decisions on production, on investments, are made at the top, and they are put into practice at successive rungs of a ladder, down to the production line.

These unremarkable facts are worth bearing in mind, as we begin to look in more detail at the tasks that production workers undertake at the Honda factories.

WHAT DO PRODUCTION WORKERS DO?

Repetitive Tasks

Production workers spend nearly all their eight-hour work day doing repetitive manual tasks, by themselves or in a pair or small group of workers. Actual tasks vary according to the production department and the particular manufacturing process. It may be picking up parts from crates, bins, racks, conveyors or machines and placing them in another bin, rack, conveyor or machine, while watching to see that a semi-automatic machine has not malfunctioned. Or it may be taking small parts from a row of little bins and attaching them to the body of a car as it moves past on an assembly line. Tasks are repeated at a steady rate, in many parts of the factory approximately every minute.

Teams and Rotation

Production workers at Honda and at nearly all transplant parts makers formally belong to a team. This is the lowest level of group organization, made up of a set of workers responsible for tasks linked together in time (that is, sequentially) or space (that is, simultaneously in the same work area). Team size also depends on technology and organization in the particular part of the production process: it may be four, or it may be twenty.

Over the course of the work-day workers at Honda and transplant parts makers exchange tasks with their fellow team members at regular intervals. The norm is every two hours but again it depends on the particular context. This job rotation is key to Honda's factory-floor group organization, which is designed to help individual workers do their tasks better:

- It relieves boredom.
- It reduces stress injuries, because different muscle groups and body joints are used. This is also why at some firms specific exercise routines – not limbering-up to music – precede each shift.
- It spreads the workload evenly: while tasks are often by nature of different physical intensities, nobody 'owns' a less difficult task or is saddled with an onerous one. This in turn has twin benefits: maintenance of a sense of equality (single status), and avoidance of resistance to change in processes from individuals jealously guarding the less difficult tasks for themselves.
- It prepares workers to fill in for absent team members with no loss of efficiency or quality.
- Workers participate in a series of processes that are linked to each other, and so gain a certain mental perspective on their work, learning through practice to envisage parts of a process and a whole to which the parts belong.

So with job rotation each worker performs a variety of tasks, all involving basic manual work and a dexterity acquired from practice. No job is officially recognized as better than any other. Workers are therefore all classified in the same grade, regardless of tasks performed or seniority, thus single status dovetails neatly with the organization of production.

Transfers

Production workers can transfer between teams or between production departments, though not on a regular basis. Transfers are organized by an internal labour market. A worker makes known his/her desire to transfer from, for instance, assembly into welding. Managers do their best to accommodate such desires, selecting workers when posts become vacant. With the exception of skilled maintenance workers, no formal qualifications are involved, and because of single status, no social barriers impede transfers. To ensure a certain level of stability, transferred workers must stay in the new department for a year before they can make another transfer request.

Transfers have several benefits:

- They allow workers to find their own niche in the factory, a place where they feel most comfortable. Workers are different from each other and management may not have selected the right niche for them when first hired. Niche refers both to the work involved and to the social environment: some people prefer to be able to talk to fellow team members as they work, while others prefer more isolation.
- To know that you can transfer, and seeing others doing so, acts as a psychological safety valve in case of stress.
- After several years in the same department, a fresh start may provide mental and emotional stimulation that in turn brings renewed motivation. Managers need to keep people as interested as possible and not thwart their desire to do something different.

Indirect Tasks, Quality Control

Beside direct manufacturing tasks, production workers are responsible for other tasks linked to production at each work-station. They clear away waste materials to maintain a clean work environment. They do routine maintenance tasks on machinery, checking it is in good working order, lubricating moving parts, reporting any worn pieces to skilled maintenance workers so that appropriate down-time can be scheduled.

The most significant indirect task takes place simultaneously with production (in fact it is no longer an indirect task). This is routine quality control, the job of every Honda worker and every worker at every transplant parts maker. First, workers assure their own quality by getting their job done properly. Any worker having a problem in finishing a job – perhaps a component does not fit properly, or a tool malfunctions – should immediately ask for aid to resolve the problem, and stop the production process if it cannot be resolved quickly.

Then, workers systematically check the quality of work that has been done upstream as they come into contact with it while performing their own tasks. They label any defects they spot. This form of permanent routinized quality control is especially effective, because workers develop a keen eye for the abnormal when they observe the same set of visual stimuli for hours on end. And without such in-process checking defects can easily become hidden from view as more processes are applied to the defective part (for example, paint), or more parts assembled together making later inspection impossible.

At some transplant parts makers workers even stamp the unexposed faces of finished parts with the date of production so that if problems arise in future they can be traced, and finished cars with components made at the same time can be recalled from the customers for checking if necessary.

Production workers at Honda are repeatedly exhorted not to fear reporting mistakes, whether their own or those of another worker. Management stresses that nobody will be blamed, that supervisors will merely want to help the worker ensure that the problem is eliminated, and that the better worker reports problems rather than ignoring or hiding them. The widespread maxim is 'accept no bad parts, make no bad parts, pass on no bad parts'. Downstream workers are 'customers' whom each worker should do his utmost to satisfy.

In some production departments, like body parts stamping, defects frequently result from problems with technology rather than from human error. In these departments internal newsletters name and commend every worker who has spotted a fault (Box 7.1). Publicity is possible because no worker is being publicly blamed. The lists are short because the faults are few, a handful every fortnight. As we saw in Chapter 6 in the case of regular attendance, performance of routine activities can be both expected of workers and specifically rewarded at the same time. This is also true of quality control. Workers who spot faults are likely to receive Quality Award certificates.

Making workers responsible for routine quality control doesn't mean that stringent testing can be dispensed with. As in most automobile factories, there are quality checkpoints at several points along the line. At Honda there are specific employees responsible for this kind of quality control, but they are described as a 'team that works with production' rather than a group of inspectors, judges and critics. Quality-control employees are likely to have undertaken production work up and downstream of their quality-control post for a period to teach them what matters and why.

Production Workers as Innovators

Routine reporting of quality faults obviously requires an alertness to the task at hand. But Honda and the transplant parts makers also utilize the brains of their workers more actively to try to improve the

Box 7.1   How to Receive a Quality Award in the Marysville Stamping Department (abbreviations refer to body parts)

Found crack in fender in a basket on way to weld.

Found hole in door skin which was not punched out.

Noticed T/L frame draw die moving in bolster during production.

Found conveyor-belt roller which was locked up.

Found crack in T/L skin.

While doing handwork on T/L skins, found cracks and short flange.

Found a very small hard-to-see crack in SE-5 front fender.

While setting dies noticed safety bolts had not been reinstalled in draw die.

Noticed noise coming from sheet loader which was caused by dry bearings.

While inspecting SPO on line, noticed crack on SPO on other conveyor.

While operating press, noticed a bolt fall off loader into die and stopped press before any damage occurred.

Source: Internal company newsletter.

---

manufacturing process. *Worker innovations* are systematically encouraged, guided by teaching, rewarded, and put into practice.

Different organizational channels allow for different kinds of worker innovation. Most firms have separate channels for individual innovations (for example a suggestions scheme) and for group innovations (invariably quality circles).

To start off the process of implementing an individual innovation, workers fill out a form describing their idea, often with a diagram, and explain the expected benefits. They are urged not to feel intimidated in doing this, and to seek help from co-workers, superiors, or – in Honda's case – full-time staff at the Associate Development Center.

There are safety awards (ideas to, for example, install safety gates, remove potential trip points), and a general suggestions scheme for improvements that save money or improve productivity. And then there are competitions to write slogans expressing worker goals: perhaps 'Working nights or working days, the first thing to learn is safety pays', or 'Quality and safety go hand in hand, let's work to make Honda no. 1 in this land'.

Honda treats worker innovations delicately. For the safety programme, workers can be nominated by somebody else, but they can also nominate themselves. Managers judge the merit of the ideas, and several hierarchical rungs are involved, not just the worker's immediate superior. Ideas that can be implemented, bearing in mind costs and benefits, are put into practice as soon as possible. The person who suggested an innovation is likely to be asked to organize its implementation. If it has wider applicability, he or she may be asked to go and explain it to other teams or other departments.

When an idea is not accepted, the department manager must provide the worker with a written explanation within two days. Such proper and correct treatment is seen as fundamental for assuring a continuing flow of ideas. (Note how much emphasis is placed on correct personal treatment each time real individual input is required, from the engineers and researchers we saw in Japan (Chapter 2) to the factory workers we're looking at here.)

Feedback is also provided in the type of award made. Ideas are passed up the management hierarchy from department manager to plant manager and to the North American company president, with a number selected for higher consideration at each stage and earmarked for 'Department Manager's Award', 'Factory Manager's Award', and so on. This process, together with the written explanations in case of rejection, allows workers to learn in practice which innovations are judged best by management, and so to hone their skills at coming up with new ideas.

Individual worker innovations are therefore rewarded in three ways:

- Ideas are put into practice by making alterations to equipment and to work organization. Slogan competition winners see their ideas all over the factory. Having your idea taken seriously by superiors and put into practice cannot be underestimated as a reward.
- Tokens of appreciation, from savings bonds to pens, are given out at ceremonies (there are no monetary rewards).
- Award winners receive a certificate that marks official recognition of their innovation. Certification, together with actual implementation, establishes individual 'ownership' of the innovation, and therefore of a piece of the factory itself (workers do sign a form transferring legal property rights to Honda of America Mfg Inc.).

This whole process can instil a great sense of pride among people whose basic production job would not otherwise receive much in the way of social recognition.

The channels for individual innovations suit immediate and small-scale improvements whose possible resolutions have already been thought up. Quality circles provide a mechanism for a group of workers to develop and promote an innovation together, and are more appropriate to complex innovations – for example, involving more than one team or production department and so requiring formal coordination – or to problems whose solution is not evident. As in Japan, Honda's quality circles in North America are called NH Circles. At transplant parts makers they can have different names, 'Pride Circles', for instance, but the principles are the same.

Production workers organize quality circles around themes they suggest themselves. The group has a certain lifetime, perhaps several weeks, during which members meet regularly outside working hours, paid (not the norm in Japan). There are no 'professional leaders'. At Honda's Associate Development Center workers learn how to organize an NH Circle from staff who advise them, and they can obtain meeting space and materials for presentations. Managers and engineers can be invited to a meeting and asked to help, but not to take control.

Running a quality circle is quite a challenge. Workers who don't possess a great deal of authority during normal working hours take on the responsibility for articulating a problem, work together with colleagues, try to resolve the problem, and publicly justify the group proposal.

Whereas some Western firms have implemented quality circles in a top-down manner, at Honda they are very much bottom-up. To organize one successfully requires an accumulation of experience and adoption of the kind of controlled puzzle-solving mentality we are seeing throughout Honda in this book. Workers have to learn how to make good innovations that also fit into the existing organization of the firm.

Most transplant parts makers have adopted quality circles or plan to do so, but some have waited several years before trying something so ambitious, until workers are bedded down and integrated into the ways of the factory. Quality circles only work when built on the correct foundations, according to the manager of one transplant parts maker, explaining why in his experience they did not work well at domestic American companies, and why his and other transplant parts makers were holding off on adopting them for a while. To function properly, they need good ideas that can really be implemented, in turn fostering the high morale that will encourage workers to form new groups. Managers have to learn too. If one or two quality circles are not managed correctly, the whole system can easily fall apart.

Quality circles present their results at open meetings in front of an audience. Members must not only arrive at a satisfactory solution to their problem but work towards communicating it at a 'big day'. They are listened to and judged by senior managers. The social mechanics of implementing quality-circle innovations are complex: hence the importance of good management cannot be over-emphasized. Hierarchies of authority are being in part reversed. Workers may come up with a solution that implies criticism of the way specialist engineers and managers have organized manufacturing processes. Project implementation often requires expenditure of resources on new or modified equipment, and there can be a strong sense of lobbying from below, publicly hoping that a project 'will attract the support it deserves'. Managers still have the ultimate say, but they have to use their position very carefully.

Winners are selected, and go forward to higher-level competitions between factories, and eventually to present their ideas at a worldwide Honda competition in Japan (this last has not been held in the early 1990s, which is one means to communicate the tighter financial situation of the company to workers).

What kinds of ideas do quality circles come up with? At least in the early years, quality-circle projects have often dealt with problems at the margins of the main flow of production, cleaning up and recycling scrap and waste materials. Direct challenges to specialist engineers and managers are avoided by treating problems that the latter have often not even tried to resolve. This has not reduced the importance of quality-circle activities as cost-saving measures. Thus Marysville now sends its stamping scrap to Anna's furnaces from where it finds its way back into Accords and Civics as mechanical components. It was NH circles that set this process up.

Honda's Voluntary Involvement Program

If NH Circles provide an element of cooperation among workers at Honda, a sense of competition is injected via the Voluntary Involvement Program (VIP), established in 1986. The VIP simply consists of keeping score of each worker's innovations in all the different channels described above – quality, safety, suggestions, NH Circles (see Box 7.2). The idea is to encourage and reward workers who come up with lots of ideas.

Some workers deliver ideas at a furious rate. The winner in 1990 made an average of two and a half suggestions every week, though input falls off significantly for those placed tenth and below; to enter the top 100 requires about one input every two weeks. Managers had

Box 7.2   The Voluntary Involvement Program (VIP) at Honda

Goals

Launched 1986. Provides a competitive framework encouraging and rewarding worker participation in a series of channels designed to promote worker innovation.

How to Score Points

1.	Participate in an NH Circle presentation	50 points
2.	Receive Department Manager's Award	10 points
	Plant Manager's Award	30 points
	President's Award	50 points

in either: Suggestion System
            Quality
            Safety

Prizes awarded on annual basis and for total accumulated points.

How Many Points Do You Need to Win?

1990 winner: accumulated 1425 points in 12 months including one NH Circle and seven Plant Manager's Awards.

To be in the top 100:   160 points in 1987 (VIP's first full year), 300 points in 1990.

Prizes

Annual winner drives Honda Accord free for six months. Since 1991, winner can opt to buy car at book value after six months.

Top 100 and guest invited to annual banquet at plant cafeteria.

Accumulate 2500 points in career at Honda to drive a Honda Civic free for six months.

Note that the VIP does not give monetary rewards.

calculated that it would take 5–8 years for any worker to win a Honda Civic free of charge for six months, but the first was awarded after two and a half years, with seven awarded by 1991, less than five years after the VIP started.

Is this a measure of success? Clearly it is. On the other hand, managers at some transplant parts makers view Honda's VIP as actually too competitive. They observe the same names each year among Honda VIP winners, and they attribute this to only a small proportion of workers actually taking part seriously. The danger is that meeker workers with sound ideas will be put off by the activities of their colleagues, and that participation will fall off to leave only a small minority involved: counter to the principle of human-using-to-capacity. And if programmes like the VIP are emphasized too much, those who don't take part in after-hours activities like NH circles (they may have young children they want to get back to) may be falsely judged to have a 'bad attitude'.

We have seen various channels for worker innovation. But a crucial question remains unanswered. Do workers have the autonomy and freedom to design their own production tasks, as some advocates of the Japanese model claim, or is their work strictly controlled in detail by specific instructions, as claimed by some critics of the Japanese model? As with most dualist questions, there is no simple answer.

In Japan, Honda prides itself on being different from 'the Toyota model', in which tasks are minutely specified down to fractions of a second by engineers. This kind of detailed organization doesn't take place at Honda. What seems to count is that the tasks are performed effectively. In many cases at least, the work-teams and their team leaders devise the details of their jobs, layout of tools and parts, where to place themselves, and so forth. On the other hand, for reasons related to technology, in some work areas there is less freedom of choice, and in other areas a job more or less has to be done in a certain way.

The same distinction between worker autonomy and detailed task specification is visible at transplant parts makers. At many, production workers at least help to design their own tasks. At others, when production was first established, Japanese engineers came over armed with thick piles of detailed papers prescribing exactly how each minute task was to be undertaken and how long it was to take, copied meticulously from their Japanese factory. In part the idea was not to waste the accumulated experiences of many years of work in Japan by asking the American novices to reinvent the wheel. (On the other hand, as we saw in Chapter 6, some Japanese managers and engineers have found it hard to 'loosen their grip' and trust Americans to do the job well.)

Why It's Worth Cultivating Worker Innovations

These complex channels for worker innovation involve many person-hours of management input in reviewing ideas and in organizing their implementation. This must be seen as a worthwhile use of resources. In fact Honda and the transplant parts makers benefit in several ways from worker innovations:

- The innovations result in real *improvements to the manufacturing process*: to quality, safety, productivity and cost.
- Worker innovations are often 'little' suggestions rather than 'big planning'. But precisely because of this they can lead to *smoother production*, by resolving so-called 'minor' problems before they interfere with work. Quality circles relieve managers and engineers of tasks that workers are indeed capable of taking on.
- *Fewer production engineers* are needed: (a) to seek out the 'little' improvements; (b) to resolve breakdowns, accidents or damage that occur in the absence of improvements.
- *'Human-using-to-capacity'* is encouraged without having to promote workers up the management hierarchy. Simultaneously, potential frustrations among the workforce at being 'helpless' to aid managers are turned into positive energies. This way there can be many engineers at Honda who wouldn't be considered engineers in the West because they have no formal engineering qualification or formal position.
- Worker innovations provide *practical evidence when candidates for promotion are sought*. They reveal 'ideological correctness' and show that a worker understands the Honda Way via real 'tests' that have actually already helped the company, rather than paper qualifications or 'classroom' skills.
- Quality circles are a vital mechanism for encouraging *horizontal and diagonal linkages* across organizational structures, which aids overall coordination and provides multiple learning paths for innovation diffusion.

Honda takes the worker as innovator very seriously, well beyond simply improving worker morale, to get the basic job done better. According to the Anna plant manager, speaking at a VIP awards ceremony as the 1990–2 recession began to bite:

Our hard work and VIP activities will see us through these hard times. We gain further strength from the main thing that makes us different from our competitors – our associates using their hearts, their heads and their hands together.[3]

The president of Honda's manufacturing operations in North America echoed:

> I am confident that at Honda we now have a definite strength in human factors as represented by VIP. It is a strength which others can hardly see from the outside and which others can hardly copy.[4]

He added that if Honda's markets were to weaken, the value of worker innovation would grow in importance. And workers would have more time to improve the factories (instead of being sent home on almost full pay in the North American tradition). Rather than a costly extra to be jettisoned when times get tough, worker innovation schemes are a core competitive tool.

MENTAL WORK AND PHYSICAL WORK

Production workers in the Honda just-in-time region do both physical work – using their bodies to construct automobiles – and mental work – thinking about how to construct them better. But let's be clear, the primary task of the production worker is physical work. He or she comes to work mainly to build the vehicles.

The primacy accorded to physical work is obvious. Production would grind to a halt if only a few workers stopped doing their tasks. It is clear from the rewards Honda gives out too. A sizeable money bonus is paid for regular attendance at work, whereas worker innovation is rewarded mostly by tokens. Finally, it is clear from the fact that most workers do not participate in worker innovation schemes or do so only irregularly. They are neither punished nor do they receive lower financial compensation.

Moreover, the mental input is intimately related to the physical work. Production workers have to learn how to innovate effectively, but they are in a very good position to do so. That's why at Honda you constantly hear phrases like 'the production worker is the expert', 'there is more knowledge in the factory than in the office', 'everyone here is an engineer', or 'associates know better than anyone how to change the process to make it better'.

The Honda worker–innovator is not a free-thinking production-line philosopher, but functions within very strict disciplines that govern, channel, and direct the innovation process. The worker–innovator role is built on a foundation of mastery of physical work, and directly taps into the knowledge that builds up, the ideas that emerge, while performing physical work.

This explains why Honda didn't want workers who had previously worked in the automobile industry: they would not only bring expectations of certain terms of employment with them (for example, labour union involvement) but also bring a knowledge of how to perform the physical work the 'un-Honda' Way. Feeling themselves to be already knowledgeable, they might end up being disruptive by seeking to impose what they already knew, regardless of Honda's particular methods of organizing production.

So, the principal role of the Honda worker – just like in Western tradition – is to get the job done. The difference is that in the Western tradition of Taylorism workers weren't supposed to use their brains, officially at least. And yet they often had to anyway, if only to find a way to get the job done with technology and organization – designed by people who never used it themselves – that didn't always make sense or work effectively but which the workers couldn't alter. The contrast is that at Honda, the worker–innovator's brain is systematically allowed and encouraged to improve technology and organization.

In the West, then, the dualist puzzle of mental work/physical work was solved by separating the tasks into separate people, some who thought, some who did. Of course the person who 'did' couldn't help thinking anyway. But his thoughts were ignored, he felt alienated, he had less interest in keeping production running even if he could have intervened to help: the whole system could so easily degenerate into a negative spiral. Honda has a much better solution, because it allows the person who does to think too, *and therefore to improve his or her physical work*. Mental work and physical work are no longer exclusive opposites: one aids the other.

At this point we can begin to see a perhaps surprising answer to the questions of whether Americans can make automobiles the Honda Way, of whether the Japanese culture of groupism is a necessary precondition whereas American individualism sabotages the system. The surprising answer is that for a firm like Honda, producing in America may be as good, if not better, than producing in Japan. The American worker may already possess the individualism which we saw in Chapter 2 that Honda is trying to promote in Japan. Once the cooperative element is mastered by the North Americans, the willingness not to conform and the individual assuredness that are so strong in American culture, combined with its competitive element (provided this can be suitably harnessed), mean that the American worker–innovators can flourish. Far from sabotaging Japanese management, Western individualism can aid it.

Honda brings to America a foundation, a cooperative environment, on which Western individualism can be structured, guided, harnessed, exploited, in the company interest. That's something its Big Three rivals have conspicuously failed to do over the last half-century.

UP THE AUTHORITY HIERARCHY

Honda's authority hierarchy is shallow. But it would be a mistake to think of its organization as therefore a horizontal structure. Vertically above the production workers are team leaders, the 'pivots' of production. Above these are four management layers in each Honda factory (plus two above, for North American operations as a whole).

Team leaders are the lowest rung of the management hierarchy. But they are also production workers, and work directly with their team all the time. Team leaders coordinate the actual tasks undertaken by team members, organize the pattern of task rotation, complete routine paperwork, and step in to work themselves when workers need to be relieved for short periods. At transplant parts makers there is no standard list of roles devolved to team leaders: it varies by firm (Table 7.1).

Table 7.1   What Team Leaders Do (at Transplant Parts Makers)

	Proportion of firms (%)
Assign workers to jobs	97
Fill in for absent employees for short periods (for example, five minutes)	86
Complete quality-control paper work	83
Represent worker suggestions to management	62
Organize safety meetings	58
Fill in for absent workers for whole shifts	52
Prepare work standardization and task descriptions	45
Organize team-member vacation time	31
Other	14
	(n = 29)

Source: Mail questionnaire.

To equip a group of production workers with a team leader is to provide them with a significant amount of autonomy for organizing routine activities and dealing with everyday problems (absent workers, quality problems, machinery difficulties). The team should therefore run itself semi-autonomously, with its leader deciding to call for help when it needs aid, but needing virtually no direct supervision.

The principle of devolving authority extends into all management roles. Each team, each department, each plant, operates autonomously to implement production targets (set centrally, of course). The idea is that it asks for help only if it needs it.

As a result, the internal organization structures of each production department do not necessarily follow a set corporate model, but have been devised or have developed over time somewhat independently from others. Orders don't necessarily come from above for everybody to start adopting fixed procedures (that all too common practice in Western firms which sets everybody rolling their eyes and sighing 'not again'). Instead, innovations come from below, and may or may not diffuse – horizontally and diagonally as well as vertically – elsewhere depending on their appropriateness.

In practice, there is plenty of supervision, but of a less direct sort. Authority is respected and – especially in the case of higher-ranking Japanese managers – almost revered. There is an almost mythical aura of past achievements, perhaps involvement in developing the CVCC engine, perhaps having been in charge of a successful motorcycle or racing-car team. As with workers, for managers too there is plenty of reference to great individual achievements.

The goal of creating respect for managers means that supervisory authority should remain in the background, alongside decision-making capacity and power to call in outside resources, rather than show itself constantly. This kind of management framework, in combination with worker–innovators, devolved teams, and some of the self-regulatory aspects of manufacturing technology and organization that we will look at below, means that very few 'indirect' supervisory workers are required to make the system run (Table 7.2).

Managers and engineers spend a substantial portion of their day on the factory floor. The manufacturing process is strictly planned, but they don't wait for something to go wrong before intervening. They spend their time scouting for anomalies, looking for things out of place that might reveal a problem, or something that could be done better.

At some factories, not only is the engineering staff office right on the factory floor, but it does not have enough tables and chairs for

Table 7.2   Management Hierarchy: Assembly Department at Marysville
(One Line, One Shift)

Associate	c. 1000
Team Leader	50–55
Production Coordinator	26
Assistant Manager	3
Manager	1
Plus 44 engineering staff, for both shifts, 10–12 of whom are Japanese.	

Source: Company employee newsletter.

everyone. The uniforms worn by managers, identical to those of
workers, play a more than symbolic (single-status) role, they make
moving between office and production area easy: there's no need to
stop and put on overalls. Thus it is that brains and brawn take steps
towards each other; the production workers get their chance to
innovate, and the managers look like workers and spend their time
in the heart of the factory.

At first, superficial, glance, it might seem that Honda has done away
with the division between physical and mental work, with the emphasis
on equality, with managers who look like workers, with the stress on
the engineering talent to be found among production workers. But the
fundamental division hasn't been done away with at all. In fact the
production worker innovates precisely to be able to do physical work
better: better product, fewer accidents, smoother process, less waste.
Worker innovation is built on foundations of physical work, and is
focused upon improving that work. It's the same in reverse for
managers and engineers. Their thinking, their organizing, is improved
because they know by close involvement how production actually
works. The production worker still makes automobiles. The manager
and engineer still organize the factory. But each does their job so much
better.

MASS PRODUCTION AND FLEXIBILITY

How is manufacturing organized from a technological and logistical
viewpoint? Are Marysville, East Liberty and Alliston carbon copies of
Sayama and Suzuka? Are they watered-down versions? How have

manufacturing processes been tailored to suit North America? Are they flexible, like in Japanese factories?

Let's start with a brief look at each factory, and at two significant aspects of organization and logistics.

Marysville: The Heart of Manufacturing Operations

Built next to the two-year-old motorcycle plant, the first automobile production line at Marysville was basically modelled on Sayama, where the Accord is also made.

There are, however, some key differences between Marysville and Sayama. The success of the first North American investment depended on Honda's ability to sell all the cars made there. So the production line was short, designed to make 150 000 cars per year instead of the 250 000 – 280 000 made at the Sayama and Suzuka lines. As we mentioned in Chapter 2, Honda Engineering had to develop new technologies in the 1970s that would reduce capital costs commensurately. The two key innovations came in stamping and welding:

- Quick die changes on body stamping presses, so that fewer of these expensive machines are needed to stamp a given variety of parts just-in-time for welding. (By 1986, there would be pairing-up of body part dies for the big body stamping presses, which means that even fewer presses are needed.)
- The creation of a general purpose welding machine that takes the place of several ordinary welding stations, so that Marysville could have short welding lines.

While the Sayama plant is built on a very cramped site, and expanding production there meant manufacturing on two or more storeys, little advantage was taken of the wide open spaces at Marysville. Certainly production is only on one floor, and aisles are wider to facilitate movement of parts to production areas, but the plant has the most efficient use of space in the United States. Indeed the output/area ratios of all Honda assembly plants are basically similar, with newer and lower-output plants and North American and European plants using a little more space per unit output, and the cramped Sayama being most efficient of all (Table 7.3).

The second automobile assembly line at Marysville was completed in 1986, again overseen by engineers from Sayama. It was built in a U-shape parallel to the first, and had to be rapidly expanded unexpectedly, towards the end of its construction (see below). The

Table 7.3   Factory Area and Output Capacity at Honda Automobile
Assembly Plants

Plant	Open	Built area (sq.m.)	Monthly capacity	Capacity/ area*
Sayama	1964	361 000	45 000	0.124
Suzuka	1967	528 000	61 250	0.116
Marysville	1982	290 000	30 000	0.103
Alliston	1986	83 600	8 300	0.099
East Liberty	1989	130 000	12 500	0.096
Swindon	1992	93 000	8 300	0.089

Note: * The higher the ratio, the more efficient is space usage. This measure
is a rough comparison since the activities undertaken at each plant
differ. Note that apparently less efficient use of space can in fact
produce better results if it permits more efficient and less costly
internal physical organization.
Source: Author's calculation from data in various company documents.

result of various such unforeseen expansions is that internal organization at the Marysville plant has become, in the eyes of one Japanese
Honda engineer, 'a mess': a bit like some factories in Japan.

Alliston: From Branch Plant to Major Factory

The engineer who qualified Marysville as a 'mess' considered the
Alliston plant a 'marvel'. The factory was much smaller even than
Marysville to begin with, at only 40 000 cars per year in 1986: initially a
branch plant for the Canadian market, served with parts from
Marysville. It has since expanded to become a fully fledged factory
with 100 000 capacity and its own presses. But even as a branch plant
appendage of Marysville, Alliston incorporated some of Honda
Engineering's latest technologies, including a production line where
cars move sideways down the track to make it easier for workers to
reach inside engine compartments, and automated installation systems
for suspensions and engines that were set up at Alliston before Suzuka
and Sayama.

East Liberty: High-Tech Future

East Liberty's single production line was built at the same time as the
third assembly line at Suzuka, and its manufacturing equipment was

modelled on Suzuka, including the latter's independent platforms for vehicles in assembly to replace the old chain-driven assembly line.

Like the Suzuka line, East Liberty was designed for a major step forward in automation of production, especially of final assembly operations. Marysville was less automated in final assembly than some Big Three factories. At East Liberty Honda caught up, with automation focused on ergonomics and linked in to the separate platforms holding car bodies.

Many components are now preassembled before installation, which reduces the need for workers to crouch uncomfortably inside the automobile body fitting little pieces. The result is a series of modules (for example, assembled doors, bumper–light modules, dashboards, steering-wheel plus pedal sets, engines with many parts already attached). Robots or other machines install the heavy modules automatically or semi-automatically. At appropriate points along the assembly line vehicles on individual platforms are lifted for workers to work in otherwise awkward places.

East Liberty was given a series of other innovative features in line with the world's best, like water-based paints, as well as Honda originals like gangways above all the production areas for workers to walk to and fro without crossing assembly lines, and an entrance drive to the car park with a specially built hill so that people arriving for work can easily see empty spaces.

Finally, bearing in mind the experience of unplanned expansions at Marysville, the layout of East Liberty was deliberately organized so that production could be expanded, or a second assembly line added, without complications. In fact, East Liberty was slow to reach anticipated full output levels as the continuing economic recession in North America and Japan prevented Honda from reaching its sales targets in the early 1990s.

Anna: Nerve Centre for Mechanical Components

The Anna factory regroups under one roof activities that take place at seven factories in Japan, including production of major aluminium and steel mechanical parts:

- Casting and machining of aluminium engine parts and assembly of engines, of which four types were made by the early 1990s: a 1.5l 6-cylinder motorcycle engine, 1.5l and 1.6l engines for the Civic, and a 2.2l engine for the Accord. Aluminium wheels for one Accord variant were cast, machined and painted at Anna between 1987 and 1989, before production was outsourced to a new transplant parts maker.

- Casting, machining and assembly of a series of steel mechanical components, including suspension parts, brake parts, automatic transmissions, clutch cases, and engine crankshafts and cylinder sleeves.

The Anna plant incorporates numerous advanced technologies, including piping of molten aluminium from furnace to furnace instead of the traditional ladles, a Honda-developed low-pressure casting system instead of traditional gravity or high-pressure casting, and use of the same machine tool lines to machine all engines: retooling between models is automatic and takes fifteen minutes.

Transplant Parts-Maker Factories

What about technology and organization at transplant parts maker factories? How do they compare to Japan? Because they all make different products, in different ways, it is hard (and it would be wrong) to generalize. But in most cases manufacturing processes have been transplanted with very little change, basically copied from Japan. If there is a pattern to differences with Japan, it lies in the adoption of some conventional Western features (Table 7.4).

Organization and Logistics

'Hard' technology – machinery, tools – is closely linked to 'soft' technology – organization, logistics. We cannot enter deep into the complexities of logistical organization at Honda's factories. But we can look at two simple methods with sophisticated results that bring out the principles involved for Honda.

1. Detailed Advance Planning: But Expect the Unexpected

The logistical system increasingly associated with Japanese automobile manufacturers in recent years has been the Toyota *kanban* form of just-in-time, in which downstream production pulls along upstream production by transmitting orders to it via *kanbans*. Honda's manufacturing strategy involves planning production schedules well in advance and adhering to them as strictly as possible; the pull

Table 7.4   At Transplant Parts Makers, Manufacturing Processes have been Transplanted without Substantial Change: Some Western Features are Adopted

Similarity between manufacturing process in North America and in Japan	Number of firms (%)
Exactly the same	15
Very similar	53
Similar in most ways	22
Similar in some ways	9
Not similar at all	0
	(n = 32)

Kinds of changes made

Organization:

Group, rather than individual, makes important decisions in Japan
Less planning and direction of projects in North America

Technology:

More advanced technology here
Less advanced technology here
More automated here
Less automated here
Work stations built higher here
More space used here
Cleaner and safer plant here
Newer equipment here, but more robotics in Japan
Less signs in production areas here
Less continuous line-oriented here

Role of production workers:

More complete job descriptions here
Long term employment not guaranteed here
Employees less evaluated here
More regulations and 'employee right to know' here
Simpler process here because employees not flexible enough
More classifications here, higher overtime pay

Quality control:

Formal quality control personnel here
Quality control outside line here

Other:

Larger batches here
Less variety of products made here
More efficient here
Smaller capacity here
Fewer people employed here

Source: Mail questionnaire.

mechanism plays only a minor role, and simultaneous production in different areas according to strict plans is the dominant force.

Despite the strict planning, schedules do change at the last moment, and in this case we see the pull mechanism at work. There may be a problem in painting, so that a particular colour cannot be used. Or a maker of certain parts may experience delivery or quality difficulties. Rather than simply stopping for a short time while the problem is solved, Honda rejigs its schedules in an effort to keep production running.

Many parts makers have to be ready to respond rapidly. They may need to change delivery timing or sequences, or alter the balance of different parts sent (for example, for Civic or Accord, different colours). Because they hold low stocks, they are unable to use inventories to provide the necessary elasticity. There may only be a couple of hours' notice to change production plans. (On the other hand, some factories don't need to respond quickly, because they don't make parts that are changed at short notice.)

One transplant parts-maker engineer previously had a job implementing just-in-time systems at a division of General Motors. Honda sometimes gives his new firm only 90 minutes to two hours of lead time, versus two days at General Motors. These short lead times, he says, force parts makers to select locations within a maximum of one hour's distance from Honda, since travel time becomes a crucial element in overall response time. By contrast, nobody at the General Motors division thought much about the location of parts makers.

And if parts have to come from Japan at short notice? They are flown into the regional airports at Dayton or Columbus, though the lead time here can be as long as five days because two or three days are lost at customs in San Francisco.

The result is a system characterized by both strict advance planning and rapid responses to problems as they occur. Flexibility keeps mass production running.

2.   *Auto Organization: The Magic Number 60*

Honda operates a simple but effective mechanism for keeping control over flows of parts, in which the lot size of 60 units guides production planning: 'the magic number 60'. Parts and vehicles are made in batches, not the line-balancing lots of one which many Western automobile assembly companies have adopted following the Japanese model. Manufactured parts are packaged and delivered to the assembly lines in lots of 60, or, if large parts, in lots of fractions of 60: for example, 2 of 30, 3 of 20, 5 of 12, and so forth. Rather than simply delivering crates full of parts, everything is counted.

A cousin of this system is used for delivery of components from Japan. Engine parts that are imported for Anna come in sets for each engine arranged in a tray, rather than in boxes of each part separately. At Anna, the tray from Japan accompanies the engine on its journey down the assembly line. The principle is the same: parts are counted exactly.

As we'll see in Part III, this tight control system at first bemused engineers working for Honda's British partner company Rover – which was making British-badged Honda cars in the early 1980s – when they found they couldn't simply order crates of small parts from Japan but had to specify the exact numbers. To the Rover engineers the system at first seemed petty in its concern for detail. But there are in fact several benefits once it is set up.

Two advantages are simply ease of logistical planning and rapidity of accounting. But a principal benefit is that the system provides a simple, effective, automatic and objective control mechanism: control over the provider of parts, and control over the manufacturing process at the point where the parts are used.

Imagine that a production worker who is using a certain part runs out before expected, or finds one left over in a parts bin (or in a tray of engine parts). This provides an immediate signal either that the parts maker made an error or that the worker has recently neglected to install a certain part. Downstream workers can quickly check the latter possibility before too much further production has taken place. And the parts maker can be informed straight away if necessary (as we saw in Chapter 5).

This simple organizational tool allows a substantial reduction in indirect staff, because the logistical system in part runs itself, performing its own accounting, checking its own quantities delivered, and permitting a routinized form of quality control built into the production process.

Making Mass Production Flexible

Honda's manufacturing process is designed to promote flexibility in a number of ways. In each case there is an unexpected relationship to the rigid mass production structures that in the dualist approach are usually labelled as opposite to flexibility. We have already seen how last-minute responses to production problems allow mass production to continue unimpeded, and this is exemplary of manufacturing flexibility at Honda.

Honda's flexibility is built on a foundation of very rigid and highly controlled organizational frameworks. Like the production worker whose mental process or innovation is founded upon physical work, mass production is undoubtedly the central and underlying theme of manufacturing at Honda. Flexibility is not, therefore, the opposite of mass production, it is not beyond mass production, and it is not lean (where that means no longer mass production): instead of these, flexibility *improves* mass production.

Flexible mass production at Honda has three goals:

1. **To use machinery more or less permanently,** making parts and automobiles with little downtime, hence reducing the capital needed per unit output and reducing costs. This is achieved by deploying flexible machines capable of making various products and which can be quickly switched. But note that simple inflexible machines are nonetheless used where possible. *Flexibility improves mass production by increasing output and reducing costs.*

2. **To introduce innovations into the manufacturing process on an ongoing basis without disrupting the flow of mass production.** This is achieved by introducing innovations – which may be major pieces of machinery or a small alteration – one at a time, and perfecting them before relying upon them. The machinery may first be set up parallel to (right next to in the factory, if there is space) the old process until it is perfected and can be slotted into the real line, perhaps over a weekend. *Flexibility improves mass production by allowing manufacturing to continue unimpeded while it is made more efficient.*

3. **To respond quickly to changes in demand.** This is also achieved with automation capable of making more than one product – even products not yet designed – with very little modification of the equipment. The balance of production can be altered between different products – Accords and Civics, for instance – with no effect on productivity or quality. This principle also makes it possible to decouple introduction of new models from introduction of new equipment (whereas in Western firms it remains common to introduce both at once, problems with one frequently compounding problems with the other to hamper the build-up to full production after a model change). *Flexibility improves mass*

production by allowing cheaper model changes – whether switching between models or introducing new ones – with little disruption to daily output. Mass production can better meet changing demands in mass consumption markets.

Let's look at some more examples of Honda flexibility in practice.

Rapid Model Changes

In the conventional Western factory, introducing a new model means shutting down for several weeks to retool, followed by a slow ramp-up of output to full capacity over several months while problems are ironed out. Honda does things differently.

In 1985 a new Accord model was introduced at Marysville. Production workers were trained to build the new model as the old one reached its final months. Even as the last of the old model was being made, the first of the new models was in production: on the same day. There was no shut-down, and hardly any production was lost.

The same thing happened the next time the Accord was changed, in 1989. Production never stopped, shortly regained full levels, and kept rising as demand for the new model increased (Figure 7.1). Then in 1993 the Accord changeover was made still more ambitious, with the new 4-door, 2-door and station wagon versions all launched simultaneously instead of at intervals sometimes months after the main changeover.

Rapid Response to Global Demand Shifts

The sheer speed of Honda's big push into North America revealed a fast response to market forces (see Chapter 3). At the height of the big push came a quick decision, quickly implemented, which accelerated the growth of North American production even faster.

During 1985 Marysville's second assembly line was being installed. The expansion plan was already ambitious. Civics were to be added to the Accords. Total output would increase from 150 000 per year in 1985 to 300 000 by 1988, with a second line constructed parallel to the first. The Accord model was changed (as above) in the midst of the factory expansion. So fast was the pace of change that another major capital investment – installing virtually a whole new welding department – took place simultaneously. All this while maintaining full production on the first assembly line.

Figure 7.1   Accord Model Changeover, September 1989

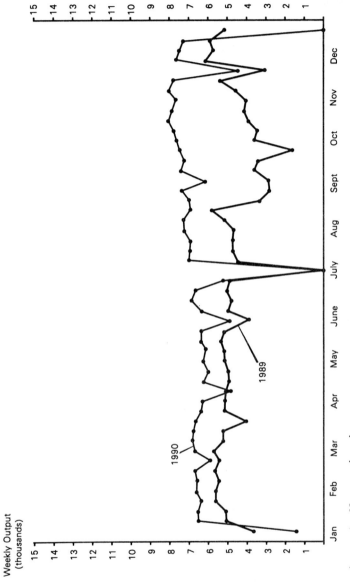

Source: Automotive News, various issues.

Suddenly, in late 1985, demand for Honda automobiles in Japan shifted upwards. But there was no way to increase production in Japan quickly enough to respond. The only expansion in the pipeline was that at Marysville, which was already proceeding at full steam. So it was that in a matter of weeks, Honda had decided to bring Marysville production up to the 300 000 level by the end of 1986, a full year and a half ahead of schedule, and to increase total capacity by a further 20 per cent to 360 000. That way production in Japan could be held back for the Japanese market and more North American needs met from Marysville. The expansion plans were rapidly modified. Here was an instance of flexible corporate planning at world level.

The Flexifactories

Honda only makes two basic models on its four assembly lines in North America, the Accord and the Civic. In 1991, the models were split among the factories as follows: Accords at Marysville, 3-door Civics at Alliston, and 4-door Civics at East Liberty. This certainly doesn't look like a paragon of factory flexibility, considering that in the Japanese model dozens of different automobiles and variants come down each production line in lots of one. Is this a sign that Honda's North American lines and workers are therefore actually inferior to the Japanese, only able to make one model with little variation?

In fact, to focus on the one-model-per-factory pattern of production in 1991 would ignore something more fundamental. The production lines are in fact very flexible, and the allocation of models to factories has regularly changed over time: sometimes one model per factory, sometimes two, with models switching back and forth between Marysville, Alliston and East Liberty to balance capacity utilization and market demand. Each of the four assembly lines can make both Civics and Accords, and each factory has in fact manufactured both Civics and Accords at some time (Table 7.5). This is a dimension of flexibility not seen in Japan, where large cars like Accord and small cars like Civic are made in different factories (Sayama and Suzuka, respectively).

Production is nonetheless kept as simple as possible. This explains why only two models have so far been made in North America. It eases logistical planning, within the factory, within the just-in-time region and in links to Japan. And it fits the pattern of market demand in the

Table 7.5   Flexifactories: Switching Models Back and Forth Adjusts Capacity Utilization to Match Demand

Year	Marysville	Alliston	East Liberty
1982	4-A		
1983			
1984	4-A, 3-A		
1985			
1986	4-A, 3-A, 4-C	4-A	
1987	4-A, 2-A, 4-C		
1988		3-C	
1989			4-C
1990	4-A, 2-A, W-A, 4-C		
1991	4-A, 2-A, W-A		4-C, 4-A
1992		3-C, 2-C	4-C, 2-C

Notes: 2, 3, 4 = number of doors, W = station-wagon; A = Accord, C = Civic

Year noted is calendar year in which the models produced at the factory were altered. No entry for a year implies no change over previous year.

Source: Various company and press sources.

United States and Canada, with the Accord such a big seller and the Civic Honda's second model.

Decisions on how to best utilize each North American factory are now made in a global context. When East Liberty opened in 1989 there was much talk that the Integra model would soon be added, but by 1992 it still had not been, even though the factory was not producing at full capacity. Examining this case, we see how decisions about what to produce at which factory are taken to balance not only various North American considerations but Japanese ones too. All the following factors came into play: on the one hand, the need to make use of North American capacity; on the other hand:

- North American demand for the Integra still fell behind demand for Accord and Civic;
- complicated logistical planning would be needed to make Integra and many of its components in North America;
- the car is already made in Japan;
- the subsiding Japanese market of the early 1990s meant that Integra production lost in Japan could not be compensated with another model;
- East Liberty's full planned workforce had not yet been mobilized.

Here was a global local corporation balancing its production and markets across the world. In fact, the brand-new 2-door version of the Civic was introduced in 1992 in a bid to boost East Liberty production to full capacity.

Honda is reacting very flexibly in North America: mass producing cars for a market dominated by mass consumption (a market that for several years wanted to consume more Accords than any other automobile model in North America), capable of making different models in one factory when only one factory was available, but simplifying its logistical structures when this became possible. At the same time, Honda is able to switch models back and forth within its network of factories to cope with rising and declining demand for each model, and so maintain high capacity utilization. This is economies of scope in pursuit of economies of scale.

The use made, the profitability, the employment levels, of any one factory, are therefore decoupled from the sales achieved by any one model. This is the principle of the flexifactory, which we saw at Suzuka and Kumamoto in Chapter 2, and which we'll also see later in Europe. It stands in marked contrast to practice at the Big Three, where even by the early 1990s, and simultaneously within one firm, some factories stand idle, some operate at half-capacity, and others are on overtime, as a result of variable market responses to the single product each is capable of producing.

MANUFACTURING IN NORTH AMERICA: THE HONDA WAY

At the beginning of this chapter we saw how Honda's North American factories are in some ways unremarkable, sharing many traits in common with their Big Three counterparts. Now we can go a step further. Honda is an ordinary automobile maker pursuing some extraordinary manufacturing strategies.

We've seen how Honda tackles and solves a series of dualist puzzles in its manufacturing process. Physical work/mental work, individual work/group work, machines control workers/workers control machines, vertical/horizontal, centralization/devolution: in each case, at Honda, both elements are at play at once without contradicting each other, for they interact so that one aids the other.

Honda's human-using-to-capacity strategy means exactly what it says. Honda is people-oriented, but it exerts very high levels of guidance over its people. The role of individuals is stressed, whether creative production workers or star managers, but all within a strict corporate framework. Workers do get to control their machinery, but only within the confines of disciplined production organization. There are diagonal and horizontal channels and links, there is devolution of authority, there is bottom-up information flow, but all within strict boundaries of vertical structure, central control, top-down management. In each case, one element of the dualism is pursued within the confines of the other, and that's why they don't clash.

As far as production organization and technology are concerned, the Honda and transplant parts-maker factories are close copies of their Japanese sister factories. The goal is clearly to transfer every possible advantage from Japan, as we saw in the case of the just-in-time region in Chapter 5. Just as many Japanese firms have established transplant parts makers, so Japanese staff have come over to run them. And just as domestic firms are being taught to operate exactly as Honda requires, so too are North American workers.

This doesn't mean we should expect carbon copies of Japan in every respect, for the same kind of flexible adaptation of production to the market seen in Japan is being reproduced in North America. What North America wants is Honda Accords, and to a lesser extent Honda Civics. And that's what it gets, made in North America. It's hard to watch 360 000 Accords all coming out of one factory every year (even if some have 2 doors and some are station-wagons), 100 000 3-door Civics out of another, and 100 000 4-door Civics out of a third, and conclude that this is not mass production.

On the other hand this is a peculiarly flexible type of mass production, one which is able to improve itself continuously and to react at short notice to market changes, both areas in which the traditional kind of mass production fell short. It keeps its productivity and quality rising, keeps its capacity utilized, and keeps its costs down, a sure recipe for success.

Flexible Honda is out-mass-producing the Big Three on their home turf, and with that, making a mockery of claims that the era of mass production is over. Only for some forms of mass production perhaps.

Notes

1. Ford official on Marysville, cited in 'Autos, a special report', *Wall Street Journal*, 15 May 1986.
2. Honda spokesperson Roger Lambert, cited in 'Honda cuts Civic hatchback output', *Automotive News*, 5 October 1992.

3. Cited in '1990 VIP Top 100 banquet topic: commitment', *Honda Wing*, February/March 1991.
4. Cited in ibid.

Part III

Fortress Europe: Inside the Walls

Introduction

The story of Japanese car manufacturing investment in Europe is both similar to and different from the North American experience. The comparison is fascinating, and has much to tell us about the ultimate shape of the global local corporation.

As in North America, most of the Japanese car makers will have a European manufacturing presence by the mid-1990s, in this the largest of the three major world markets. As in North America, it is the emerging Japanese global Big Three – Nissan, Toyota and Honda – that have taken the lead. There are also several joint ventures involving Japanese and Western firms, where the output is shared between the partners. Finally, as across the Atlantic, strong voices have spoken out against the Japanese presence and Japanese business practices. The Japanese have to pay close attention to the political context and to the political ramifications of their strategies.

The differences between Europe and North America reflect the different market and political context of Europe. The big European car making countries are still emerging from a long history of separate national markets each dominated by one or two 'national champion' car makers that governments have supported and protected when necessary. While most of Europe's major car makers do own factories in more than one country, national roots are still plainly evident, even for the American multinationals Ford and General Motors with their British and German bases. The European Community's Single European Market policy is now accelerating the interpenetration of markets, but the past still weighs heavily on production and sales patterns.

Whereas in North America the main split on policy towards Japanese competition has been between the automobile assemblers and the parts makers (see Chapter 4), in Europe the industry is more polarized on national grounds. National attitudes to Japanese competition reflect histories of different national policies towards local car industries. In the southern European countries, Spain, Italy, France especially, there is a strong tradition of government willingness to protect markets by erecting trade barriers to keep out imports. Other countries, Germany in particular, profess a market-oriented approach which is shared by those northern countries with no car industry to speak of, like Denmark.

The free-market/protectionist split explains much of the wide divergence in Japanese sales across Europe (Table III.1). In some free-trade countries without their own car industry, Japanese sales are very high. In the southern protectionist countries, they are very low. In between, the variations largely reflect a balance of national policy and Japanese political calculation about what is 'safe'.

Political factors also partly explain the relative lateness of Japanese investment in Europe compared with North America. The other major factor is simply that there was no comparable upsurge in demand for small cheap Japanese cars during the 1970s: several European

Table III.1   Japanese Sales Vary Across Europe

Country	Vehicle imports from Japan: 1990	Japanese import market share (%)
Germany*	467 279	14.4
United Kingdom*	234 499	11.5
Netherlands*	143 557	25.1
Belgium*	127 107	22.5
Austria	110 357	
Switzerland	106 643	
France*	87 051	3.2
Greece*	68 484	47.1
Sweden	60 455	
Finland	57 448	
Ireland*	46 033	42.2
Denmark*	42 929	41.3
Turkey	41 117	
Norway	39 123	
Portugal*	31 506	10.9
Cyprus	25 334	
Yugoslavia	23 424	
Soviet Union	7 895	
Malta	7 323	
Iceland	5 878	
Italy*	4 476	0.2
Poland	4 353	
Spain*	3 407	0.3
* EC total	1 256 328	
Europe total	1 750 497	

Source: JAMA, Economist Intelligence Unit, author's calculations.

companies already made similar cars, if not of the same quality (which the Big Three American firms didn't). To expand Japanese sales, creating the basis for local production, was correspondingly more difficult in Europe. Moreover, other European companies made very high-quality cars, and so that market too has been more difficult to penetrate. Average Japanese car market share in Western Europe stood at 12 per cent in the early 1990s, compared to 30 per cent in North America.

Returning to the political context, until the early 1990s it was unclear what policy the European Community as a whole would adopt towards Japanese competition: would the free traders prevail, allowing full Japanese access, or would the protectionists succeed in imposing barriers for the whole of Europe, resulting in the building of a 'Fortress Europe'? A crucial question that hung in the balance was whether transplant production would count as Japanese or as European in trade agreements the two sides struck.

In the end, a compromise was reached in 1991. All of the European Community markets would be opened up in stages over the course of the 1990s, with the Japanese being 'encouraged' (that is, they could avoid political controversy by following this path) to invest in transplants with high local content levels and to use these to increase their European sales rather than imports from Japan.

Japanese transplant investment in Europe was pioneered in 1986 by Nissan's British factory, which was the first to open, remains the biggest in output terms, and has attracted the most attention and interest. But Honda was actually the first Japanese company to have its cars made in Europe: the British company BL first assembled Honda Ballade CKD kits in Britain, rebadged under its own marque, as early as 1981. That was the first of a series of collaborative ventures between Honda and the British company (now called Rover) which have seen the latter making Honda products for sale under the Honda badge too, well before Honda's own car assembly plant opened in 1992.

The main wave of investments by Japanese car producers arrived in the early 1990s, after the European political situation became clearer, and after the transplants in North America were up and running (Table III.2). Whether a flood of Japanese parts makers will follow remains to be seen. Most European observers don't expect it, citing high quality levels and high overall capabilities (for example, R&D capacities) at Europe's domestic parts makers, in tandem with continuing political pressure on the Japanese companies. The issue of local content simmers on, however, and may still come to a boil later in the 1990s.

Table III.2   Japanese Production Capacity in Europe: Plans for Mid-1990s[1]

Company[2]	Production starts	Country	Forecast Capacity (approximate)[3]	Comment
Suzuki	1982	Spain	60 000	4WD vehicles
Nissan	1986	UK	300 000	Passenger cars
Isuzu	1987	UK	50 000	4WD vehicles with GM
Nissan	1990	Spain	150 000	Commercial vehicles, 4WD with Ford
Honda	1992	UK	100 000	Passenger cars
Toyota	1992	UK	200 000	Passenger cars
Daihatsu	1992	Italy	35 000	Small vans/trucks with Piaggio
Suzuki	1992	Hungary	50 000	Passenger cars
Mitsubishi	1995	Netherlands	100 000	Passenger cars, with Volvo Car BV

Notes: 1 Table does not include ventures that may have ended by the mid-1990s, such as Rover's production of Hondas.
2 In some cases vehicles are sold by Western partners under their own marques.
3 Capacities are as announced or forecast: the North American experience tells us that they may be revised upwards during the 1990s.
Source: Various press sources.

That could happen if European economic growth fails to keep pace with expanding car-production capacity, leading to an overcapacity crisis like the one in North America, with all the ramifications in terms of plant closure and unemployment which would follow. The issue will be sensitive enough already, as many European producers plan to cut their workforces drastically as they increase productivity to cope with the Japanese competitive challenge over the 1990s.

By the early 1990s there was growing nervousness about increased Japanese competition across Europe, as the southern Europeans began to feel less protected as their barriers came down, as the Germans felt less and less protected by the reputations of their cars, and as speculation mounted that one of Europe's own major producers – but whose? – might eventually go under as the economy continued to weaken. The United Kingdom, on the other hand, had placed itself in a different position, becoming what Peugeot's outspoken protectionist chairman had called a 'Japanese aircraft carrier' off Europe's coastline. (Recall the similar dive-bomber imagery evoked in the United States.)

Now the Japanese have freer rein to break with the old European dualist view which held that cars had to be either cheap and of poor quality or high-quality but expensive. The 1990s will see the Japanese increasingly set their high-quality inexpensive cars – now made in Europe – against the cheaper European competition, and their high-quality higher-priced cars – brought in from home base – against the even more expensive German competition.

Have the Europeans purchased enough time by controlling Japanese market penetration to reform themselves? Will they have learned enough from the American experience to move sufficiently quickly to keep the Japanese at bay? Will the Japanese take better advantage of the Single European Market than the Europeans themselves? And will matters come to a head with a major crisis somewhere in Europe as early as the mid-1990s, as they did in North America?

Most of this story is still to be told. But whichever way events develop, the 1990s is set to be a decade of enormous significance for the European car industry in every aspect of its operations. And the new Japanese multinational car makers like Honda will be playing a key role in breaking up the old patterns and in setting up the new.

8 Working with a Western Partner

> To negotiate with the British in English in a typical English plant is not easy. They discuss, discuss and discuss, but they do not reach a conclusion . . . . The greatest thing we learned from Austin Rover is how much we can be internationalized. We learned little technically, a lot culturally.[1]

For contextual reasons both political and economic, and for reasons of corporate strategy set within that context, Honda's attack on Fortress Europe has been inevitably more complicated than the relatively straightforward push into North America we saw in Chapter 3. The immediate conclusion to be drawn is that global local corporate strategy varies greatly depending upon market, social and political contexts. But that much was already known to Ford and General Motors, with their European organizations quite separate from North America, and making car models unknown in North America. For Honda the real question is how to localize in Europe and still maintain the global linkages that the Americans companies had dispensed with as they set up their separate subsidiaries.

The key differences between Honda's strategies in Europe and North America lie first in the speed of its market penetration, much slower in Europe, and second in its close relationship to the British car maker Rover (previously called BL and Austin Rover), which has no equivalent for Honda in North America. We focus on understanding these two aspects of Honda in Europe in this chapter. Then in the following chapters we investigate Honda's own manufacturing operations in Europe, and look at how Rover has been developing and restructuring internally in the context of its links with Honda.

The link to Rover is especially fascinating and we will spend most of our time looking at it:

- It is one example – a splendid one given its longevity and complexity – of a much larger phenomenon whereby Japanese and Western firms in the car industry and beyond have become increasingly

closely entwined in recent years. Naturally, each inter-firm collaboration proceeds somewhat differently, but each raises the same
questions. Is there a transfer of Japanese technology, organization,
managerial prowess, to the Western firm? How can the Western firm
best learn from its partner? How does the Japanese firm learn from
and otherwise benefit from the collaboration? Does one firm
effectively gain more than the other? In short, what are the long-
term implications of collaboration for respective global competitive
capabilities?

• The case of the Honda–Rover collaboration is important for these
  reasons and others besides. First, Rover and its predecessor BL were
  widely known as one of Europe's weakest mass car producers:
  poorly designed cars, poorly made, by an unreliable workforce that
  was poorly managed. So what could Honda hope to learn? Why not
  form an alliance with a stronger European firm? Second, compared
  to North America, Honda has effectively entered into European
  production backwards: through Rover learning to deal with parts
  sourcing before it had started car assembly. Looking at this process
  will show that the quotation at the start of this chapter is a little
  misleading.

SELLING CARS IN EUROPE

By the early 1990s, the European market was still not very significant
for Honda compared to Japan and North America. Even more than its
Japanese rivals, Honda had focused during the 1970s and 1980s on its
big push into North America, leaving European sales trailing behind
(Table 8.1), and consequently lay only in fifth place among Japanese
firms in Europe.

The global geographical unevenness of Honda's markets has been
paralleled inside Europe. Marketing arms were established in various
European countries beginning in the early 1960s, often starting with
motorcycles, moving to cars later on. With the exception of France, the
dates when Honda car sales subsidiaries were established closely reflect
Honda's response to the evolving political map of policies towards the
Japanese, with Southern Europe lagging behind: Germany, 1961,
Belgium, 1962, Netherlands, 1963, France, 1964, United Kingdom,
1965, Switzerland, 1974, Portugal, 1986, Spain, 1988, Italy, 1990.

If we take the year 1988 as a benchmark, when almost all Honda's
European sales were imports from Japan, the importance of the

Table 8.1   Honda's European Sales are Minor Compared to Sales in Japan
and North America (1990)

Market	Honda sales, Ybn, % in brackets	Honda sales, units, % in brackets	Honda's share of market (%)
Japan	1 110 (32)	669 000 (35)	8.7
North America	1 849 (53)	952 000 (50)	6.2*
Europe	370 (11)	173 000 (9)	1.2**
Others	146 (4)	121 000 (6)	
Total	3 476 (100)	1 915 000 (100)	

Notes: *   United States
          **   Western Europe
               Sales figures in first two columns for the fiscal year April 1990–
               March 1991, as Honda reports them. Europe is defined widely by
               Honda, referring to its regional marketing division.
Source: Company reports and author's calculations.

German market is clearly evident, but equally apparent are tiny sales in
Spain, Italy and Portugal and low market share in France, all due to
government limits on Japanese imports. Several of Europe's smaller
markets – those without their own car industry to protect – have higher
sales figures (Table 8.2) than the much larger southern countries. Put in
global context again, even Honda sales in Europe's economic power-
house Germany only reached 55 000 in 1990, compared with 855 000 in
the United States that same year, proving just how far Honda had been
able to increase sales in North America, compared to Europe.

Remaining at the global level, we can see how Honda has supplied
the European market from a number of sources:

● **Exports from Japan**: by the early 1990s this remained by far the
  major source of vehicles.
● **Exports from North America**: since 1991 Honda has imported the
  Accord station-wagon/estate from Marysville, becoming the first
  Japanese firm to sell American cars in the European Community.
  The Accord coupé followed in 1992. Questions were initially raised
  by the French government over whether these Hondas were

Table 8.2   Honda's Western European Sales Vary Widely (1988)

Country	Sales	Honda market share (%)
Germany	44 023	1.57
United Kingdom	26 214	1.21
Netherlands	12 669	2.63
France	9 449	0.43
Belgium	8 704	2.04
Switzerland	8 373	2.61
Austria	7 825	3.09
Finland	5 044	3.56
Sweden	4 958	1.62
Norway	2 241	3.30
Denmark	1 619	1.83
Italy	987	0.05
Ireland	983	1.83
Portugal	757	0.40
Spain	236	0.02

Source: Company reports.

really American in origin or in fact Japanese (and therefore included
– and excludable – under import quotas). The United States
government strongly protested that these were genuine American
products (even as its Customs Service was criticizing Honda's
Alliston Civics as not North American enough!), and the British
government joined in too, fearing a bad precedent for the transplants
located in the United Kingdom (France had already tried to hold
back Nissan's British cars on the grounds that they were fundamentally Japanese, not European). But as the European Community and
Japan reached their own accord in 1991 the issue subsided.

• **Production at Rover**: Rover (and BL before it) has manufactured a
series of Honda-designed cars since 1981, for sale in Europe under
both Honda and Rover marques. We'll be taking a closer look at
this collaboration below.

• **Production at Honda's own European factory**: Honda's own car
factory, located in the United Kingdom, opened in 1992, with the
first output of an Accord version specially tailored for Europe
despatched immediately to Germany to test the reaction in the
hardest European market to crack in quality terms. A Honda engine
plant had been in operation on the same site since 1989, supplying
Rover's main assembly plant. We'll return for a closer look at
Honda's European manufacturing investments in Chapter 9.

So Honda was already using a global network of factories to supply the European market even before it started manufacturing at its own car assembly plant there. For the rest of this chapter we'll examine one of those sources in detail, the British firm Rover, posing questions about how – and why – such a leading Japanese firm has collaborated closely with a company seen as one of the West's worst car makers.

THE ROVER CONNECTION

In the late 1970s Britain's domestic mass car maker British Leyland (BL) was in deep financial trouble. The government had just taken over ownership to prevent its complete collapse. Sales were tumbling, employment too. The future looked bleak because no money was being set aside for new product development. Management began to look around for a partner firm to supply BL with a ready-developed model to plug one of the yawning gaps in its model range. That would help keep the company afloat while it drastically restructured its operations.

For BL to get involved with an American or a European company would have been very difficult for domestic political reasons: fears of 'loss of national sovereignty' would have squashed that. But Japan was still viewed differently: a new arrival in world competition, a curiosity, but hardly a threat. And in Honda BL management found what they considered to be the ideal firm. Honda was medium-sized, like BL, and so wouldn't be able to dominate BL or push it around. Moreover, Honda was the only Japanese firm that had adopted the same technical basis for its cars as BL: transverse-mounted engines with front-wheel drive.

1. Ballade/Acclaim

So it was that in 1979, BL and Honda signed a deal for BL to assemble CKD kits of the Honda Civic's sister model, the Ballade, which BL would market under the name 'Triumph Acclaim'. For Honda the timing was very appropriate: the press conference with BL came only a few days before the announcement of the automobile assembly plant at Marysville. Production of the Acclaim began at BL's Cowley, Oxford plant, in 1981: a year before Marysville car production began, and a full five years before Nissan opened the first Japanese transplant assembly plant in Europe.

In the event the relationship between Honda and BL turned out to be far less evenly matched than the early discussions supposed. Honda has continued the march towards becoming a global local corporation which was just beginning in 1979. BL, on the other hand, was in the midst of a brutal decline, pulling out of its overseas manufacturing operations, retrenching at home.

The Ballade/Acclaim was a revelation for BL manufacturing staff, parts-maker liaison managers and workers alike. The manufacturing side found the Ballade very easy to assemble, the most simple car ever built at Cowley, due both to its design and to the fact that the parts received from Japan always fitted together as they were supposed to. The car 'came in a box and went together like a Swiss watch', in the words of one engineering manager.

For parts-maker liaison managers used to poor-quality British parts that didn't always meet specifications and were often packed in approximate quantities, dealing with Honda came as a shock. The kits of parts Honda sent from Japan to Cowley turned out to be almost always perfect, of meticulous quality, always meeting specifications, and always in exactly the correct quantities. Indeed, even for parts such as simple bolts, which BL managers wanted to order from Japan in large boxfuls rather than spend time calculating precisely how many they needed, Honda seemed unable to supply anything but exact quantities, a meticulousness that some BL people viewed at the time as bordering on the absurd.

The high-quality finish and reliability of the resulting vehicle was not lost on British consumers, and the model proved very popular. A decade after they were manufactured, many Triumph Acclaims could still be seen running on British streets, often in remarkably good condition for their age.

Over time BL increased the local content of the car by taking over some subassembly tasks previously done in Japan, and by making some changes, such as new seats with new materials, more suitable for larger European drivers. Only at that point did BL run into a major problem with the Acclaim: how to obtain parts of high enough quality to match those from Japan.

For Honda, there were immediate financial gains from the licensing agreement, particularly from the sales of the CKD kits. Not unconnected, there was talk for a while that France would refuse to let BL sell the Acclaim in France, again on the grounds that the car was still effectively a Japanese import and therefore subject to France's import quotas on Japanese cars.

2. Legend/800

Soon after assembly of the Acclaim began at Cowley, BL and Honda signed a second agreement. Remarkably, looking back on it, they decided to jointly develop and manufacture a new executive/luxury car. If the Acclaim collaboration was a simple CKD proposition, now the pendulum swung to the other extreme, to what remains the most ambitious single collaboration ever agreed between a Japanese and a Western automobile producer.

The basic agreement behind what became the first generation Honda Legend and Rover 800 involved the joint development of two cars with as much commonality as possible. Honda would then produce both the Legend and the 800 at Sayama. Austin Rover Group (BL had since changed its name) would produce both the 800 and the Legend at Cowley. The idea was to launch both companies into the high-quality executive and luxury car market, in which neither enjoyed any real reputation in the mid-1980s.

Was the Legend/800 project too good to be true, too complex to succeed? Both firms got their new cars, so to that extent it worked out. But beyond that the project was plagued with a series of revealing problems. Those problems reflect the challenges of designing cars for consumption in quite different markets, for production by quite different firms.

In fact the first difficulties arose as soon as the designers started work, because the two design teams actually wanted quite different cars to meet quite different market needs: Honda essentially wanted a car to launch it into the upper echelons of the American market, while Austin Rover wanted an upmarket 'executive' car for the British businessman. The cars 'drifted apart from day one', according to one Rover engineer, because 'two engineering teams had two different goals'.

In the end, mechanically the Legend and 800 were similar, all with Honda engines except for the 2-litre and diesel versions of the Rover 800. The size of the cars was the same too, with the same basic subframe. But beyond that there was little commonality at all. The two firms had run into exactly the problem of varying tastes and marketing goals in different world regions that was bedevilling other attempts to make a 'world car'. Like Ford and General Motors before them, the different teams with their eyes respectively on North America and Europe simply went their separate ways when they couldn't agree.

The design divergence resulted in what Rover managers consider – to look on the positive side – as one of the more successful attempts to build separate versions of a common car, vehicles quite distinct to the consumer's eye. On the other hand, that same distinctiveness was to sabotage the joint manufacturing plan. In Japan, Honda engineers were designing their own cars specifically to fit the manufacturing equipment at Sayama and Suzuka (see Chapter 2). All of a sudden, along came a Rover 800 at best designed to be made at the very different Cowley plant in Europe, at worst not really conceived with manufacturing in mind at all. Moreover, its components came from Europe too, and frankly didn't meet the standards Honda workers were used to dealing with.

An incident that occurred in Japan underscored the differences between the Western and Japanese design-cum-manufacturing processes. Austin Rover had designed its own seats for the 800, but in Japan they were to be made by Honda's seat supplier, the independent Tokyo Seat Co. British engineers, including the seat's designers, visited Tokyo Seat to finalize production arrangements.

Instead of the cordial welcome expected, the British contingent was treated to a dressing down by Tokyo Seat engineers. Rather than adopt the role of willing subcontractor manufacturing to specifications given by the assembly firm – the typical Western model – the parts maker's engineers lectured their visitors on the poor design of the seat from a manufacturing viewpoint. Tokyo Seat engineers took the opportunity to show the British seat designers the inferiority of their seats, and by implication Tokyo Seat's own prowess.

After only two years' production, with fewer than 2500 of the Rover 800s made at Sayama, the project was cancelled: a decision made easier for Austin Rover by the same sharp rise in the value of the yen in the mid-1980s that was propelling Honda's shift towards more local sourcing in North America, and which made it cheaper to simply import the finished Rover 800s from Europe. The moral of this story? If a factory is expected to be flexible enough to make different models on the same production lines, then the models have to be designed with the factory in mind too.

On the other side of the world, production of Honda Legends at Cowley also hit a series of problems before it too was cancelled in 1988. The Rover 800 had already been launched a year behind Honda's Legend. By 1987, however, Austin Rover was proudly showing off the Cowley production line, with the Honda Legends mixed in among Rover 800s. Manufacturing managers pointed to all their investment in new technologies, including welding robots, computer-integrated work-stations, advanced doors-off assembly, automatic guided vehicles to carry components, and partly robotized final assembly operations.

But something went wrong with the arrangement. By the early 1990s the visitor to the Cowley factory could see – alongside the expected Rovers filling employees' parking spaces – dozens of Honda Legends too. Were these evidence of such a success that Rover employees were buying the Legends too? No, they didn't belong to the employees. These sleek, large and comfortable cars, loaded with options, were being used simply to drive about the sprawling Cowley complex from one part of the factory to another. Surely a less expensive model might have been used.

What was going on? Wait for this: under the terms of the joint-production agreement, each firm could decline to purchase any car the other company had produced for it, and that's just what Honda had done. Honda opened an inspection facility in Swindon, close to Oxford, to coincide with the start of Legend production at Cowley, so it could put the cars through a series of tests: mechanical, electrical, paint, squeaks and rattles, and so on. Much to Austin Rover's shock, Honda simply refused to accept many of the finished cars. That's why they were still at Cowley years later.

While officially this is a sensitive area, some Rover engineers are still aggrieved by what turned into a major fiasco, in which Honda would sometimes reject all the Legends produced in a day at Cowley, and then accept several at once, for reasons that baffled the Cowley staff who could perceive no difference between the accepted and rejected cars.

Rumours abound as to why. Honda rejected some cars because 'the paint was too thick', it is explained, as though this were absurd. (Without offering any judgement, paint on car bodies can in fact be too thick, so that it tends to crack over time when exposed to temperature extremes.) A less acceptable explanation is also widely believed at Rover: Honda took or rejected cars largely as a function of its own sales requirements, and varied the standards, using supposed poor quality as a reason not to purchase the cars, because it was too proud to admit it couldn't sell them.

At this low point the collaboration between Rover and Honda must have seemed destined to collapse. But in fact from here on the relationship improved rapidly. However, it moved to a rather different footing. Honda ploughed ahead, reorienting the *nature* of its relationship with Rover rather than annulling it. Rover could both supply Honda with cars – so long as the manufacturing process was carefully monitored – and become a vehicle through which Honda could learn how to localize in Europe. Since 1988 Rover has taken up a distinctly secondary position to Honda in matters of product design.

Honda has therefore built learning opportunities into all aspects of its relationship with Rover. An example comes from a 'real-life experiment' during Legend production at Cowley, in which Honda took the opportunity to learn about Rover's major body parts stamping factory located at Swindon. Honda insisted that it would subassemble its own bonnets and boots out of the Rover-made steel pressings. It set up a little workshop in its own Swindon inspection facility for this purpose. There was no other manufacturing process there at the time.

With manufacture in-house, Honda got direct access to every steel bonnet Rover's stamping factory manufactured. That allowed systematic checking of both the steel used and the quality of the pressings before Rover covered them with paint at Cowley. Moreover, Honda engineers also gained direct access to the stamping factory itself, since Honda was now the direct purchaser of the parts and so could legitimately visit it. This experiment may have played a key role in Honda's later decision to buy more body parts from the Rover stamping factory: but only after adoption of a big new programme of investment including capital equipment from Japan.

3. Ballade/200

The third collaboration between the two companies rejected the implied equality of the Legend/800 project, and built instead upon the concept behind the Ballade/Acclaim. Rover was to act more independently, but firmly within parameters set by Honda-designed models. This third project in fact ran parallel to the Legend/800 venture, but was located at Austin Rover's central production base at Longbridge in Birmingham.

The next-generation Honda Ballade model became the basis for Austin Rover's first '200 series' cars. The cars were based squarely on the Honda Ballade, but Austin Rover's active involvement progressed beyond the CKD-with-some-attempts-at-local-sourcing that had characterized the Ballade/Acclaim. Rover redesigned the bonnet and boot for its version to give the car 'a more Rover look'. It also supplied its own engines, and as years went by progressively sourced more and more of the parts in Europe instead of importing them from Japan.

Austin Rover reached 'job four' on the 200 series cars before the model was replaced, meaning four annual steps of increased local input, whereas the Acclaim had only reached job two. In practice, job four meant local sourcing for such parts as rear lamps and door handles. The 200 series nevertheless retained quite a high Japanese content.

As part of the Ballade/200 deal, Austin Rover agreed not to sell its 200 model in Japan. More significantly, neither would Honda sell its Ballade – nor its similar 4-door Civic – in Europe. By 1986 Honda was chafing over the restrictions. That year – before the problems involved in Legend/800 production had surfaced – the two firms agreed that Austin Rover would also manufacture Ballades for Honda at Longbridge. The Honda Ballade was introduced into Europe later that year.

Honda was therefore able to sell the Ballade outside its import quota, gaining real local production in Europe for the first time with virtually no investment. This strategy of minimizing direct Honda investment in European production facilities by allowing Rover to make the capital investments has been pursued by Honda on several occasions. But it was hardly as though Honda was taking no risk. Indeed as with the Legend (an even stranger case given the high quality standards expected of upmarket vehicles), Honda was confiding assembly of its car – and thereby confiding its reputation as manufacturer of near faultless vehicles – to one of Europe's worst-reputed car makers in terms of product quality.

Honda did have its own Japan-built 1.5-litre engines installed in the Longbridge Ballades, thus assuring high-standard mechanical parts. However, in the meantime, Austin Rover had been progressively adding European sources for 200 series components, many of which were identical for the Ballade. Trouble arose when Honda engineers took a closer look at the European-sourced 200 series parts that Austin Rover now proposed to assemble into the Longbridge Honda Ballades. That was when, as one Austin Rover engineer delicately explained, 'engineering standards first became an issue'.

How should we interpret such clashes? Were Honda's engineers being fiercely protective of their car, and by implication their traditional Japanese suppliers? Viewed from outside, perhaps they were simply looking after their own. But at least some on the Austin Rover side are inclined to be more generous. The whole Honda manufacturing system and culture militates strongly against the slightest reduction in parts quality: we've already seen how Honda dealt very strictly with domestic firms in North America (Chapters 4 and 5), and it would hardly be surprising to find similar situations arising in Europe. But there were tensions within Honda too. Corporate strategists wanted a high level of local content for the Longbridge Ballades, and the mechanical components were already coming from Japan. How was the firm to maintain superior quality production whilst achieving high local content?

Honda inspected the Ballades in Swindon. As with the Legend, Austin Rover found that Honda accepted some vehicles but rejected others for reasons it couldn't fathom. Still, Ballade production continued until 1989. Output never rose above 5000 cars per year: hardly a significant amount in market-share terms, but quite significant as a further step towards deeper collaboration. Ballade production was another *real-life experiment* for Honda, in this case testing out the Longbridge plant, and testing out more of Rover's European suppliers. At the same time, the deal allowing Honda not to accept cars it considered to be substandard provided a considerable safeguard.

4. Concerto/200/400

The fourth collaborative venture was launched in 1987 with the agreement that Austin Rover would replace its 200 series and Ballade with a car it would base on the Concerto model which Honda was developing for Japanese launch in 1988. The Concerto would be made by Rover too: and this time in greater numbers, up to 40 000 per year. In fact the initial agreement was for Honda to build Austin Rover versions in Japan too, but that plan was shelved after the problems of Rover 800 production at Sayama became apparent.

This time Rover (another name change for the British company) became more adventurous, making various versions of its car, from 2-door to 4-door with boot (400 series) to 5-door to coupé, several of them versions with no sister Concerto. For Honda, the Concerto was a car of minor importance: a total of only 70 000 were made in Japan between 1988 and 1991 (versus 1.5 million Civics in the same period). Rover's 200/400 became the central model in its whole range.

The collaborative deal for the Concerto/200/400 took on a new dimension in complexity, but this time (unlike with the Legend/800) a complexity that worked. Honda supplied engines for the Concerto and some of the 200/400s from a new engine plant it built on its Swindon site (which we'll look at more closely in the next chapter). That put Honda in the peculiar position of owning an engine plant but not a vehicle assembly plant in Europe. Rover built a new engine of its own, the 1.4l K-series engine, for most of the rest of the 200/400 cars.

In the design process, the companies learned from the Legend/800 and Ballade experiences. Honda's Concerto became the basis on which both companies worked. The companies set up a joint purchasing structure, with Honda now establishing its own local purchasing office and stationing engineers at Longbridge.

For the parts that had to be shared in common to make joint manufacture viable, the principle became to set common standards according to whichever company had the highest. This meant that while Rover desired European sources for as many components as possible, for some parts it proved impossible because of the clear superiority of Japan-sourced parts. On the other hand, many easily substitutable parts weren't shared and there was wide variation in sources. Thus while the anti-lock braking system (ABS) on some Rovers was made in Europe by Bosch, for others Honda's 'ALB' system was imported from Japan.

While Rover versions mushroomed to fill a wide range of market niches (the car eventually accounting for over one-third of total sales), Honda stuck to a very simple two derivatives (4- and 5-door) with a 1.6l Swindon engine for Longbridge production. In part this let Rover concentrate on making one Honda car well, but in fact – and going against the idea some people associate with Japan of customizing cars and offering a wide choice of options for the buyer – it is common Honda practice to offer few choices within a model type: few colours even. Many of what other firms might include as optional features are simply made standard by Honda.

Reaching agreement on common parts sourcing still meant overcoming numerous difficulties. When a component was to be sourced in Europe, the parties worked together to ensure that the parts maker met high standards. But even some apparently simple parts raised unexpected problems. For instance, Japanese and European bolts have slightly different thread forms, which can cause difficulties in assembly operations when the thread exceeds 10mm in length. The problem in finding local sources was that the capital equipment used by European bolt makers, however modern and flexible, couldn't accommodate Japanese thread forms. Many bolts and fixings – apparently simple parts easy to source locally – were therefore initially sourced from Japan.

Sometimes, an obvious technical difficulty like thread form allowed agreement on the best place to source parts. In other cases, different histories, different standards, different demands that might be 'legitimate' but were difficult for the other party to understand, did lead each team to insist on its own source. For instance, Honda insisted that radiator fans and petrol-filler caps for its Concertos should be brought from Japan, while Rover considered them to be straightforward parts, easy to source in Europe.[2]

Honda systematically used the Concerto/200/400 parts-purchasing process to learn about Rover's traditional parts-maker base. Even when Rover engineers had been made responsible for sourcing a certain part they frequently found Honda engineers coming with them to inspect factories. As with the Legend, Honda purchased stampings for Concerto bonnets from Rover's Swindon stamping factory and subassembled them itself before they went to Longbridge. Honda says the idea was to teach manufacturing techniques to the engine plant workforce. More likely is that once more Honda was getting independent access to the product and to the stamping factory.

So the Concerto/200/400 model became another real-life experiment in which Honda's people seemed interested in far more than simply the current project. Rover engineers knew that the Concerto was a 'stepping stone' to something bigger.

That something bigger was in part Honda's own European car assembly plant, which we'll look at in the next chapter. However, to have the Concertos to sell (not restricted by quotas) was far from negligible. For a firm with only 150 000 sales in Europe, an extra 30–35 000 vehicles was a significant increase. By 1990 Concertos (all from Longbridge) already represented 15 per cent of Honda's European sales.

What did Honda do with its new European cars? Most were retained in the United Kingdom. But nearly all the rest were sent to precisely the markets with the tightest restrictions on cars imported from Japan itself, in Southern Europe. Addition of the Concertos accounted for sales being more than quadrupled in Italy, Spain and Portugal between 1989 and 1992, and over 50 per cent higher in France (where sales were already greater). Honda was beginning to carve out its foothold in Southern Europe from within the fortress walls. Of its Japanese rivals, only Nissan could yet do the same.

5. Accord/600

The fifth collaborative project, code-named Synchro, gave Honda its first car specifically designed for Europe, and gave Rover a car to slot in the gap between its 400 and 800 series cars. The original scheme was launched in 1989. Honda simultaneously announced the construction of its own assembly plant at Swindon.

Under the original plan, Honda and Rover would both derive models from the basic Honda frame, the Honda Accord and the Rover 600, and Honda would make them all at Swindon. The Accord itself was derived from a new Japanese model (see Chapter 11). Then in 1991, a year before production was to begin, the plan was modified in a highly significant way. Rover would build its version at its Cowley plant where it also made the 800, leaving Honda the whole capacity of its new Swindon plant for itself.

When this book was written the Accord and Rover 600 had only just been seen publicly, and the two firms have been understandably reluctant to discuss them. But there are already hints of further interesting stories regarding the design process. Some observers have suggested that Rover could not physically fit its own new 2-litre engine under the low bonnet, and has been obliged to buy one from Honda instead, at least to begin with. On the other hand, Rover engineers think Honda has been surprised to find Rover's 600 is a much more attractively designed car, which will also be positioned further upmarket than the Accord. While we don't know the whole story yet, in Chapter 11 we'll come back to the highly significant role these particular cars are playing in Honda's development of a 'global local car' as successor to the 'world car' idea of the 1970s and 1980s. Suffice it to say at this stage that the European Accord is no longer to be the same car as that in Japan, or in North America.

The importance of the 1991 modifications to Synchro plans is that they portend a new phase in the joint manufacturing arrangements between the two companies. Just as they were becoming ever more complex – Rover had made three Honda models at two factories in Europe (Legend, Ballade, Concerto), Honda had made Rovers (800) in Japan, and now Honda had been to make Rovers in Europe – there was a sudden turn to a simpler arrangement, with Rover and Honda only to make their own cars. If the next generation Concerto is also made by Honda at Swindon rather than Longbridge as seems likely, there will have been a whole cycle just like at Honda's factories in North America, with a period of complexity – each factory making various models at once – followed by a return to simpler arrangements (in Europe back to one marque per factory even if different models at each factory).

HONDA AND THE ROVER RELATIONSHIP

A series of five joint manufacturing projects has spanned more than a decade. The core of Rover's range consists of modified (albeit often very much modified) Hondas (200, 400, 600, 800). The exceptions are the Metro/100, and the niche Land Rover 4 wheel drive vehicles, a type Honda doesn't yet make. (In 1993 Honda announced that it would purchase Land Rovers for sale in Japan with a Honda badge.)

But not until 1989 did the two firms formalize their relationship to give it a sense of semi-permanence (discussed below). Paradoxically, that formalization coincided with Honda building its own assembly plant: just the time that it could have dropped Rover if it wanted to. So just what has Honda been doing tied to one of the West's weakest mass car makers? And why has it chosen to maintain the relationship when it no longer seems necessary? Needless to say, the answers lie in business and politics.

Honda's ties to Rover developed step by step over the course of the 1980s. It is doubtful whether Honda had expected them to last any longer than BL did, with the Ballade/Acclaim seen as a short-term stop-gap. Indeed different camps within Honda's management have continually argued for and against maintaining the link to Rover.

Let's take a closer look at the potential business advantages that have underlain Honda's relationship to Rover:

- *Design?* It is a commonplace at Rover that Honda has used Rover to learn how to improve the interior design of its cars – a Rover specialty – along European lines. But there is some room for scepticism here. Honda's public position is that nothing has been learned about how to make cars from Rover. And if Rover's interiors are superior to Honda's, then until the early 1990s at least, Honda seemed to be paying no attention, if we are to judge by the uninspiring and often criticized interiors of most of the cars it sold in Europe. Anyway, as we'll see in the next chapter, as far as design for Europe is concerned, Honda's eyes are fixed not on United Kingdom tastes but on those in Germany.

In several other areas, however, there have been clear-cut benefits:

- *Sales of CKD kits and parts*: Honda has increased its sales in Europe beyond the political quotas by manufacturing substantial portions of Rover cars: the whole CKD kit of the Acclaim, the Japanese engines in many Rover 800s, the Swindon engines in the 200/400 cars, and other Honda mechanical components like gearboxes. In the financial year 1989–90, for instance, Honda sold the equivalent of 37 000 whole cars to Rover in the form of parts for the Rover 200/400 models. That alone boosted its European sales by 20 percent over the official numbers.

- *Sales of Honda cars produced by Rover*: while Legend and Ballade output was insubstantial, the addition of 30–35 000 Concertos per year after 1989 provided Honda with the resources to start a push into the protected southern European markets ahead of all its Japanese rivals but Nissan. And minimal capital investment was needed: that was taken care of by Rover.
- *Learning about parts makers*: the series of joint arrangements with Rover provided a direct conduit to learn about Europe's infrastructure of parts makers long before Honda's own European production began, as we saw illustrated in the case of the Rover stamping factory in Swindon and the joint planning for Concerto/200/400 parts purchasing.
- *Learning how to do business*: multiple linkages between Honda and Rover personnel over a decade have provided Honda with an ongoing lesson in how business is normally done in Europe.

Throughout the series of collaborations, Rover appears to have allowed Honda access wherever it wanted, rarely rejecting Honda requests. Some managers think the firm has been quite naïve in this respect. It's here that we see an advantage for Honda of partnering a weaker company. It is far from clear that one of Europe's larger and more entrenched car makers would have been so open. Rover's very weakness made it an ideal partner for Honda.

Has Rover profited equally? The fundamental ambiguity – from a dualist perspective – remains whether Rover has been saved from complete collapse, or whether Honda has exploited Rover to the hilt. At this stage of our analysis it will hardly be surprising to hear that the answer is: both. We will return to how Rover has been learning from Honda in Chapter 10.

Politics has also played a key role, and Honda has engaged in a clever game to guard its interests and to gain political points at the same time. It was not for a decade, until 1989, that Honda renounced the possibility of easily dropping its connection to Rover. In 1989 Honda agreed not only to purchase a 20 per cent share of Rover from

Rover's corporate parent, the industrial conglomerate British Aerospace, but also to let Rover purchase a 20 per cent share of Honda's new British manufacturing operation, Honda of the United Kingdom Manufacturing (HUM).

That exchange sounded more equal than it was, since Honda ceded minority control only over HUM, not even over Honda Europe. Nevertheless, in another gesture of reciprocity, Rover and HUM each appointed one of the other's directors. An alliance sealed in very Japanese terms, then: apparent mutuality, no take-over or merger, yet a clear statement to indicate a long-term relationship between separate firms. (Will Honda purchase back Rover's 20 per cent share of HUM now that Honda's Swindon engine output is increasingly kept for its own use as the 1990s progress?)

Many observers had expected Honda to strike out on its own in 1989, after wringing all it could from the last joint-production projects with Rover. Some British observers now argued that Honda had cast its lot in with Rover entirely. Others argued that Rover would no longer be an independent firm, and was destined in future to simply make Honda cars under subcontracting arrangements. Still others feared that the last major domestic car manufacturer was no longer independent.

But these are typical dualist-type interpretations. As we will see in the next chapter, Honda has in fact *both* cast its lot with Rover and struck out on its own. Neither is it true that Rover has become merely a cog in Honda's global local corporation, even though it is clearly tied in to it. However dependent Rover has become on Honda in terms of new product development, it seems equally clear that Honda has no intention of taking over Rover formally. What would be the point, with all the responsibilities that would entail?

Instead, a Japanese-like swap of interests and board members suited Honda fine, and was just the right touch politically. Honda could honestly deny that it intended to take over a symbolic British company. Damaging political repercussions might have followed a Honda decision to pull the plug on Rover completely, just – around 1990 – when the European Community was still formulating its policy towards the Japanese car industry for the decade to follow. Honda ended up well-positioned politically as having 'saved' a European company, at the very time the Europeans began to fear that the Japanese were going to inflict the same kind of damage on their car industry seen in North America.

Notes

1. Honda R&D President Kawamoto (later President of Honda), cited in 'Brits are long talkers, says high-up Honda exec', *Ward's Auto World*, July 1988, p. 32.
2. The case of the petrol-filler cap recalls an interesting incident experienced by the author during North American research. At an automotive industry conference I met the sales representative of an American company that made petrol-filler caps. He was having great difficulty, despite several attempts, in selling them to Honda. As he explained, the caps that Honda used did not have a device for releasing the vacuum created as petrol was pumped out of the tank to the engine. I knew this was a problem because the petrol-filler cap on my own Honda was sometimes difficult to open, and then moved with a whoosh of air. The sales representative wanted to sell Honda a cap that opened more easily, but Honda apparently didn't want to know.

9   Honda Builds Its Own Base

Throughout the world, Honda strives to work in harmony with its host nations. The goal of each Honda business within these countries is to develop and perfect independent technology. This policy helps create products of even higher quality, designed from global perspectives. In Europe, Honda is building a truly European business.[1]

We've already seen some key differences between Honda's North American and European strategies. In Europe, sales remain significantly lower, with the pace of market penetration slower and several years behind. Honda has developed close ties with a European car producer, whereas it has kept its distance from virtually the whole domestic automobile industry in North America.

On the other hand, reading the quotation above raises many of the same questions we posed for North America. Let's use it to guide this chapter's analysis of Honda's own investments in Europe. What kind of 'harmony' is Honda seeking in Europe? What does 'independent' technology mean? And what does Honda mean in practice by a 'truly European business'?

We will investigate: the extent of Honda's own investments in Europe (beyond those with Rover); how Honda is dealing with European – British in particular – social structures and ideas; the question of trade unions in the United Kingdom; what Honda expects from its European workers; how parts are being sourced; whether there is a just-in-time region in Europe; and finally, what kinds of research and development are taking place in Europe. That will let us draw some useful conclusions on the questions of harmony, independence, and Europeanization.

One note of caution needs to be sounded. We're dealing with Honda at a much earlier stage of investment in Europe compared to North America. For a start that simply means we have less information, because less activity has been taking place, and the investments are less developed. But it also means that we need to remain sensitive to the dangers of drawing hard and fast conclusions from one stage of a phased process: one lesson from North America is just how quickly Honda can move (indeed that is one of this book's striking findings) so let us not jump to false conclusions. Some answers may have to be left open, but that would be true to form, because that is just what Honda has been doing all along.

HONDA'S EUROPEAN NETWORK

By the early 1990s Honda had built an extensive network of facilities spread across Europe, each playing a special role in the car-making business. With one (partial) exception, they all opened after 1985. An overview will help us see the breadth of activities involved.

Swindon, Manufacturing Complex in the United Kingdom

In 1985 Honda acquired a former airfield on the outskirts of Swindon, a small city in the south of the United Kingdom, where it established Honda of the United Kingdom Manufacturing Limited (HUM). The first activity on site was pre-delivery inspection (PDI) of vehicles, which started in 1986. Honda began to test all cars imported from Japan into the United Kingdom as well as Honda models made by Rover (Legend and Ballade, later Concerto).

The PDI facility consists of a series of checkpoints where detailed tests are undertaken. By 1989 Honda was inspecting about 20 Ballades built at Longbridge each day, increasing to 190 Concertos per day in 1991. Honda managers refuse to reveal the rate of defects in Rover-built Hondas, but the implication is that Honda's requirements generally exceed Rover's, because Rover is used to supplying the less-demanding 'company car' market. Rover has its own employees stationed at the PDI facility to communicate any problems directly to Longbridge.

As we saw in Chapter 8, Honda built its engine plant before there was a car assembly plant, in order to supply engines for the Longbridge-built Concerto/200/400. The engine plant opened in 1989 to coincide with the introduction of those models. The original plan had been to build 70 000 1.6-litre engines per year, for all 40 000 Concertos and a proportion of Rover's 200s and 400s. However the success of the new Rover models exceeded expectations, and in early 1990 Rover was asking Honda for a significant increase in engine output. In a striking example of the kind of rapid flexible response we saw in North America, Honda agreed to raise capacity to 100 000 per year later that same year, and by early 1991 was already making more engines for Rover models than for Honda Concertos.

Showing still more classic Honda manufacturing flexibility, engine plant output is now likely to switch by the mid-1990s away from the Rover 200/400 – Rover to make a 1.6-litre version of its own new K-series engine – to a 2-litre engine for the Honda Accord and its sister car, the Rover 600.

Just after the Concerto was launched, and with production also about to commence across the Atlantic at East Liberty, in 1989 came plans for a new car assembly plant at Swindon, together with the joint Synchro project with Rover which yielded the Accord and the 600. A team of Honda engineers experienced in factory start-ups – East Liberty and an expanded Alliston plant being their most recent achievements – arrived in force to get this latest new plant up and running.

The new factory was to lack one significant manufacturing process: it had no body parts stamping facility. Honda had learned what it needed to know about Rover's Swindon stamping factory – literally just down the road – and Rover had invested adequately in new technology at the factory, so that Honda decided not to invest in its own stamping presses. Here is a revealing glimpse both into the versatility of corporate strategy at Honda – which makes its own major stampings in North America but buys them from supplier companies in Japan – and into the ability of a European parts plant to satisfy stringent Japanese demands.

The new assembly plant was finished three years later, ready for launch of the Accord in 1992. Honda had not been in a great rush: more important was to get production right from the start, and further sales growth in Europe would be steady and not too rapid. Anyway, Honda's first goal was the top: to test reactions to the new cars in the German market. Full two-shift production was not due to start until 1994, only then reaching the announced 100 000 annual capacity.

We can safely predict a high level of Honda-style flexibility at the Swindon factory in future. The car assembly plant is capable of mixed-model production, with Honda to recall the current Concerto's successor from Rover and make it on the same production line as the Accord: as we saw earlier, these are two cars made at separate factories in Japan.

Aalst: The Belgian Flexifactory

Honda's pioneer overseas manufacturing investment was in fact the little known and now eclipsed motorcycle factory at Aalst, a small town in rural Flanders, Belgium, not so different from Marysville. That plant opened as long ago as 1962, which made the Aalst plant the first factory built by any Japanese manufacturer in either Europe or North America: a first taste of what was to come twenty to thirty years later.

Indeed for Honda Aalst was to provide many lessons in operating outside Japan, and the factory has a fascinating history of its own that we simply don't have the space to tell here. That history is one of cooperation and conflict with trade unions – curious to note that Honda has learned to live alongside the Belgian trade unions, organized along party-political grounds, Christian, Socialist, Liberal – and of all manner of lessons in how Flemish and Japanese employees could get on with each other on a personal level. There have also been developments in parts purchasing that foretold many of the practices repeated later.

Unlike its Japanese rivals, then, Honda already had a twenty-year experience of manufacturing in the West when the Marysville plant opened, which taught that it was indeed possible, at the same time revealing some of the difficulties involved.

What does this thirty-year-old motorcycle plant have to do with car manufacture directly? Honda's motorcycle production network mirrors – indeed preceded in many cases – the automobile production network on a global scale. It too operates flexibly, with factories across the world supplying products to the other markets in criss-cross fashion. And the factories are continually changing the mix of their product lines to accommodate market needs.

In this context it hardly comes as a surprise to find that the Aalst factory is slowly but surely being incorporated into the new car making network. By the early 1990s Aalst was poised to make the same 'flexifactory' transition we saw earlier at Suzuka, from being a motorcycle plant to a car plant (or in the Aalst case a car components plant). The first product was plastic fascias (dashboards). From 1986 it made fascias for Rover 200s, and since 1989 for all Concerto/200/400s. From 1992 Aalst began to add production of fascias for the Swindon

Accord and Rover 600 too, making that product a major line of business.

By the early 1990s Aalst was ready to become involved in engine parts manufacture too. A new site near Aalst will house an aluminium foundry from 1994 to make engine parts that will be machined in the Aalst factory itself and then sent to Swindon. Later on a variety of other metal parts are planned, from oil pumps to anti-lock brake components. Machining starts first, with the foundry work to follow.

Honda is retraining the same workers who used to assemble motorcycles: after all, they have years of experience with the Honda Way that would otherwise go to waste. The same people are turning from welding and painting steel, plus two-wheel vehicle assembly, to plastic moulding and assembly plus aluminium machining, jobs that in Western tradition would normally demand different skills, different people and a new factory. But this is Honda's flexi-factory principle at work again: keeping the same factory and the same workers but making a completely different product.

Finally in Belgium, Honda imports its vehicles for continental Europe to a facility at Genk, near Aalst. Here they are inspected, and locally purchased trim and accessories, like car radios, are installed.

Honda R&D: Several Centres for Different Tasks

There have been some Honda engineers stationed at Longbridge, starting in 1988 to facilitate the launch of the Concerto/200/400, which is also a convenient base for liaison with the many West Midlands parts-making companies around Birmingham. And there are some Honda engineers who work at Swindon. With Europe's national markets each still retaining so much different character, Honda also opened a small design centre in Milan, Italy, in 1988, to help it understand trends in Southern Europe.

But the major Honda R&D operations for Europe are in Germany, near Frankfurt. The seeds of Honda R&D Europe (HRE) were planted in 1985 when a small office with five staff was opened, to start 'sensor' work on behalf of Honda R&D in Japan. The HRE office expanded quickly during the early 1990s. Its mission became to learn more about the cars made by what Honda considers the best European manufacturers, to compare the cars Honda has been selling itself, and to propose design modifications suitable for Europe. (We'll take a closer look at these activities below.)

Honda's European Headquarters in Southern England

Honda set up a full European headquarters to coordinate activities within Europe (as opposed to each still being controlled from Japan) in Reading, in the south of England, in 1989. Both the Frankfurt HRE facility and the Reading European HQ are located conveniently close to major international airports (Frankfurt and Heathrow), and Reading is also en route, by motorway, to Swindon: all of which considerably eases travel.

Honda now claims that it has established all aspects of car manufacture in Europe ('top-to-bottom' facilities, in current parlance), all the way from R&D and engineering to engine and component manufacture to car assembly, sales and finally to headquarters activities. Honda clearly wants to leave an impression of 'independence', or 'self-reliance' in Europe, as we saw in the North American case.

That's all well and good for fending off accusation of Japanese 'screwdriver plants'. But does it give an accurate interpretation of what is actually happening, how the Honda organization in Europe functions? Let's now take a closer look at Honda's two main European operations, at Swindon and Frankfurt, to see what's going on: how they fit into Europe, and how they fit into Honda's global local corporation.

A CLOSER LOOK AT SWINDON

Questions of Location

Judging by the American experience, Honda's choice of the southern English city of Swindon for its manufacturing operations is something of a puzzle. Here is an urban area with a strong history of trade union organization and a long history in the motor industry too, as the site of Rover's main body parts stamping plant. Local politicians and officials didn't even go on a recruiting campaign: they were a little surprised themselves at Honda's decision to come to Swindon.

On the other hand big industrial sites are not so easy to find in Europe, with its often strict planning laws, as in the United States. An old airfield site offered the chance to build a vehicle test track easily. Moreover, Swindon's communications are very good, on a major motorway, half an hour from Rover's Cowley plant, an hour from Heathrow airport, and about two hours from Rover's Longbridge plant.

Finally there was that stamping plant just down the road. Perhaps an apparently disadvantageous history as a car industry site could be turned to advantage. Even so, Swindon's differences with Marysville are testimony to the way Honda makes individual strategic choices rather than following a set pattern or model.

Just as important was why Honda selected a United Kingdom location for its European manufacturing operations in the first place. Use of the English language is often suggested, but this is a rather trivial explanation (the working language at HRE in Frankfurt is also English). Presumably the liaison with Rover played an important role too, but on the other hand the United Kingdom also has several weak points, notably its relatively poor industrial infrastructure of domestic parts makers.

What were the alternatives? A political welcome mat was assured in the United Kingdom, but far from certain in Italy. Spain might have been welcoming but it too has a poorly developed parts-maker base. French and German trade unions may have appeared too daunting: after all, in France, strikes are still common, and the trade union IG Metall still plays a determining role in the German car industry. That really only left Belgium or The Netherlands, neither of which held particular advantages.

In fact the recent poor industrial climate of the United Kingdom proved an advantage. The Japanese car makers were welcomed in, especially as it seemed that they would be exporting most of their products to the rest of Europe and so helping reverse the declining trade balance. Moreover, the British trade unions had now been weakened by years of attack on them and by new legislation to control them from a Conservative government and would therefore be easier to cope with, whether or not they represented Honda workers.

Employees and Terms of Employment

Full employment for the whole Swindon complex was planned to be 2000 by 1994 (including PDI, engine production and car manufacture). Let us analyse what some of those employees are doing. We start with the managers and engineers, and look at the production workers afterwards.

There are several clues that the pattern of management we saw in Ohio is being repeated at Swindon, that is, that top plant management is in local hands but Japanese staff are responsible for all aspects that are technical in nature, from production equipment to parts purchasing to manufacture itself. In short, it is the Japanese who manage the process of actually making the cars. Take the case of the plant manager, who is British. As in North America he argues fervently that he, a local citizen, is in charge of operations. But like his North American counterparts he has never worked in the car industry before (he previously worked winding down closing businesses). It's his strong sense of organization, determination, and ability to deal with difficult problems inside and outside the plant that Honda prized; and which lets the Japanese staff get on with organizing the manufacturing of cars while he takes care of other business.

So while the 'Britishness' of the Honda factory is continually emphasized, in the upstairs offices there are rooms full of Japanese staff. Managers are twinned, Japanese/British, with the latter learning from the former by example, and the former shadowing the latter to make sure they do what they're supposed to.

As far as production workers are concerned, Honda has the luxury of steadily recruiting them, first for the engine plant and then for the assembly plant, over a five-year period between 1989 and 1994. What kind of people is HUM looking for? There are some very clear requirements:

- Nobody is recruited against a job description: all necessary training takes place in-house, so Honda has complete control over it.
- Recruits are not viewed as 'moronic clay' to be moulded to Honda's requirements but as people who have *achieved* and will be able to *achieve*. They should therefore be strong individuals; but Honda avoids those with pre-formed 'mindsets'. Open minds, flexibility, commitment, these are the keys.
- Who would be the ideal recruit? 'A farmer would be ideal,' according to the engine plant manager, 'he is probably used to having to rely on his own initiative when he repairs his tractor.'

Some local observers think Honda will find it hard to recruit the production workers it wants. The local labour market has been quite tight, for Swindon is in the prosperous south of England. Moreover, factory work is increasingly unpopular locally, with parents steering their children away from it because it is seen as 'insecure'. Swindon has had plenty of office jobs for those who feel that such work is superior for status reasons. Will Honda be able to show that factory work can be secure over the long term and can in fact be good-status high-tech work, skilled work?

In practice Honda has recruited production workers from a variety of backgrounds, some from factories, some from farms, some from services. People with work experience are preferred over school-leavers. The workforce is young, but not very young: the average age was 27 in 1991. People with motor industry experience are explicitly avoided, precisely because they would bring those 'preformed mindsets' with them.

Honda wage levels began below those prevailing locally, rising later, but are not considered particularly generous in Swindon. Centrally, though, equality of conditions for all employees – single-status – is emphasized. In its terms of employment, Honda has therefore mounted a frontal assault on British social practices, in which status and rank differences are deeply ingrained in many people.

All staff are called 'associates'. They all wear the same uniforms: Honda caps and no tie are obligatory, leaving little space for any personal expression or expression of status. All share the same car park, canteens, number of days off. There are no plush offices or special facilities for management staff. When air-conditioning was planned for some southwards-facing offices, it was installed for the whole factory so that all employees could benefit. In a country where most factory workers would normally use the public National Health Service, the Honda benefits package included private health insurance for all employees starting in 1991.

Security of employment is stressed to new recruits. They will not be made redundant even if the market drops, instead being busy with other tasks around the factory such as 'building their own equipment', apparently possible because employees are developing multiple skills.

For those hired early on, the prospects for promotion are high. The plant manager likes to tell the story of a person hired as a production associate in 1986 who by the age of 31 was in charge of a whole area of the engine plant. Even if such a meteoric rise isn't possible for all, the chances of good associates being promoted to team leader were high as production and employment expanded for the assembly plant, whose cadre of team leaders was being trained in the engine plant long before construction of the car assembly line was completed.

What Chance a Trade Union?

Honda already seems set on following a unique path in the United
Kingdom as far as trade unions are concerned, much as it did in North
America. There would seem to be every intention of running Europe's
first car plant for many decades to have no trade union.

Local and national officials of different trade unions with members
in the British car industry approached Honda early on. The local press
seized on a brewing battle among the different unions for Honda
recognition. But inter-union competition hasn't warmed up because
Honda won't play.

The company told the unions that the union question should wait
until all the workforce had been hired (which could be in 1994), at
which point it would be up to the workers to decide, not for
management and union leaders to come to agreement first. Without
Honda's acceptance, British legislation on trade unions is going to
make it more difficult to gain representation, because there is nothing
to compel the employer to recognize a union no matter how many
workers join, and there is no organized election system like that in the
United States either.

Not even the tie-up with Rover, with its 20 per cent ownership of
HUM, seems likely to have an impact, with Rover telling the trade
unions that HUM's policy is none of its business. To put this in
context, all the Japanese transplants in North America where a Big
Three company has some involvement recognize the United Automobile Workers' union. And Toyota and Nissan, neither of which
recognize the UAW or the Canadian Automobile Workers at their
North American plants, have both signed deals with British unions for
their United Kingdom factories. Even Honda's own Aalst plant in
Belgium is unionized.

Local union officials differ on whether they will eventually be able to
represent Honda workers. The 'optimistic' view holds that work
conditions in the car assembly plant will be considerably worse than
in the spotless engine plant, and that disillusioned workers, subjected to
spot-weld burns, grime, and a rapid and regimented work-pace, will
turn to unions for support. Moreover, the beneficial role of union
recognition will dawn on Honda: a union can be a source of stability,
acting as a policeman for the employer.

The 'pessimistic' view holds that Honda will be determined to avoid
union representation at all costs, to the extent of firing substantial
numbers of workers, or even relocating its operations, if necessary.

Moreover, it is still a bad time to organize workers at Honda. There is a steady flow of new employees, there are opportunities for promotion, and workers with negative experiences are likely to simply leave Honda, as some have already done.

The company has already made it plain that there is no place, no role for unions to play, in its labour relations framework. But let's not assume that Honda will stick to its anti-union stance come what may. Serious organizing efforts might lead to a preemptive move to recognize a favoured union, one selected by the company, not by the workers.

What is clear is that any serious attempt by trade unionists to organize Honda's British workers is going to need a fresh and innovative approach. As we saw in North America, Honda has all kinds of anti-union strategies ready to play. The British unions would be well-advised to take a trip to Detroit and learn as much as they can from the United Automobile Workers before they start. The key will be to not fall into the trap of assuming Honda to operate just like any other (western) car maker.

What Role for the Workers?

The Swindon manufacturing complex has a full engine-production facility, including aluminium casting, machining, and assembly, together with car assembly, including welding, painting and final assembly, plus a final test facility. All that is 'missing' is the body parts stamping, which, as we've seen, takes place at Rover's nearby factory.

But what kind of manufacturing processes is Honda introducing at Swindon? What roles do workers play? Have these been modified to take account of the European or British environment? Are workers adhering to plans laid down in Japan, or are they able to actively design their own work? Are there the suggestions schemes, quality circles, team meetings, the panoply of organizational devices associated with Japanese-style manufacturing?

Heaven or Hell?

Two local viewpoints on Honda are presented in Box 9.1. According to one, HUM is a photocopy of a Japanese factory, run by a hidden group of Japanese managers and engineers, with the British personnel just a front, employing hundreds of tightly disciplined local employees who have no input of their own and simply obey strict instructions from above. According to the other, HUM is a profoundly British operation in which local input is positively encouraged, to the extent that Japanese influence is quite restricted, with the whole organization functioning like a close-knit team of people treated equally, creating their own organization and developing their own manufacturing plant.

Which of the two viewpoints is true? Here is a classic dualist dilemma, and it is one being posed not just about Honda but, now, about Japanese companies the world over. Briefly put, is working for the Japanese hell, or is it heaven?[2]

And yet, is it possible that both viewpoints are correct at HUM? Consider the following statement by a British Honda worker:

> You are left to do a lot on your own and expected to show initiative. And yes there is discipline. If a coffee break is 10 minutes they don't mean 11, because production is production.[3]

Here it is, discipline and autonomy at the same time, discipline providing general bounds within which autonomy can be exercised: just what we saw in North America. Thinking in terms of dualist opposites, as many people in Europe are still doing, is not sufficient for understanding Honda.

Honda-Specific Skills

How is Honda developing its workers' skills to operate in this environment? Rather than attainment of formal qualifications, skill at HUM refers to the ability to undertake a specific task, coupled with a mental perspective on the way that task is undertaken and on how new tasks are learned. While for some skilled mechanical and electrical tasks, HUM has hired people who possess formal qualifications and work experience, there are few employees whose skills are measured in this way compared to the traditional Western firm, since Honda production workers undertake many routine maintenance tasks themselves, which also reduces the number of equipment breakdowns that require qualified technicians to resolve.

Some staff have been sent to Japan and to North America to learn from Honda factories there. But training for production workers is largely 'on the job'. Learning by doing at Honda is directed towards the ability to perform multiple relatively simple tasks rather than a single complicated one. Within each production team 100 per cent task-

Box 9.1   What People Think About Honda in Swindon

Viewpoint 1

Technology

The Swindon engine plant is a carbon copy of Honda facilities in Japan: 'big blocks of technology have been dropped in to Swindon; apart from the faces, it strikes you at first that you could be in Japan'.[1]

Management

In an upstairs room dozens of Japanese engineers study and discuss plans with British counterparts.[2]

'British managers would reject and not want to work in the Honda system because they believe that everything has already been decided in advance (in Japan, or in Europe by Japanese staff), leaving them no space to undertake management themselves. And Japanese managers tend to sit separately, in a clique, even in the restaurant they all share and which is supposed to symbolize a team spirit and lack of barriers.'[3]

Workers' Roles

'Honda workers are subjected to overbearing discipline, with alarms telling people exactly when to leave the canteen to return to the factory floor, and then when to start work again. This system is profoundly alienating because workers are treated inhumanely. While Honda says it wants to cultivate worker initiative, regimentation like that neither demands nor allows it. In fact, Honda doesn't really want initiative from its workers, the firm believes that the Honda Way is the only way. Work conditions in the assembly plant will be worse than in the engineering-oriented engine plant, and Honda is going to face significant problems recruiting workers.'[4]

Viewpoint 2

Technology

This is not just a clone of a Japanese plant: 'we devise our own production systems and write our own training manuals'. 'Associates' have designed their own work-stations: 'there are no industrial engineers or work study people on site'.[5]

Management

'This is a British plant, under British management. Status distinctions do not exist at the plant, everyone sharing the same conditions. British people hired as production associates were soon promoted to control production equipment worth £6m.'[6]

Workers' Roles

'Production associates at HUM very much "own the process on the track"; they're in control of the manufacturing process where they work.'[7]

'About workers who have left Honda already, there will always be some inexperienced people who decide that they don't like factory work after all; that isn't necessarily specific to Honda.'[8]

'British workers have designed their own equipment and work-places. Production associates, returning from trips to Japan, were put in charge of installing whole areas of machinery. Worker involvement in the manufacturing process shows, far from an alienated workforce, a high level of input into the organization of the factory: employees in one section designed and built their own hopper system for cleanly collecting waste from machining operations.'[9]

Sources: Author's interviews:

1. Rover engineers with experience at Honda in Japan.
2. Personal observation.
3. Swindon trade unionist.
4. Swindon trade unionist.
5. Honda plant manager.
6. Honda plant manager.
7. Rover engineers with experience at Honda in Japan.
8. Second Swindon trade unionist.
9. Honda plant manager.

flexibility is expected. Boards displayed on the factory floor list workers' names against an array of tasks, with coloured indicators to show what tasks each worker has learned.

Training for specific production tasks therefore requires no specialist trainers: workers and team leaders teach each other tasks they have already mastered. And there are incentives to learn more tasks, and quickly, because the names of laggards are clearly visible for all to see. Moreover, promotion decisions depend partly on progress and attitude in this regard.

But there is also training to teach general principles: how work should be approached mentally. As we've seen, attitude, not qualifications or experience, is the key to hiring in the first place. And meetings, with their person-to-person communications, are the key to ensuring that that attitude remains correct, is enhanced even. There are all sorts of meetings: shift-start meetings, shift-handover meetings, monthly meetings for all staff, and 'birthday meetings'. In the last, a cross-section of people randomly selected because it is close to their birthday all meet for open discussion: typical topics seem to include car parking, temperature, canteen food.

At Honda, what Westerners sometimes see as the Japanese preoccupation with meetings in fact reflects a programme of continuous training of the associate's mental approach to work. While some meetings, of managerial and technical staff, are designed to resolve problems, the majority, involving production workers, are for information flow, to keep them up to date with what is happening in the factory, interpreting changes 'correctly' for them. In the same vein, more open meetings allow for immediate resolution of outstanding problems or for clarification of uncertainties: the production worker's mind is thus free of anxieties, ready to concentrate on work.

For non-production staff, from team leaders to managers, HUM has developed its own lengthy training manuals from scratch. According to the plant manager everything has been created internally for this formal aspect of training. Training therefore develops workers with Honda-specific skills.

Worker Innovations

At least to start with, Honda management did not adopt a formal suggestions scheme. That would apparently be too cumbersome, a 'stultifying wooden box': why not simply get on with the job of implementing good suggestions? On the other hand, there was already a system of NH circles: 14 circles functioning in 1990, 40 in 1991, with 80 anticipated for 1992. The best Swindon NH circle went to Japan in 1990, spending a day at the company-wide competition, three days at other Honda factories, and three days sightseeing. Other people who participate in quality circles are rewarded with pens.

As in the United States, the early quality-circle activities focused on resolving problems outside the main flow of production. A favourite example comes from a group of workers in engine-block trimming (where excess aluminium is shorn off before machining). This NH circle designed and built its own hoppers to collect waste instead of spending time sweeping it up: all at a cost of £66. The double benefit was that the scrap would be clean and reusable.

Because training is Honda-specific, worker innovation can be channelled into well-defined Honda goals. Hence the importance of

(a) training workers well on the job, (b) developing flexible workers who rotate tasks, and (c) training workers from scratch. Learning 'on the job' teaches workers through practical examples how the manufacturing process works. Flexible rotation teaches people to understand a whole production process even though at any one time they only undertake part of it, thus giving them a global vision. Training in quality-circle techniques orients the way in which people try to resolve problems. Finally, internalized training from the start eliminates the 'interference' that would likely accompany reliance on outside qualifications.

Now we see why Honda avoids ex-motor industry workers. While, as some local trade unionists argue, local ex-Rover workers possess a wealth of experience that Honda might mine, those same years of experience in a Western firm could create a tunnel vision, worsened if the worker thought he already knew how to work in a car factory and had little to learn: this in turn carrying an obvious risk of disruption.

Worker innovation is not, therefore, to be confused with worker autonomy. Major changes to equipment designed by Honda Engineering are out of bounds, as are many decisions relating to investment, production, quality and so on. But where worker innovation plays its role is at the vital 'margins', that is the last 2–3 per cent of the manufacturing design process, where significant errors can occur, where there are little inconveniences that cause major problems, where machines break down. Early worker innovation has also been channelled to the margins of the actual flow of production. Likewise, topics brought up at open meetings appear often to relate to general conditions, to the canteen, to the car parks, and so on.

As in North America then, innovation does take place within a very strictly controlled production process. One local trade unionist thinks it is a military-style regimentation. If so, this may have its negative aspects, but on the other hand it makes crystal-clear that management cares very much about what happens on the shop floor: and that's not always the case in the Western work-place. Rather than leading directly to a sense of alienation, tight discipline may instead provide something for the worker to respect and belong to (again not always the case in the Western work-place).

The key lies in exactly how the non-dualist combination of worker innovation and strict discipline is designed, and how the two elements fit into place, the goal being to make production function smoothly all the time and to improve it at the same time as keeping workers content enough to keep coming up with the innovations.

Breaking Down Class Barriers at Work

The single-status system provides terms of employment designed to minimize internal status barriers. But daily practice at work plays a significant role too. Again, attitude is the key word, and that applies to non-production staff, not just to production workers. Every visitor hears the story of the people hired as receptionists whose first job was to build gearboxes on the line. Engineers with university degrees are also expected to spend several weeks in direct production before moving on.

The goal of these exercises is certainly not to teach the specific tasks – these people are never (or very rarely) likely to repeat them – but to teach what it's like to actually work on the factory floor. That runs directly counter to the classical British and European tradition of a strict separation between the worlds of the blue-collar and white-collar worker, distinguished by place of work, clothes, language, and, yes, attitude, communicating largely via an intermediary, the foreman, who moves between the two worlds.

Honda's aim is once more to eliminate the 'false' barriers among the different groups of the very kind that form the essential stuff of the British class and status system. Honda wants to 'get rid of any status feeling', according to the plant manager. Practical experience on the production line and lack of barriers will in turn make for better management and engineering: as we saw in North America, physical work in order to improve mental work (as well as the inverse, the production worker's mental work to improve physical work).

So Honda, far from adopting the root class ideology of the United Kingdom as it did the – very different, equality- and individual advancement-oriented – root class ideology of the United States, is determined to stamp out the traditional British system. All who meet Honda's chief British manager come away with the impression of an abrasive character determined to break down anybody's feelings of 'superiority' (for example, by making all visitors take their ties off and wear Honda hats just like the workforce). Some think he goes too far. But continually breaking up the behaviours that people 'naturally' fall into because of their culture is no small part of his job. Localizing in the United Kingdom doesn't mean adopting local traditions of status and class difference related to jobs done at work.

Honda management believes that it has a mission to dispense with the job demarcation and class differentiation that have caused so much disharmony in British industry for decades. Self-development, participation, good communication, fair treatment, no political infighting, achievement orientation, single status, broad job flexibility: these are the buzzwords at HUM.

Getting beyond the deadlock of the opposing viewpoints on Honda is nevertheless made more difficult by Honda's one-sided approach to its British public relations. This presents a particular view of life and work at Honda, which emphasizes the Britishness of the operation, the team spirit of its workforce, the general sense of togetherness, the lack of internal hierarchy, how workers are so important that they design great parts of the production process by themselves, and so on: taken at face value, the ideal workplace democracy, a concept captured in the idea of the gearbox-building receptionist.

Less important than how we, outside, judge the accuracy of this vision is how it plays within. How does it stack up against reality on the production line? Will workers come to resent the disciplines of production when the system is publicly described so one-sidedly? Or has Honda in fact got the combination of discipline and worker innovation right, the two working in tandem and more or less harmoniously? These are some of the questions for Honda's European operations in the 1990s.

EUROPEAN PARTS SOURCING

As we saw earlier, Honda parts sourcing in North America has been controversial. Is the same pattern set to develop in Europe, or is localization of parts sourcing in Europe a different affair altogether?

To begin with, there are two key differences in Europe as a whole. First, on the political level, Europe's parts makers have more weight on their side. That's not because the car makers themselves are necessarily overly concerned with the survival of domestic parts makers (some are, some clearly aren't). It's more that the car makers and politicians see pressing for high local content levels as a politically legitimate – even if it is strictly illegal in international law – way to place obstacles in the Japanese path. The French government and the French car makers, for instance, have taken the lead in asking questions about the Japanese content of cars made outside Japan all the way along, from the BL Acclaim to Nissan's British cars to Honda's American models. That questioning came much too late in North America.

The second key difference is that there are widely accepted to be a number of European parts makers, especially the larger ones organized as multinational corporations in their own right, that are capable of undertaking their own research and development, and supplying high-quality products too. Whether they all do so at low cost, or along Japanese lines, is another matter, but the point is that the risks versus the rewards of bringing in a wave of transplant parts makers weigh up differently in Europe compared to North America.

From the start, Honda stated its intention to include high levels of local content in its Swindon cars. When the Swindon assembly plant was first announced in 1989, Honda also signed a 'statement of intent' with the British government according to which the cars made in Europe would attain 80 per cent local content, and that within 18 months of starting volume production.

That sounds unimpeachable, fit for a model European company: as indeed it was meant to. But what exactly does it mean? To begin with, the apparently harsh British government condition turns out in fact to be a form of political protection for the transplant investment it had encouraged. The government was effectively announcing that it would be 'taking care' of the local content issue: no need for France to become involved this time.

Taking care? The British government has used the most simple method of accounting for local content possible, which is also the most liberal. It allows Honda (and the other Japanese transplants) to calculate local content by merely subtracting the cost of direct parts imports from the cost of the finished car. Everything else is assumed to be local. So 80 per cent local content means no more than that 20 per cent of the car's value is composed of direct parts imports from Japan. Overheads, advertising, local profits and so on are all counted as local content. That may be acceptable. Stranger however, R&D in Japan, production equipment purchased from Japan, second-tier parts purchasing from Japan, may all appear on the local content side of the equation as 'made in Europe'.

So 80 per cent is a political measure that translates into 'European beyond doubt', with the stamp of the British government to provide authority. In practice, measuring real value added for each stage of the development–production process for each part, the figure would doubtless be substantially lower. And that still leaves aside the qualitative issue: whether the really high-technology aspects of car production – R&D for core drive-train and overall design, production equipment manufacture, electronic components – will remain in Japan even with 80 per cent European content.

Honda seems ready to play tough on local content if it needs to. At the Swindon manufacturing complex visitors can see cutaway drawings of the Accord model, coloured according to the source of the components: red for the United Kingdom, blue for internal HUM, green for continental Europe, and so on. But where is the colour for Japan? There isn't one. The unmistakable visual impression is that the car will have 100 per cent local content. With this kind of information manipulation Honda may be ready to keep a lid on all potentially controversial facts.

Now we have reviewed the context in terms of the politics of local content, let's take a look at Honda's strategy for European parts sourcing. The strategy is already different from that in North America in key respects.

Honda entered Europe 'backwards'. In North America assembly operations were established first, and learning about domestic parts makers came later. In Europe Honda has had ample opportunity to learn about domestic parts makers – the good, the bad, how to do business with them – through its tie-up with Rover. That gave it a great head start even before it was making cars.

Honda has been capitalizing on its links with Rover to find high-quality supplier firms in the United Kingdom. We saw how the Swindon stamping factory was investigated at length. Since 1989 there has been systematic investigation of Rover's parts-maker base, using lists of firms already graded on quality by Rover's own purchasing department. And as we noted above, Honda engineers have accompanied Rover visits to parts makers connected to production of the Concerto/200/400.

Honda has also approached British parts makers directly, and quietly. Some firms don't even want Rover to know they have been approached by Honda, as they have 'gained the impression' that they may be switching their output from Rover to Honda. But Honda has also been hard, even though it knows European content has to be found, wielding prices charged by its own suppliers in Japan as a means to bid down prices in Europe. And parts makers are surprised that the bidding is based not on the announced full capacity production of 100 000 cars per year, but on 200 000: an indication of future plans at Honda.

At that output level, by the end of the 1990s Honda could be planning to make a mix of Accords and Concertos at Swindon as its mainstream mass European models, accounting for perhaps half of

European sales. The other half would be composed of upmarket more expensive niche models imported from Japan (Legend, Prelude, CRX) or North America (Accord and Civic derivatives).

Over 100 parts makers based in the United Kingdom had been contracted by the time Accord production began in 1992, including major British parts makers and small companies alike, manufacturing a wide range of parts, from driveshafts to small clips, though mostly supplying exterior and interior trim and external engine parts (cables, fuse-boxes). Some of the parts makers are subsidiaries of American or other multinationals. There is also clearly a move to purchase parts from continental European countries for political reasons: each part purchased is a potentially hostile voice silenced. There is clear evidence too that in some cases Honda has purposely selected second-best European parts makers in order to spread its purchasing around Europe.

There is little sign yet of a substantial wave of Japanese parts-maker transplants, though it shouldn't yet be ruled out. More common is Japanese investment in, and new technology supplied to, existing European firms, a policy Honda avoided in the first years of North American production. Several of Honda's United Kingdom-based suppliers are majority- or minority-owned by Japanese firms even though not new investments.

Another intriguing pattern involving Japanese firms can be seen in Honda's seat sourcing. This involves the first new factory to be built close to the Swindon manufacturing complex, owned by Bertrand Faure, the major French multinational company specializing in auto seating. (Bertrand Faure is a prominent example of a special type of 'transplant' increasingly common in the United Kingdom by the early 1990s: one owned not in Japan but in continental Europe.)

The company has developed a strong reputation for constructing separate plants across Europe to supply seats to assembly factories according to sophisticated just-in-time manufacturing and delivery systems. Honda's Japanese seat maker, Tokyo Seat, prominent in North America, becomes technical collaborator with Bertrand Faure, for seat-design matters.

In a further model for parts purchasing arrangements that comes as little surprise, even with a low 100 000 output level Honda is purchasing some of its window glass from the Belgian subsidiary of Asahi Glass (owner of its transplant window supplier in Ohio), and some from the top-ranked French firm Saint Gobhain: a dual-sourcing arrangement like those we saw in North America.

Will there be a Honda just-in-time region for Europe? To start with, spatial scales tend to be smaller than in North America, so maybe a new one isn't needed. Most of the United Kingdom's West Midlands core automotive industrial area is within two hours of Swindon already. Many of Honda's British suppliers are located in the West Midlands or scattered across southern England, few more than two hours from Swindon. On the other hand, purchases from continental Europe are necessarily over long distances, by ship. There is a major warehouse facility in Swindon to store parts from overseas and prepare them for just-in-time delivery to the Honda factories.

But we can envisage a regionally concentrated production network – perhaps an infant just-in-time region, emerging in Southern England west of London (Figure 9.1). Whereas only a few years ago many local people believed that the Rover factories at Swindon and Cowley were destined to close in the near future, now the Honda connection has certainly saved them. Rover at Cowley makes the 600 and 800, both derived from Honda models. Rover at Swindon makes Honda's and Rover's body stampings. Now, located in between the two is Honda's production complex at Swindon, with its engine plant producing for Honda and Rover, and its car plant too. Halfway between Swindon and Oxford is the rural site of Bertrand Faure's new seating factory, and Honda Europe's Reading headquarters is close by. The whole network is located with best possible access to Heathrow international airport.

EUROPEAN RESEARCH AND DEVELOPMENT

Localizing research and development activities has come to be considered virtual proof that a company is not just building screw-driver plants, because R&D is associated with high technology activity and with a sense of a locally integrated, autonomous process of car making. Honda has indeed localized R&D operations in Europe. But what exactly are their functions?

There are R&D activities at Swindon for liaison with parts makers, and there are some development activities there for model launches. But the central Honda R&D subsidiary in Europe isn't in the United Kingdom where the manufacturing is located: as we've seen, it is at Frankfurt in Germany.

The geographical location is revealing for two reasons. In the first place, this is a marketing-oriented research and development centre,

266

Figure 9.1 Map of Southern England Showing the Honda–Rover Infant JIT Region

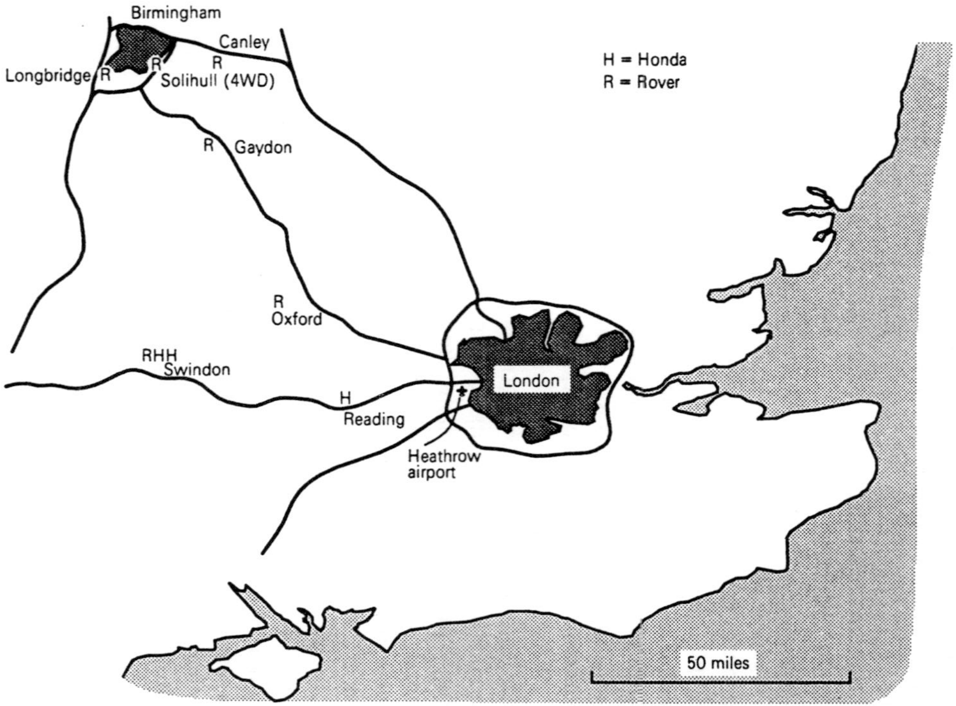

H = Honda
R = Rover

50 miles

Birmingham
Canley
Longbridge R
Solihull (4WD)
R
R
R Gaydon
R
Oxford
RHH
Swindon
H
Reading
London
Heathrow
airport

not one for undertaking basic research. It is located in Germany so as to be physically and psychologically as close as possible to the home market of what Honda considers to be the finest European car makers in terms of product development and quality. Honda engineers view Mercedes, BMW, Audi, and Porsche as their targets in terms of product quality and product concepts. They also profess admiration for the French company Peugeot, but that's where the list ends.

So the German location, diplomatically explained by Honda's Japanese engineers at Frankfurt, has to do with the 'atmosphere', the 'culture', of car design and car driving. For Honda, the United Kingdom, like the United States, is no longer a global centre of innovation in design: there is really only Japan and Germany. Besides, Honda has plenty of people in the United Kingdom at HUM, working with Rover, to pick up ideas about the UK market. If the United Kingdom isn't exactly small fry in market terms, then it's not the prime target market either; that's why Honda's first British-produced Accord models were left-hand-drive, exported straight to Germany.

The second reason the German location is revealing is that HRE is a direct subsidiary of Honda R&D in Japan, and is not linked primarily to HUM in the United Kingdom. Its key mission is to help understand European, German especially, driving habits and conditions, so that Honda R&D in Japan can design cars more suited to Europe (whether made in Japan or in Europe). In fact, HRE staff profess surprise when asked about their links to Rover, because there aren't any.

So what exactly does HRE do? HRE's first input into Honda design came in the late 1980s, in the form of a commentary on the 5-door Concerto to be made by Rover (only a 4-door version was made in Japan: 5 doors has not been a popular variant in the market there, rather like the 2-door and estate cars Honda exports to Japan from North America). But HRE input was hardly enough to make the Concerto a properly Europeanized car in conception: Honda engineers admit that its design was 'compromised' for Japan, even though far more of them have been manufactured in Europe.

Still, it was at this stage in the late 1980s that Honda R&D first began to properly internalize some of the major differences between the North American and European markets, something to which it had paid little attention before. There are simple things like the speeds at which cars move, which are much higher in Europe than in North America. And European drivers use their cars differently from North Americans, with myriad implications for the mechanical and interior aspects of car design.

The Accord had far more input from HRE. Besides testing Honda cars against various European standards, and testing the cars of competitors to 'get the feel' of them, by the early 1990s engineers there were concentrating precisely on getting design aspects like seating and suspensions right for European drivers and driving conditions. In the 1980s Honda suspensions had been frequently criticized in the automotive press as quite inadequate (too soft) for European driving. In the early 1990s that criticism began to turn to praise as a result of HRE input. The European Accord was given a series of features especially for the European market, from rotary heating controls to indicator stick on the left and even to ease of attachment of a tow-bar (said to be very difficult in previous Accords).

But a 'full' R&D facility for Europe is still a long way off: sales of over 400 000 per year would be required to justify one in cost terms, and that goal hasn't even been announced yet. By the early 1990s HRE had no prototype-building or full computer-aided design facilities, and sent all its reports back to Japan. For the next few years at least, HRE's job will be to concentrate on improving the weakest aspects of Honda products as far as Europe is concerned, and on helping Honda R&D design cars to compete directly with the likes of Mercedes and BMW. That means that HRE is more akin to Honda's California R&D design offices, a location in the midst of the hottest and most innovative market, than to the Marysville R&D facilities, with their development focus: there's no real parallel to that in Europe coming yet.

HONDA AND EUROPE

We've now seen how Honda has established its own organization for car making in Europe. This has important implications for Honda's relations to Rover. Some British commentators argued that Honda had thrown in its lot with Rover in 1989 when it agreed to purchase a minority shareholding. But at just that point Honda was in fact launching its own organization, one that could stand alone, operating separately even if the link to Rover was severed entirely. And now we've seen that the two companies are moving to separate their production again, likely no longer to make each other's cars after the mid 1990s.

Far from becoming dependent on Rover, Honda established its independence even as it became more closely linked financially. It is that kind of complex corporate strategy we have to get to grips with when we analyse firms like Honda, and this is why it is necessary to get beyond the dualist 'choices' that so often limit our understanding.

We have covered a lot of ground in this chapter. That's been possible because Honda's European operations are still not as developed as they are in North America. But this in turn means it is a little too early to draw definitive conclusions, because we don't want to mistake a phase of early development for the finished model. On the other hand there are several fascinating trends emerging, which give us important insights into how Honda's global local corporation works as a whole.

Let's begin to compare Honda in Europe with what we discovered in North America:

- **Location:** manufacturing locations in North America tend to be greenfields sites near small towns. But Swindon is an urban area with a trade union history and a large existing car parts plant.
- **Human resources:** in the United States Honda has grasped core parts of American culture and ideology and used them to motivate its workers: money, individual advancement, competition, equality. At Swindon, by contrast, the plan is to squeeze out many of the basics of British culture, especially class differentiation and status divisions. However, in both North America and Europe the goal is the same: to achieve a task-flexible workforce that both works in a disciplined way and plays its part in the innovation process.
- **Trade unions:** here Honda has so far adopted the same policy at Swindon as in North America: it is constructing a labour relations framework that has no place for trade unions. But we also noted that in Belgium, at the Aalst plant which is now becoming a car components factory, Honda does negotiate with the local trade unions.
- **Parts sourcing:** in North America Honda moved first to establish assembly operations, and local parts sourcing was a slower process of exploration followed by a wave of transplant parts-maker investments. In Europe we've seen Honda entering 'backwards', the link to Rover providing an entry point for learning about European suppliers before car assembly had started.

We can see a cluster of facilities emerging in Southern England around two Rover factories and a set of Honda facilities, but we don't yet see a full North America-style just-in-time region developing, because Honda is purchasing parts mostly from a group of firms scattered across the southern United Kingdom; it's far from clear that any will have to relocate to be closer than they already are.

- **Research and development:** the main development activities in Europe are helping with new model launches at Rover and Honda factories. The major research facilities are in Germany, working on design matters but firmly linked to Honda R&D in Japan. The critical mass of sales in Europe that is needed to proceed further may yet be several years off. The result is that the interrelation of R&D with manufacturing in Europe may take a different form from the more locally integrated operations in North America, at least for the next few years.

What we see then are some key differences emerging between Honda strategy in Europe and North America, besides the obvious difference that we examined in the previous chapter, the link to Rover. Localization in Europe shares some features in common, but it's not at all the same process as in North America. The moral here is that even if the goal is the same in terms of setting up the same manufacturing system, how you get there may be quite different in different places. That's a moral which need not apply only to Japanese firms.

So is Honda becoming a truly European firm? As we've seen, the company wants to argue that the answer is yes. But that's actually a bit too simple. Here we see Honda's *public relations* becoming fully European, fitting in with the dualist way Europeans want to see things: either you're European or you're not! In fact we have to answer the question in several different ways, and so we get several answers at once. Honda is becoming European, but by the very same process it's also becoming a global corporation. Perhaps most intriguing, however, Honda is actually changing what it means to be European.

To start with, let's agree that Honda has indeed established a wide set of activities in Europe. Any accusations along screwdriver lines would be inaccurate: there is research and development, manufacturing, parts sourcing in Europe; and parts sourcing largely involves domestic companies and factories, even if Japanese firms are tied in with some of them. In this sense there is a true localization, and Honda can justifiably claim as much. Moreover, Honda is now designing cars specifically to suit European tastes.

But that is only part of the picture. The situation is inevitably more complicated than this in reality. The comparison with Ford's or General Motors' European activities has often been made. But with

Honda there is a clear difference, because Honda in Europe remains far more fully integrated into the corporation's global structures of R&D, manufacturing, parts sourcing. And it could be the turn of the century before Honda makes as many cars in Europe as it imports from Japan. Here we come to a central argument of this book: the global local corporation is not about setting up separate subsidiaries, each with the gamut of car-making facilities from research to sales via manufacturing of quite different models, as in the traditional multinational corporation. The global local corporation is a different animal. We return to this idea in the final chapter.

But we don't want to become embroiled in the political debate, and conclude that Honda is not in fact 'truly' European. The point is that this question doesn't make much sense any more for firms like Honda. Even as Honda tries to play along with, fit into, Western ideas for public relations purposes, even while it really does localize several activities, employs Europeans, targets its cars at European consumers, it also has a home base in Japan, and other new bases at places across the globe. Why would Honda want to cut off the resources available in these bases from each other? Rather than setting up a separate subsidiary in Europe, Europeanization for Honda means targeting global corporate resources on selling cars in Europe. It makes sense to locate many of the resources needed to do that within Europe. But it makes sense to locate others in Japan, and others again in North America.

How, then, is Honda changing Europe? One key area is technology transfer. We've mentioned Honda's relations with domestic parts makers, and Honda has been moving to ensure that these come up to its standards. But just as important is European society. Here Honda is playing a potentially significant role.

The company is doing its best not to adopt a whole set of traditional European social and class relations, including status differentiation and trade unions: all aspects of European society that it views as European problems. In their place it is building new structures, hammering away at themes of equality, single status, the important role of the worker as innovator.

So Honda's European activities are designed to change Europe, not just to fit in with what already exists. And yet we have to emphasize that these changes don't mean Japanization either. The question is very complex, and the final results have yet to emerge. We can't even predict that Honda will 'discover a Europe undiscovered by Europeans', as we saw in the American case; at least to begin with there is a lot of knocking away of the old to be done. Is there a strong enough existing European culture and ideology that Honda can tap into and fit together with its production system? That is a vital question for Europe's domestic car makers too.

Notes

1. Honda of the UK Manufacturing Ltd, *Honda: 4th Decade in Europe*, Reading: Honda, 1989.
2. Critical examinations of this topic are Joseph Fucini and Suzy Fucini, *Working for the Japanese*, New York: The Free Press, 1990, and Philip Garrahan and Paul Stewart, *The Nissan Enigma*, London: Mansell, 1992. Both these analyses conclude that factories purported to be exemplars of humane working conditions with worker autonomy – according to managers and unionists alike – are in fact riddled with top-down discipline and high levels of mental and physical stress for the workforce. An example of the positive analysis against which they are reacting is Peter Wickens, *The Road to Nissan*, London: Macmillan, 1986.
3. HUM quality coordinator, cited in Andy Wilman, '. . . batting for Britain', *Auto Express* 26 January 1991.

10 Rover Learns How to Make Cars Again

> We had our share of problems with Honda to start with. Then, after a while, it all sank in. Why all the aggravation? They're right, we're wrong. All of a sudden the concept changes, and things fall into place.[1]

Apart from our discussion of Honda's domestic parts makers in North America, we've been concentrating on the strategies of Japanese firms: mostly Honda, sometimes its parts makers. But Honda's close working relationship with Rover, which we saw in Chapter 8 from Honda's standpoint, gives us a fascinating opportunity to look at the other side of the coin: instead of asking how a Japanese firm is operating in the West, how is an existing Western firm adopting and adapting lessons from Japan, and how are its relations with a Japanese partner implicated in this process?

The Rover case is especially interesting because for so many years the company was viewed as a classic case of all that was wrong with management at Western car makers. Obviously each Western company has its own history, problems, strong and weak points, but they also share much in common. The Rover example allows us to ask whether and how it is possible for one of the West's worst companies to turn itself around, and whether this amounts to 'Japanization'.

No Western automobile manufacturer has had a closer relationship with a Japanese counterpart than Rover. Starting with discussions on the Ballade/Acclaim project by Rover's predecessor BL in 1978, the links became more and more complex, as we saw in Chapter 8. It has become possible to visit Rover factories and see manufacturing equipment made by Honda Engineering, to go to Rover research and development offices and see Honda engineers working, to go to Rover factories to see Honda products being made. Inversely, Rover engineers have worked at Honda factories, Honda has made Rover products, and Honda has hooked itself into Rover's parts-maker network in Europe. Moreover Honda and Rover engineers now scour each other's factories to look for innovations and to study different ways of organizing manufacturing.

While Rover has been integral to Honda's strategy for Europe, Rover has its own complex history that unfortunately we cannot do justice to here, a subject that would require a book by itself. So rather than present an inevitably shallow sweeping overview of change at Rover, it makes more sense to focus our resources and look in detail at key areas. Several aspects of Rover's activities have been influenced by Honda, from new product development, to manufacturing technology, to sales and marketing, to relations with parts makers, to financial structure. But here we're going to focus on how Rover has been learning from Honda, then zoom in on its latest innovations in human resources and labour relations strategies. It is nevertheless apt to start with a reminder of the legacy of Rover's past.

ROVER'S PAST

Rover represents the last of the United Kingdom's domestic mass car makers, the result of a long history of mergers of smaller companies like Austin and Morris that culminated in 1968 with one large company – British Leyland Motor Corporation – which was supposed to become internationally competitive because of its size, but instead proved unwieldy to manage and eventually floundered into financial collapse in the mid-1970s. The company was taken over by the British government in 1975 as a nationalized industry, and shrank to half-size between the early 1970s (1.1 million cars per year and 200 000 employees) and the early 1980s (500 000 cars per year and 100 000 employees). As we saw in Chapter 8, successive reorganizations and shrinkages were accompanied by successive name changes, BLMC became BL (British Leyland), which became Austin Rover, which became Rover. A Conservative government sold the company to the aerospace industrial conglomerate British Aerospace in 1988 to get it back into the private sector.

As the United Kingdom's 'national champion' car maker, the company had become synonymous with the many ills of British manufacturing. Its product development was patchy, depending on cash availability, sometimes simply not taking place at all (hence the product gap that was filled by the Acclaim). The quality of the products was widely known to be poor, with vehicles suffering from mechanical breakdowns and from poor fit and finish. All the problems of 'big business disease' hampered change.

The company's use of human resources and its labour relations framework were central to its problems. Management was solely a top-down affair, instructions and targets coming from on high like tablets of stone, for implementation lower down, what Rover people today call simply a 'supervisory' system. As far as the production workers were concerned, their job was to come into the factory and do as they were told, no questions asked. The last thing management wanted was for workers to use their brains (though they frequently had to, in order to get often poorly designed manufacturing equipment to function at all effectively).

The division between worker and manager/engineer, blue collar and white collar, physical and mental work, them and us, was crystal-clear. Categorization of employees into different groups, each assigned to specific tasks that were theirs and theirs alone, was simply accepted to be the system. Engineers were professionals with degrees from universities. Managers wore suits and worked in offices, many rarely visiting the factory floors. Skilled workers belonged to various skilled trades – mechanical, electrical, fitters, setters, doorhangers and so on – often reflecting family connections and long apprenticeships spent in teenage years in preparation to join an 'elite' working-class group. Production workers who had missed out on apprenticeships when young were condemned often to occupy the very same monotonous post and job for year after year.

Nobody else was allowed to do the skilled worker's job: if no skilled worker was available production ground to a halt. If somebody else dared intervene the particular trade would stop work and paralyse the factory. And skilled workers refused to do any tasks other than their own: mechanics, for instance, would usually sit in their room and wait for machines to break down before they considered actually working.

The labour relations framework fitted this human resources strategy like a glove. There were separate trade unions for the different categories of worker. These negotiated separately with management, to protect and enhance their 'rights' (for example, pay differentials over production workers, monopoly rights over certain jobs). The key union organizers on the factory floor were the shop stewards. Under a system called 'mutuality' their agreement was necessary each time management wanted to alter the manufacturing process in the slightest way.

Many stewards rarely trusted what management said, and saw their job as protecting workers from management manipulation and management attempts to get them to work harder physically in order to increase productivity. Strikes, official and unofficial, were the shop stewards' most potent weapon.

So difficult was it for managers and engineers to get the manufacturing process changed that they often waited until a whole new production line, and a whole new model, was built, every eight to ten years or so, before trying to start afresh with a big leap in productivity. The temptation then was to look to technology as a way to replace a workforce that was simply not trusted. So many changes were made all at once that it often took many months to iron out all the problems and reach target quality and productivity levels. After that the production line might remain basically unchanged for another decade.

So inflexible was the whole system that something was always going wrong: technology breakdown, workers refusing to work, quality problems requiring rework. At one BL factory in 1978, management built the following extras into their production cost estimates: 5 per cent for breakdowns, 8 per cent for labour relations problems, and 6 per cent for problems due to poor parts quality. When something did go wrong, fixing it could mean hours of production downtime. Short breaks were a welcome respite for the production workers. Longer breaks meant they were sent home, laid off work.

By the early 1980s, with production and employment cut in half over the course of a decade, the old system for car making at what was by that point Austin Rover was beginning to change. In body parts stamping, for instance, seven separate skilled trades, who used to come in one by one and take up to 36 hours to change and set up a stamping die, were amalgamated into one. The shop stewards' right of 'mutuality' was taken away by an aggressive top management brought in by the Conservative government. But change was still piecemeal, and riven with contradictions. Supposedly 'Japanese' innovations were being introduced without changing the old social structures, only to fail dismally. There were discussion groups and quality circles to promote worker involvement, but they were introduced top-down. For production workers that meant little more than little time off from production. For shop stewards it meant suspicion of another management ploy and sooner or later refusal to participate. Early suggestions schemes foundered when workers made often-impractical suggestions because they had little idea of what was going on outside their own work area.

LEARNING FROM HONDA

Surely the opportunity for a troubled Western car maker to collaborate closely with an important Japanese firm like Honda would have been grasped with both hands? But don't forget that when the relationship with Honda started in the late 1970s, Japanese success was still frequently being put down, in the West, to cheap labour, to exploitation of suppliers, to copying Western technology. Many viewed Japan as little more than a third-world upstart.

The people at British Leyland who had most contact with Honda during the Ballade/Acclaim project – like the Cowley plant's manufacturing engineers – soon began to realize that something more was going on with Honda. They were seeing first-hand the results of Honda's product development process, and they had never seen anything like it: as we saw in Chapter 8, the car's parts, imported from Japan, were so well-built that they 'went together like a Swiss watch'. Why couldn't British Leyland come up with such a car? And the engineers were perplexed by Honda's accounting system for even small components, which they had to order in exact numbers – because there would be no defects, no extras were needed – rather than the cratefuls they were used to.

Yet the lessons hardly diffused at all within BL and Austin Rover. Honda was still seen by top management as merely the short-term provider of a stop-gap for the model range. As we saw, Honda made front-wheel-drive cars with transverse-mounted engines, the same as British Leyland and unlike other potential partners from Japan. Japan was still not seen as a real competitive threat. Anyway, in 1978, when the Ballade/Acclaim deal was first being contemplated, Honda was at best seen as an equal partner. After all, that year Honda made 740 000 automobiles and trucks while British Leyland manufactured 800 000. There was even talk early on that Honda would make British Leyland's Mini model in Japan for the Japanese market.

British engineers who visited Japan found it difficult to accept at first that Honda would have much to teach them. They treated with scorn instances of different practices at Honda that they saw as illogical, and some tried to persuade Japanese counterparts how to do things 'better'. And when some of the visitors progressed to trying to learn more, the lessons were confined largely to what they could see visually, to organization and logistics, to how the hard technology was arranged. Beyond that they found themselves running into 'cultural and communications gaps'.

Not until the later 1980s did the Rover attitude swing. At that point the organization began to grasp fully the gulf in productivity, quality, cost, product development – in short almost every indicator – between Rover and Honda, and to realize there were lessons to be learned here. The succession of joint projects had allowed a growing number of engineers to gain considerable insights into Honda, both in Japan and with the 1989 launch of the Concerto/200/400 at the Longbridge factory, which saw 'swarms' of Honda engineers come in to make sure all went smoothly.

On the other hand, most of the lessons were confined to the technical side, to product development, to manufacturing technology and to logistics. As late as 1990 some of Rover's manufacturing managers in the factories were wondering why the company still didn't seem to have a plan to learn from Honda on the labour relations front, and especially why Rover wasn't taking advantage of its Honda link to learn how Honda was handling a Western workforce, in the United States in particular.

In fact, not until 1991 did Rover organize systematic comparative studies of human resources and labour relations strategies at Japanese transplants. In the United Kingdom, frequent visits to Honda's Swindon factory – which made engines used at Longbridge – were now supplemented with proper study, and a Rover team was able to make two visits to Nissan's factory in Northeast England which had been making cars since 1986.

But it was Honda's factories in the United States, making automobiles now for nearly a decade, that Rover now really wanted to learn about. There were lengthy negotiations to convince Honda headquarters in Japan – especially the Japanese who viewed Marysville as a child still learning the ropes, and so with little to teach anybody else – that it was sensible, for 'cultural' reasons, for Rover to study from the American experience rather than the Japanese one. Honda's Swindon management too argued that Rover ought to want to learn more from them (even though they only had an engine plant, running for only two years).

This supposed 'cultural' barrier is worth thinking about for a moment. Could Rover learn much from Japan directly? In the first place there is the problem of language: unless all the British participants knew fluent Japanese they would never be able to grasp fully what was happening. True, they might learn Japanese – and some have done so – but the investment would be very long. Second, there is the question of whether to learn what Honda does in a Japanese social context would actually be as useful as to learn what it does in a Western context, albeit the rather different case – despite the language commonality – of the United States. Finally, there are some of the same difficulties we mentioned that are experienced in Japanese–American interactions in the United States: culture on a very personal level. The very particular interpersonal practices of the Japanese can seem so different to Rover managers and engineers, who sometimes feel it difficult to get a 'straight answer to a straight question'. Different Japanese and British cultures seem so ingrained in personalities that communications are difficult to sustain, and easy to spoil on both sides by 'inappropriate' behaviours that break down trust.

Eventually a small team from Rover spent several days in Ohio, sitting in on meetings, watching training exercises, working on the line with production workers, generally trying to absorb how the Honda Way was being implemented in Ohio and how human resources were being utilized there. For the British, the Americans turned out to be very open, willing, patient partners in discussions. We can speculate that to converse with other Westerners also deeply involved in car making was a form of release for them from the tight grip of Honda ideology. Now the British from Rover and the Americans from Honda are planning regular exchanges of experience, and working out what and how they can learn from each other: beginning to create diagonal and horizontal learning links across the Atlantic.

HUMAN RESOURCES STRATEGY FOR THE 1990S

While changes in the way human resources were perceived and used were already taking place little by little during the 1980s, not until the early 1990s did a clear new structure crystallize on the ground in the Rover factories. What does the new model look like? We can start by studying the changing roles of the different actors in manufacturing, from the production worker up to the lower rungs of the management hierarchy.

The Production Worker

The key change for the production worker is the addition of new tasks so that work becomes more varied, plus the delegation of a certain authority to the worker so that he or she takes on new responsibilities.

Variation means being trained to do a series of different tasks and moving between them within a small work group. Delegation of authority means taking on routine maintenance tasks and pointing out any quality and other problems observed. This may mean something as simple as giving workers in a certain section a green pen, with which they mark the vehicle around any dents, scratches or imperfections they see, which doesn't seem so radical until you recall that in the past they just ignored them, because quality problems were the job of quality inspectors to find – or not, it hardly mattered – later on.

Exactly what is involved in widening the sphere of what people do depends on the particular work process in different parts of the factories. Let's look at an example from body parts stamping at Rover's Swindon factory. In the past, the production workers had little to do except load and unload body parts between the giant presses, set up in a line, that formed the shapes, and hang them up on racks afterwards. When there were problems, or when dies were changed, they stood back. Now, however, management wants production workers to learn the basic skills involved so that they can change dies too. Instead of a structure of work divided according to skills – unskilled, setters, fitters, mechanical, electrical – it's divided by lines of presses, so that workers on a line of presses do most of their own tasks, only calling on outside help if they need it.

Among most production workers such changes are greeted positively, for they reduce boredom and create a sense of everybody 'mucking in' together. Younger workers are especially keen; on the other hand, the older ones may have got so used to doing the same job for 30 years – quite possible on the Longbridge lines where the Mini model is made – that they are reluctant to accept changed responsibilities.

Production workers are also fed more information at their workstations: graphs showing production goals and trends, quality problems, and so on, are posted for them to see. Information-sharing is intimately linked to getting workers to begin to use their experience and brains to improve the production process. Some managers believe it is now management's task to ensure that the majority of the workers participate in an active way, as opposed to the minority they think Honda succeeds in getting fully involved. But this means ensuring that the processes of worker participation are taken very seriously and function properly. Any lack of worker participation should be seen not as a worker problem but a management problem. At the Longbridge factory, the suggestions scheme developed bottle-necks – ideas simply weren't dealt with promptly – and suggestions dried up. Now it is being reorganized (see below).

At Longbridge worker suggestions have resulted in new designs for rest areas: perched on platforms above the production area, where they can be close to the workers who use them, where belongings can be safely left (instead of by the production line), where rest areas can be large enough to be comfortable without taking up any space on the factory floor, and where they can be left untouched when the production area is reorganized.

Accompanying the new strategy for utilizing production workers is a new management philosophy designed to confer dignity on them. Now, managers tell you that their people *want* to build cars well. Now, 'the lads' are the experts, it's they who work on the job and know how to make the product. Part of the idea is to confer a sense of ownership on the workers. It's a big change simply to *allow* them to participate, instead of preventing them from doing so.

Team Leaders

The Longbridge factory moved to a team-based system, each group composed of about 15 workers with its own team leader, in 1991–2. While the team leader, as organizer of the collective effort on the production line, is effectively the lowest rung of management, in fact production workers in each team were allowed to elect their own team leader from among their ranks. However, management had chosen a set of candidates it approved from among those who applied for the new position. That way, both management and workers could choose. But letting the workers vote means that the team leaders possess a vital natural authority over their colleagues.

The team-leader system is seen as the key to replacing the old supervision system in which orders came from on high for implementation at the bottom. The team leaders are to be the fulcrum of day-to-day manufacturing. One of the first tasks has been the introduction of all kinds of measures of production which the team leaders collect. It is they who draw up the graphs and charts showing daily progress on production and quality, which are hand-drawn at Longbridge, as opposed to the computer-drawn charts seen at many other factories (produced by more distant engineers).

First-hand involvement with creating the data should help the team leaders to really reflect upon the manufacturing process. The team leaders have also been responsible for drawing up manuals of practices in their work area. The goal is ostensibly for anybody coming from outside the area to be able to quickly understand procedures. But in fact, the team leaders themselves are the first beneficiaries, having now systematically investigated the whole production area they are in charge of. Managers hope that the real leap will come as the team leaders start to *use* the information they have begun to collect, both to solve existing problems and to make improvements to production processes.

One innovative responsibility given to team leaders at Rover's Longbridge factory has been control over costs from scrap in their work area. This way production workers can participate ('take ownership') not only in increasing quality but in reducing costs. Now, people take care of their tools instead of leaving them lying around, they clean them and maintain them, because they can't simply go and get another one without incurring a cost. Now, problems that recur are noticed, measured in cash terms, and the expensive ones can be studied and hopefully dealt with.

Scrap per car is graphed alongside production and quality levels. While the money amounts are quite small, for the Longbridge assembly lines it fell by over 50 per cent between 1990 and 1992. This programme has been a great confidence-booster for people who not so long ago weren't supposed to be actively involved and were often made to feel worthless. In parallel, it has been a learning process for management.

One of the early lessons drawn from appointing team leaders had to do with what managers call their 'enthusiasm'. Because they are still classed as production workers (receiving the same salary, plus a new fixed sum, each week) they could participate in the suggestions scheme. They had an unfair advantage however, and anyway their basic job was now supposed to be similar to coming up with suggestions full-time. Moreover, 'enthusiasm' included comments that various people above them in the hierarchy were incompetent, or were simply thought to be unnecessary. There's a fine line here between getting the old structures to move, become flexible, and disrupting them. Clearly some fine-tuning was called for after the first experiences were in, which means that the innovations took on an experimental aspect rather than being cast in stone from the start.

New forms of horizontal and diagonal communication also begin with the team leaders. At one point Longbridge assembly workers experienced continuing trouble fixing bumpers on to vehicles because they wouldn't fit. In the past the problem would have been passed up the management hierarchy in hopes of a response and meanwhile the workers involved would have used their brains – 'unofficially' – to come up with a solution to get the still poorly fitting parts assembled.

This time, however, a series of horizontal meetings was set up. There turned out to be several problems, all linked, that had to be solved. For a start, it wasn't the bumpers that were wrong but the previous welding together of the car body. Another problem was that the shifts in the assembly building and the body-making building rotated on a different basis, so those involved in the meetings frustratingly came across different colleagues each time they met. Now the shifts have been changed to rotate in unison, so that you always know who your counterpart from the other area of the factory will be.

The Skilled Trades

Some skilled trades are disappearing entirely. Some weren't necessarily based on hard-to-learn skills in the first place, but there was a trade union monopoly over them. Many routine maintenance jobs can be done by production workers with a minimum of training. For other skills, technology has changed, displacing the skilled workers. Fitters and setters who used to be needed to change stamping dies are no longer necessary. As production workers take on more tasks and develop wider skills, so the old-style skilled worker sees the areas he 'controls' diminish.

Other skilled trades will still exist, but the relationship between their jobs and those of the production workers is shifting rapidly. In the past skilled workers were in many ways largely their own bosses, working on their own terms, and insisting that they and they alone undertake a certain task. Now management wants them to evolve into *outside experts*, called in by the production teams and factory areas to solve problems they can't deal with.

The shift required can be as simple – not to be confused with easy – as getting maintenance workers to talk to production workers when they come in to work and ask them if there have been any problems in recent hours. In the past maintenance mechanics believed they should wait in their room to be called on. The change is as straightforward as getting maintenance workers to come out of their room and walk around the factory a little, looking over and examining machines that have not yet broken down.

The benefits of having skilled workers patrolling the factory floor can be substantial. Their skills can be used to spot problems before they lead to disruption and production down-time, so that preventive repair time can be scheduled. Take the case of lines of robots welding car bodies. The robots tend to shift slowly off their programme over time, with the result that their welds move out of place. In the past, workers at the end of the line would have noticed the results, but several cars further up the line, the off-target welds could have become so bad that whole welded bodies had to be scrapped at high cost. Now, the robots are watched and adjusted on the spot.

Foremen and Manufacturing Conformance Engineers

At Longbridge, the old category of foreman no longer exists. Instead, three or four team leaders work under a production coordinator. This person in turn works under a manufacturing manager.

Like the team leader, the coordinator position is new. It has been filled by the foremen from before and by a number of manufacturing conformance engineers. The coordinator's job has folded in the old jobs of the foreman and conformance engineer: it is a broad job with responsibility for both the people and the manufacturing equipment. The coordinator looks after a budget that he is measured against, is responsible for line-balancing (that is, that the workers and tasks are evenly distributed), and assigns people to teams.

With the coordinator role, the old sharp dividing line between where blue collar ended and white collar began disappears too. Moreover, the daily functioning of authority hierarchies is altered as well: now it is the team's responsibility to call in the coordinators if needed, as they do the skilled workers, instead of it being the foreman's and engineer's responsibility to survey and control everything going on. Responsibilities devolved to teams and coordinators free up the manufacturing managers from having to deal with many routine concerns.

Devolving Management

Amongst the more progressive-minded managers at Rover the notion of devolution of power is very strong. In principle this 'empowerment' means giving people the tools to do the job and letting them get on with it, so that higher levels of management intervene more at the request of those lower down rather than doling out orders, along the same lines as we've just seen. While it appears that until quite recently top manufacturing management at Rover was still operating in rather autocratic style within the ranks of management, there is some considerable evidence that devolution is now a powerful impetus from the shop floor upwards.

Under the old system manufacturing managers were given targets and told to reach them. If you failed, you sweated. Now they are asked to say what they think they can achieve and told to give it their best shot. Moreover, if they find that for unforeseen reasons the targets cannot be reached or the planned programme cannot be implemented, they are able to switch their attentions elsewhere to things that can be achieved without having to ask permission or fear being criticized.

This whole management approach is quite central to the new human resources strategy. Not only are manufacturing managers able to pursue some of the innovations that directly interest them, but without higher-level managers breathing down their necks they are less apt to act harshly with their own subordinates in turn and thereby jeopardize newly constructive relationships.

For the manufacturing managers it all means more autonomy, more authority for them, and more flexibility and decision-making powers, which in turn makes them more efficient, because they don't have to get the approval of a whole organization each time they want to change something. However, devolution is not to be confused with the much talked-about 'flat' management structures. That was tried in some areas at Rover, but hierarchies had to be reinstated because it simply didn't work not to have people you were responsible to and who in turn were responsible for certain areas.

Finally, what was that managerial solution to the suggestions scheme that dried up? Again, devolution of authority: now, the production manager in each area of the factory is responsible for designing his own suggestions plan and implementing it, and he will be evaluated on his success in attracting suggestions.

Learning How to Make Cars Again

With so much restructuring of roles and relationships, it seems that everybody in the Rover factories is learning how to make cars afresh. Not only are they undertaking different tasks, but they're doing a different *mix* of tasks, each of them inevitably therefore done in a different way. Among many there is clearly great excitement as the new system begins to gel and actually works.

But we cannot ignore that change is a very political process. While for some people – many production workers – the changes seem for the better, other people's traditional positions are clearly under attack. Many middle managers are reported to have resisted and criticized the team-leader concept. In fact, for all those who used to be in the middle of the hierarchy – skilled workers, foremen, conformance engineers, middle management – everything seems less clear. Are they capable of grasping new responsibilities as power is devolved to them, just as people from below – whom they used to order about and perhaps feel superior to – seem to be reaching up to take over many of their old tasks?

What can we conclude about the new human resources strategy at Rover? It seems that many years of tinkering with the old system, trying to get it to shift, is over. The old system has been overthrown, and now there's a new system to tinker with: hopefully one that will prove far more amenable to constructive tinkering by those at the 'sharp end'. The old dualist categories of thinking work and physical work are now more subtly intertwined: the same goes for unskilled and skilled work, and for the relationship between top-down control and devolution of authority. The whole system looks remarkably like . . . Honda.

MANAGING THE CHANGEOVER

There's no doubt that the hard commercial realities of working for a company with an uncertain future provided part of the context necessary for people to be willing to adopt new roles and find new ways to organize making cars. But that is clearly not enough: after all, years of decline previously had not done the trick. Some of the most significant changes have come since the mid 1980s, after a period of relative stability in output levels. An additional factor is that new industrial and labour relations laws introduced under the Conservative Government made alternative, more militant, options for trade unionists who wanted to resist change far harder to put into practice.

But it is also apparent that Rover's own management has gone through a sea-change in attitude and strategy, and has taken up its own responsibilities in a way quite remarkable for the car industry in the United Kingdom. Let us examine management strategy more closely – in the context of the triangular interplay between managers, workers and trade unions – as management tried to effect the transition from the old system of human resources to the new.

Management and Unions

As we saw earlier, the historic structure of trade unionism at Rover was intimately linked to the way human resources were utilized by management. Different unions represented the various unskilled and skilled categories, each fighting to maintain or expand the 'rights' their members had won *vis-à-vis* management and each other. Shop stewards tried to contain the negative impacts of management's top-down efforts to get people to work harder and to periodically restructure the whole manufacturing process.

A moment's thought about the new human resources strategy, with its breakdown of barriers, with its bottom-up improvement mechanisms and devolved powers, shows that the whole role, even the rationale, of trade unions organized along traditional lines is placed in great doubt. So how have the unions reacted to the new changes? What has been management's approach to dealing with them? And what does the Rover experience so far portend for their future?

Different trade unions have reacted in different ways. Let's take the example introduced above of reorganizing the stamping-press lines. The union representing most production workers (TGWU) has tended to support teamwork since it should mean more varied jobs for its members, and also more chance of promotion to team-leader level and beyond, paths previously blocked by the skilled workers' union. The union representing the skilled workers (AEU, now AEEU) opposed the changes until the early 1990s because they threatened the very rationale for the union's existence, even though union representatives believed that the team system was coming anyway, and they would have to get on board sooner or later and get what they could out of it.

In this context, managerial strategy has been composed of a series of approaches, all having in common a positive and cooperative appearance, with all labour relations confrontation avoided. This is very important, because cooperation is also what the new human resources system requires. How much harder – impossible perhaps – to introduce the new system if management had tried to enforce it by attacking the unions and the shop stewards head on, creating an atmosphere of mistrust that would undermine the purpose of reforms.

Hence managers routinely inform union leaders of their plans, taking them 'on board'. This tactic diffuses the resentments that used to build up about 'unilateral actions' by management that were frequently resisted by unions more or less on principle. Moreover, management consults with unions about how (not whether) to make certain changes, to the point of asking union leaders to come up with a better way if they are dissatisfied.

When the Cowley plant workforce was to be considerably reduced as part of a complete restructuring of the factory in 1990–1, local management put great effort into joint planning with local union leaders, not only of the rationale of the cuts – saving the jobs that would remain – but coming up with the means to encourage people to leave voluntarily.

On the one hand, there is direct communication to explain, and to a limited extent to plan jointly, the new human resources strategy. On the other hand, there is a bypassing of confrontation in ways that are likely to result in undermining union power. For instance, the skilled workers' unions may be circumvented and isolated when management appeals to the interest the unskilled workers' union has in more varied work, undercutting the skilled worker's 'right' to certain jobs. And the shop stewards are bypassed by the appointment of team leaders.

Likewise, Rover management does not intend to push for a 'single union' deal like Nissan, Toyota and some other Japanese plants in the United Kingdom, nor a 'no-strike' clause in contracts, because these would simply be too confrontational. But it does intend to obtain the benefits of both of these, by negotiating with all its unions together, and by insisting on binding arbitration to prevent strikes in disputes.

Management and Workers

The key to bypassing the unions has been the powerful strategy of direct communication with the workforce. If this can be established so that workers believe what managers say, and if bottom-up communication actually works too, then the union role of representing workers, of ensuring management doesn't trick them, simply evaporates. This is not to argue that direct communication with workers has as its sole aim to undermine the union role: far from it, it is integral to the new human resources strategy. But the medium- and long-term effect is that the trade unions become increasingly sidelined.

As far as teamwork is concerned, managers appeal to its positive aspects when explaining it to production workers, in terms of more interesting work, of working together as a group, of sheer common sense, and in terms of new opportunities for promotion (to team leader and above) for production workers. Rover management has also promoted 'adult apprenticeships' to increase the supply of skilled workers by allowing older production workers to train for skilled jobs that they might have missed out on at the age of 16 simply because the intake of apprentices was reduced that year. The result is that skilled workers and their unions are trapped in a pincer movement by an implicit alliance between managers and production workers both hungry for change.

Fundamental to the open communications strategy is for management really to say what it intends to do, and then to do exactly what it said. Union leaders report that this is what managers have been doing now at some of the Rover factories for several years, and that it has already built up management legitimacy with the workforce to previously unheard-of levels.

Beyond this, when management has implemented difficult policies, like cutting down the workforce of a factory, it has deliberately done so in the manner least likely to antagonize either those going or those staying, sometimes offering severance benefits beyond those required by agreements. The goodwill engendered by positive approaches to difficult problems again contributes to a changed atmosphere. Union activists who in the past would have been able to oppose certain elements of management strategy find themselves facing potential isolation with little support.

Freeing up communication must also be a bottom-up process. Workers at one Rover factory, attending an obligatory three day 'Total Quality Involvement' course, strayed from the intended topics and spent part of the first day venting their frustrations about what they perceived as the dismal standards of management at the factory. The next day the schedule was disrupted again, this time for the managers to be brought in and hear the complaints for themselves. There's no downplaying the psychological effect of workers simply knowing that they are allowed such expression as a safety valve.

Importantly, training courses are increasingly being internalized within the company. In the past, external consultants and trainers were routinely hired to organize and implement training programmes at all levels. Now, managers design their own training programmes along with Rover's own professional trainers. 'Keeping it within the company' enhances the integration of training with the actual needs and experiences of participants and means that the training process itself also functions as a bonding mechanism.

All sorts of daily practices within the factories are changing to provide real substance to otherwise abstract philosophies about teamwork and treating workers with dignity. Key among these is the internal job market for workers no longer needed in certain work areas because of productivity improvements. In the past, people whose jobs disappeared were simply passed on by the manufacturing manager to the factory personnel department, which in turn dispatched them elsewhere, with little or no choice.

Now, the displaced person stays within the work group to begin with, doing odd tasks though still expected to be productive. There is a proper internal job market, in which the displaced person gets an 'employee availability card' filled out with personal characteristics, and the personnel department offers a list of vacancies elsewhere in the factory. If these are rejected, other members of the group will be offered them, in order to reduce the numbers in the group commensurate with the workload. Seniority with the company is used as a still acceptable way of making decisions when there are no volunteers.

Another way in which simply treating people properly is vital to making the new system work relates to quality control. On the one hand, the philosophy that accompanies getting workers to undertake routine quality control is one of thinking of downstream colleagues as 'customers' who should be passed only top-quality products. On the other hand, workers asked to point out quality problems they notice, caused upstream, would be disinclined to do so if they thought that 'their mates might get into trouble'. Management is therefore obliged to ensure that this doesn't happen, precisely in order to reassure the downstream workers so that they will be willing to perform their new quality-inspection tasks.

Finally, various elements of single-status terms of employment are being introduced, including having all canteens open to all employees for the first time. Managers are being persuaded (not without resistance from some) to wear overalls instead of suits: a move in the direction of a company uniform. But the kind of strict adherence to wearing a uniform seen at Honda (that is, overalls, company hat and no tie for all) has been viewed as counterproductive for Rover (so far, at least). Managers wear their suits into work and then don overalls, often just the jacket. They may or may not wear a tie. Anyway, a casual, 'no tie', rule would be opposed by some of the production workers who also like to wear ties to work.

So far we have seen how management has adopted direct strategies in its dealings with workers on a daily basis within the factory. These are in fact the fundamental, core changes to have taken place in labour relations at Rover, and they were adopted gradually and quietly over several years. More publicity, however, has been given to the apparently dramatic changes taking place in official terms of employment at Rover.

During 1991 and 1992 Rover and the trade unions negotiated what was called a 'New Deal', which was given formal sanction by votes of approval by union negotiators, shop stewards, and the workforce itself. The New Deal officially crystallized the human resources and labour relations strategies we've been looking at above (and it wasn't put forward for formal acceptance until workers had already had experience with many aspects of it). Single-status conditions were formally recognized, with production workers getting the same conditions as white-collar employees (for example, sick pay, receiving salary, one month's notice of dismissal). In return, flexibility and removal of barriers in the factories was accepted as an organization principle. The press hailed the agreements as the adoption of revolutionary Japanese methods by Rover workers.

One central feature of the New Deal at Rover is striking: the new understanding on redundancies and the 'job for life' idea so often associated with the Japanese model. Rover management has now committed itself to two principles. In the first place, it will no longer resort to compulsory redundancies if it wants to cut the workforce. It will seek voluntary redundancies instead, with people encouraged by financial means to resign if necessary. This is a major change. With forced redundancy no longer a legitimate tool, management relinquishes its ability to control the size of the labour force at short notice.

The new policy is of great interest in the context of the popular idea of the need for increased corporate flexibility, because here Rover's human resources strategy gains a rigidity it did not have before. Has management tied its own hands? Clearly it hopes that the benefits obtained in return for this signal of goodwill will mean it doesn't need to resort to redundancies anyway.

The second aspect of the new understanding on redundancies is that the workforce is no longer to be sent home when there are short-term problems (strikes at parts suppliers, for instance), but kept at work for further training, working together to improve manufacturing for when it restarts. This is the same approach adopted by Honda in North America. Naturally, management hopes that all the other changes it is introducing will mean sharply reduced production downtime anyway compared to the past.

What Future for the Unions?

Let's return to the issue of the future of trade unions. The general management approach on labour relations at Rover is an offensive along very positive grounds, with management taking action itself to try to prove itself sincere. According to one manufacturing manager, the best way for managers to think about labour relations is to adopt policies that will make workers not want to join a union. He sees part of his job as doing things oppositely from what would make his workers look to a union for support. Now he is asking his workers to sweep up their work areas. When they hesitate, on the grounds that it should be the – somewhat humiliating – job of a person 'lower down the scale' (a classic cause of union-management confrontation in the past), he – a person higher up than them – sweeps up himself in front of them.

Indeed management had been pursuing the basic on-the-ground changes so far that by the early 1990s it believed the level of trust built up on the shop floor, and the willingness of workers to adopt the new human resources strategy wholeheartedly, was far ahead of the official trade union position. With unions leaders the last to convince, once the single-status New Deal was officially accepted, reform was expected to proceed at an even more rapid pace.

So how does Rover management now view the future of the trade unions? On the one hand, it does not foresee their disappearance, having selected not to confront them or challenge their right to represent workers. On the other hand, changes to working practices have removed many of the grounds on which unions have actually represented workers in the past, particularly on the shop floor. This leaves only major issues such as wage negotiations. Some among Rover management now expect a stepped change in union attitudes by the mid-1990s, insofar as the unions become more proactive in reinforcing company goals, working within management's labour relations framework. In this view, all that remains is to 'tidy up' the company's relations with the trade unions.

Unions representing skilled workers are particularly challenged. As the production workers take over more tasks, the role of skilled workers will need to change significantly, through multiskilling and the acquisition of additional technical competencies.

Why, then, have the unions accepted reform, even recommending it to their members in 1992? Management embarked on a lengthy process of persuading the leadership that this was the only way to safeguard the company and its jobs. It presented the results of its benchmarking studies showing how far ahead the Japanese were in productivity terms. To begin with, some union leaders still thought the answer was then to simply keep the Japanese out of the British market altogether and get the government to close down their European factories.

But a combination of factors has undermined this old-style trade unionism, including: reduced power on legal grounds to carry out action against the company, progress made under the company's strategy of reaching out directly to the workforce, and the success of the company's consultative attitude in gaining allies among union leaders who are anyway more middle-of-the-road in their approach.

Radical unionists and shop stewards find themselves in a double bind: on the one hand appearing antiquated to their own members who are attracted by the company's new human resources strategy; on the other hand appearing weak and ineffective to those who are losing old privileges and have received little union protection from their union's new relationship with management.

Some union leaders certainly have a sense of willingly participating in their own demise. For some, not only is the old style of trade unionism dead and buried, but there is no obvious new style to replace it and so define what the union role should now be. The villains in the piece are not so much teamwork, flexibility and so on, but the parallel communications structures management now uses to talk directly to workers. The unions themselves appear to be redundant.

And not only is the rationale of the unions in question, so is their fundamental power base. Shop stewards have faced waning power since the early 1980s, with their influence over various aspects of the manufacturing process progressively removed. Management strategy has been to marginalize the shop stewards so that if they were to decide not to cooperate with a certain management scheme, nothing would happen because they would have no power to wield.

For the shop stewards, the team-leader concept may be the final nail in the coffin. Now an ordinary production worker has been elected to represent the others in getting management to address problems, and management listens to him and responds by helping him: it sounds remarkably like what stewards used to do, except that management was rarely willing to help the shop stewards get their problems fixed. The stewards have generally proved antagonistic to the team-leader concept. But so much do the stewards face complete marginalization that Rover managers talk about working with the unions to re-orientate the role of the shop stewards into such areas as health and safety and environmental issues.

Rover management has engaged in a clever and complex social power game to get the whole social structure of Rover to change itself inside out, even as it doesn't stop churning out cars at full production. The old structures are left in place, but even though they were the central defining characteristics of the past, they face growing irrelevance now. The new framework for labour relations is wholly coherent internally, and fits tightly on to the human resources strategy. Presuming the latter delivers the goods in terms of productivity and quality and cost, the old structures are set to wither away.

But won't management simply wait until those old structures have gone and then turn the screws on a now unprotected workforce? That's the argument of some unionists. And of course there is certainly a danger to consider here. Some Rover managers may revert to acting the old way. On the other hand, what's so fascinating about the new human resources strategy is that – quite unlike the old system – it requires that management adhere to certain basic standards of human dignity just to make it function properly. We've seen some clear instances already: the need for a proper internal job market if people are not to resist being displaced by productivity increases, the need to ensure that workers are not punished for quality errors if their colleagues are to continue pointing out those errors to management.

We can finish here with a simple comment that nonetheless opens up many questions for future investigation. What people accept in terms of human dignity, what management has to do to ensure that workers want to cooperate, is linked to the values of the wider society, and so it is likely to vary across the globe, to be different at Longbridge in Birmingham, at Marysville in Ohio, or at Sayama near Tokyo.

IS THERE A 'ROVER WAY'?

Is a unique Rover Way, 'Roverism', emerging? Is Rover in fact essentially becoming 'Japanized'? On the one hand, neither an entirely unique Rover Way nor a slavish Japanization is on the cards. On the other hand, there are elements of each of them to be found in the new equation at Rover.

Rover management has been following its own path, but so must every firm, given their different histories and existing people, organizations, and so on. To keep the organization functioning through the tumultuous change necessary to get from A to B requires a very individual approach tailored to the actual situation: there's no textbook manual, Japanese or otherwise.

At the same time Rover has also been incorporating myriad lessons learned from outside into its own evolution. The overall human resources strategy we've seen in this chapter bears a remarkable resemblance to Honda's, in its organization, in the management approach which accompanies it, in the principles behind the new roles for different groups, even in the names given to the new groups (team leaders, production coordinators, and, increasingly, 'associates' for production workers). But it still wasn't modelled directly on the Honda experience. The main thing to be learned from Honda on the human resources front is an overall structure, and the confidence – on an individual and organizational level – to try to implement it that derives from knowing that it works at one very successful firm, and that it works in a Western country too.

Besides that, there are many management techniques, the details which make the human resources strategy work on a daily basis. But at this level, Rover management is picking and choosing: will it require its workers to clock on and off when they come to work? Nissan workers in Northeast England don't clock on, but Honda workers in Swindon do. Rover workers won't. Nissan's and Honda's British operations didn't have suggestions schemes going by the early 1990s: Rover does. One thing that's worth noting here is that Rover management hasn't chosen to mimic Honda's Swindon organization or style, but to learn as much from elsewhere, from Nissan in Northeast England and from Honda in Marysville.

Lots of innovations in terms of particular techniques have been invented at Rover in the process of starting with one structure and changing to another. Honda's teams and team leaders don't have exactly the same responsibilities as Rover's: a novelty at Rover, not seen at Honda (but seen in different form at Nissan), is Rover's devolution of financial control over scrap on the production line right down to the team leaders. So there is variation, unevenness, and complexity in the adoption of a very similar general management approach. The managerial key is to understand how to unlock the door to the same result even if the form, the appearance, is different.

That the new ideas are both borrowed and invented is reflected in the way changes at Rover are portrayed as Japanese-influenced but also as 'best business practice' and as locally rooted. The Japanese threat is used frequently: 'this is the only factory without a team structure and Honda doesn't like it'; 'if we don't change to Japanese methods then only the Japanese will be left in the business, so it's Japanese methods whichever way you choose'. On the other hand the new ideas are portrayed more abstractly as representing the most advanced business practice, and frequently as 'pure common sense', necessary to become 'best in class'. Here is a denationalized approach pitched at the level of intercompany competition.

There are variations in the pace of change at the level of individual factories, with some Rover plants moving at different speeds, trying out their own ideas. What's then fundamental is to develop the horizontal and diagonal links that will ensure that innovations developed in each factory, at each work-station, are truly fertile and are diffused elsewhere in the company where they can foment improvement. That's why Honda's Americans are keen to pursue their links with Rover and vice versa, and that's why Rover needs to allow the middle-level management, down to the team leaders, to visit and study other factories, other work areas, within Rover and at Honda too, in the same way the Honda people have used Rover's factories.

It is in creating the diagonal and horizontal links, as much as through the top-down and bottom-up structures of the management pyramid, that a Rover Way will develop through practice, reflecting the company's particular achievements, its particular strong points, and phrased in language that is culturally appropriate. In the United States Honda lays emphasis on monetary rewards: that may not work so straightforwardly in the United Kingdom. On the other hand, pride in the quality of actual vehicles being manufactured may come easily. And the underpinnings of collective solidarity, the pride in being a skilled worker – which caused management so many headaches in the past – can be mobilized to other ends.

The result should be a Rover Way that is unique taken *in toto* – reflecting history, culture, language, specific management techniques – but which overlaps considerably with the Honda Way in some of its elements and in its actual impact as a philosophy. Even its form of presentation may be different: it is far from clear that the same kinds of metaphors, abstract statements and slogans that carry the message in Japan will work in British culture. Here too is room for invention.

The best path forward won't be to impose a Rover Way from above but to encourage its development from below. That's why Honda spent time in the United States finding out what the Honda Way *could* mean in practice for the Americans. There needs to be a set of ideas that make sense, that are coherent, that function as explanations, so that people know what they are doing and why. They have to be reflected in daily work and personal interactions, because if they come from on-high, with the risk of not applying accurately to reality, they will soon be simply dismissed as 'propaganda'. But if they can be created, then the organization can begin to function seemingly by itself, coherently, liberating the kind of manufacturing and organizational flexibility that Honda has attained.

Now we're speculating on the future. How far is Rover along this path? There isn't yet an overarching philosophy like the Honda Way in place. In part that's because people are still feeling, inching their way along. The documents the company developed by the early 1990s on the New Deal still looked more like specific rule-books than a general approach. And yet if you're learning how to make cars over again it all starts by learning specifics and concrete practices, and it is those that will later give rise to new ways of thinking too.

Does Rover's new direction, with its home-grown input and ideas, therefore amount to watering down the Japanese model in the process of hybridization? If you think so, think again. The Japanese learned in the 1960s and 1970s – Honda was a key firm here – that if they simply copied Western products and production methods, the inevitable result was a watered-down and poor version of the original. Doing that gave the Japanese their early postwar reputation as makers of cheap and shoddy manufactured goods that wouldn't stand up to international competition. To make progress, innovation and adaptation were the key: that is the lesson of the Honda story.

The paradox in so many discussions about how imitating Japanese practices will lead to 'Japanization' (or how not imitating them exactly will lead to a watering-down of the original version) is that actually it would be unlike the best Japanese management practice for Rover, or Honda itself, to have implemented photocopied blueprints of Japanese management methods. More in keeping with the cutting edge of Japanese management would be to keep them but to Westernize them. True Japanization isn't imitation of some supposedly fixed model, it's the process of adapting and innovating. That's what Rover wants to do.[2]

Notes

1. Rover manufacturing manager, author's interview (1992).
2. I am grateful to Tony Villiers of Rover Group for allowing me to adopt and adapt several of his ideas, particularly in these last two paragraphs.

Part IV
Global Local Corporation

11 Global Local Corporation

One of our biggest challenges is how we will establish the 'Honda Global Network,' a system whereby Honda production facilities around the world become complementary supply bases for world markets.[1]

Eventually this will mature into a 'global supply network' which will flexibly respond to the diversification of demand and the unique circumstances of each country. This approach transcends the conventional concept of manufacturing in a particular area simply because demand exists. But the most vital aspect is that each Honda organization will lay its roots deep into each locale to become a responsible corporate citizen.[2]

And also foreseeing the worldwide market at the same time. We want to fix everything at the right time. From there on, everything goes more smoothly and more efficiently.[3]

For most of this book we have concentrated on how Honda has built up its operations outside Japan, in North America and Europe: in short, localization overseas. In this final chapter we swing the pendulum back to look at globalization. How does Honda's global local corporation function, as a whole?

We've already emphasized how localization has taken place within a global framework. By the same token, in this chapter's discussion of globalization, we see how important the foundations of localization are. This will be our final pair of opposites, our final dualist puzzle solved, as we get to grips with the question: how does Honda manage to combine the global with the local?

We start by looking at what we can think of as the 'physical' structure of the global local corporation: the organization of manufacturing and its linkage to sales on a global basis, where it is that automobiles are made, and where they are sold. We will also analyse what the 'global local car' looks like, as well as how R&D is organized on a world scale. Examination of physical structure leads us into looking at mechanisms for transfer of Japanese management techniques and manufacturing methods abroad. Like Honda, we can already progress beyond thinking of a one-way flow of innovation out of Japan, and start thinking of the global local corporation as a multidirectional global learning network.

Then we move on to look at the organizational issues of global local management. Who are the new managers at Honda? What are the problems that arise when you bring Japanese and Western managers together? How is Honda evolving new organizational frameworks to make management work effectively at the global level?

Finally, we return to the vital theme of politics, to compare what we've learned about Honda with some of the recent theories which argue that a new breed of 'stateless' or 'post-national' company is emerging, operating in a 'borderless world': a breed that many believe Honda exemplifies. Are these accurate descriptions of Honda's global operations?

The global local corporation is still evolving. At each step of our analysis we make a note of the level of understanding we have arrived at, and with that what stage in the creation of a global local corporation Honda has reached. But it is also important to use the analytical position developed here as a jumping-off point to pose some of the vital questions that will arise during the remainder of the 1990s, as Honda's global organization evolves and deepens. It is time to prepare for the future. That means making sure we ask the right questions and stop getting caught out by underestimating what leading Japanese companies are capable of doing. Honda is not resting on its laurels, and the 1990s promise further dramatic innovations in its organization and functioning.

GLOBAL LOCAL MANUFACTURING–SALES NEXUS

As we pointed out in Chapter 1, traditional efforts to manufacture automobiles on a world scale have come up against various difficulties. Where separate subsidiaries make separate models for separate markets, potential economies of scale in research and development and in manufacturing are lost. With this system too, when some markets are booming while others are in decline, you can't switch production and trade flows at a world level to even out supply and demand because the models made in each region are too different, and because the factories aren't built in such a way that they could switch to make each others' products. It is just the same problem found at many Western producers *within* North America or Europe: because each factory only makes one or two models, some factories work overtime to meet high demand, but others are only partially utilized because 'their model' is selling poorly.

Moreover, when this traditional type of multinational organization makes efforts to globalize R&D and manufacturing it runs into more inflexibilities. The 'world car' has failed to materialize because the different R&D operations can't agree on what it should be like. At best the world car risks being a watered-down compromise that satisfies nobody, including the customer. And global sourcing of components – while it is undoubtedly a bold attempt to create a worldwide manufacturing network – doesn't make so much sense when wild exchange rate fluctuations can wipe out the benefits overnight. Finally, in the traditional type, real global links are limited to moving people – top management especially – and money around, but not automobiles.

New strategies for how to create true global manufacturing have been proposed recently. One idea is that a company should make separate models in Japan, North America and Europe to meet the mass-consumption needs of those markets, and then export these models to fill niche roles in the other two regions. This sounds nice, but is not so easy in practice. Differences between world markets aren't great enough – and they're of the wrong sort – to allow imports of mass models from other regions to conveniently complement local production.

Why? Because mass cars the world over are medium-sized 4-door saloons/sedans, and niche cars are derivatives of these or sporty or van-like cars. So to follow this idea to its logical conclusion would mean that each region made its own mass-market 4-door cars and sold the other regions' mass-market 4-door cars in its niche slots. The only way that makes sense is if one market needs mostly big cars, the other mostly small ones, or one needs mostly luxury cars and the other mostly simple ones. And that kind of difference between the world's major markets is in fact less and less apparent as vehicle sizes and quality expectations continue to converge the world over.

So how does Honda fit in? We will shortly examine the company's strategy for worldwide automobile design. But let's first see if Honda has made any progress on the question of interlinking its global production sites and markets. This is what Honda's strategy looks like so far.

Mass Manufacture for Mass Markets, Niche for Niche

We might be tempted to look at Honda's mass production of two basic models in North America, compare it to the wide variety of models made in Japan, and come to the conclusion that Honda has watered down its flexible Japanese production system for implementation abroad. But that would be misleading. As we saw in Chapter 7, Honda has introduced a flexible mass-production system, tailored to its mass markets in North America. Niche markets in Japan and North America are supplied from the niche base in Japan.

Different concepts of factory flexibility are needed to supply (i) the Japanese market (where nine producers offer a multiplicity of models to a market half the size of North America or Europe) (ii) the North American market (where single models attain very high sales) and (iii) both markets at once. What Honda did during the 1980s was basically to shift mass Accord production firmly to the United States but to keep production of all the lesser-selling models in Japan (City, Today, Beat, CRX, Concerto, Prelude, Accord's Japanese spin-offs, Legend, NSX: fewer than 100 000 of each are made per year). Within this pattern Civic and Integra have played balancing roles. Civics round out the numbers in North America, but more are still made in Japan (where the Civic accounts for over one-third of production and is the closest Honda has to a mass-sales model). Integra might have been shifted to North America – East Liberty was ready for it – but its sales haven't warranted the added cost and logistical complexity.

North America therefore gets flexible mass production suited to market conditions: (1) ability to move models between factories to balance capacity utilization within the North American factory network, and (2) addition of niche derivatives to the mainstays, targeted specifically at North America and not made in Japan (Accord coupé, Accord station-wagon, 2-door Civic).

Trade Between the Production Bases

Rather than export *mass* models as niche products for other markets, in the 1980s Honda's strategy became centralization of production for *niche* automobiles and *niche* derivatives for worldwide markets. However, we can't discount partial adoption of the first strategy during the 1990s with discontinuation of Accord production in Japan where sales are low, and all derivatives of the Accord then exported to Japan from North America.

Balancing Quantities

The ideal would be to elevate North America's ability to switch models from factory to factory to the global level. The goal would be to cope with a world whose market regions were continually out of economic synch, by diverting exports to and fro across the globe to match production with sales. That's just what we saw in 1985–6, during expansion of the Marysville factory, when that factory was expanded more than planned to cope with sales growth in Japan, thus allowing Japan to retain some output that would otherwise have been exported.

Global Local Parts Sourcing

This is a very complex question. Take the case of the Japanese parts makers. On the one hand, high levels of parts localization is essential for efficient just-in-time manufacture, not to mention political considerations. On the other hand, Japanese parts makers have to consider production volumes in making their decisions whether to go abroad. In North America output has been high enough to warrant parts-maker transplants. In Europe low output combined with local political pressures has meant greater reliance by Honda on domestic parts makers. There are clearly wide variations in the strategy adopted to meet the same goals.

However, one thing is clear from our investigations: Honda neither runs screwdriver operations nor has built entirely independent – close to 100 per cent local content – subsidiaries. Instead there is a complex global networking pattern emerging, one that begins to challenge the imagination. Some parts will be built strictly locally for inclusion in local cars. Others will be brought in from Japan to Marysville, Swindon and so on, and still others will flow from Europe to North America, from North America to Japan. What's more, the vehicles these parts end up in might then be sold in any market! It is already possible to purchase Honda cars in Europe, made in Japan, incorporating components from North America.

Also relevant is the qualitative issue: what kinds of parts will be made where? Local sourcing outside Japan began with the less complex and easier-to-make parts, so most local sourcing is concentrated in the parts the customer can actually see (outside and inside), plus some major mechanical parts. How far up the ladder of technology and complexity will local sourcing go? That's a question we don't yet have a full answer to, but there are strong tendencies to keep some parts manufactured only in Japan.

Reacting to Simultaneous Global Recession

This is one of the key tests for the global local corporation. One theory has it that Japanese automobile producers have been able to achieve rapid productivity gains coupled with lifetime employment for their workers because they have only operated in growing markets since the 1950s. As we've just seen, recession in one market can in principle be tackled by shifting output around in a global manufacturing network. But the ultimate test is how you respond to simultaneous recessions in all major markets.

That was just the challenge being faced in the early 1990s, with the American recession continuing seemingly without end, with Japan slowing sharply after the late 1980s boom, and with Europe too entering slowdown. There's no doubt that Honda has been affected by the global recession. Profits were down in 1991, 1992 and 1993 (though without slipping into loss). Sales began to subside in Japan, and demand for niche models like Beat and NSX collapsed, forcing a suspension of Beat production. Daily output at Sayama was cut back to 1700 per day instead of 2200 with only one shift operating on one of the two production lines. For the first time ever, there were non-production days at both Suzuka and Sayama to reduce output. For the first time since Marysville opened, in 1991 inventories of unsold Hondas built up, requiring production to be reduced to match. The build-up to full capacity at East Liberty was postponed until after the 2-door Civic was introduced in 1992. Marysville Accord output sagged in 1993 as a new version was awaited for the autumn.

Several observers – journalists especially – were keen to interpret Honda's apparent difficulties as signals that Honda too is vulnerable, that it faces the same problems as its Western rivals. And that may be true, to a certain extent at least. The deteriorating operating environment is the same. Yet Honda's problems also seem far less worrisome, far less threatening, than those of some Western rivals. Global local balance plays an important role. For instance, Honda is well-positioned in the North American market, and so reduced sales have not meant actually losing money as in the case of the Big Three. And introduction of new models was widely expected to rescue the situation, certainly in North America, and likely too in Japan, where there is now a constant stream of new Japan-oriented models like Today and Domani.

To judge from events so far, Honda plans no radical solution or action specifically in response to the global recession. A brief phase of consolidation was coming anyway in the early 1990s after the expansion boom of the 1980s provided Honda with its new worldwide factory network. Profits may be down, but then so too are investments in production capacity, with Swindon the last of the new factories to come on line, in 1992, and no such major investments yet planned to follow. Here Honda's timing has been excellent, and much better than that of some Japanese rivals, its ability to get the plants built so swiftly during the growth years leaving it able to cut capital outlays sharply during the slump just as the rivals' expensive new factories in Japan came on line. Moreover, as we have seen, East Liberty was able to increase output more slowly than first projected, with relative ease, since its full workforce was not yet hired. The new Swindon factory is in a different situation, because it will support growing market penetration in previously impermeable southern European markets even if overall European sales decline.

Resources and personnel have certainly been pulled back into automobile product development during the early 1990s, from other branches like power products and motorcycles, and from Formula 1 racing. But it is far from clear that this is purely reaction to recession: just as likely, it represents the acceleration of a change in corporate direction, part of a move to deepen rather than further expand Honda's global local corporation during the 1990s. We return to this theme below.

Timing and flexibility are the keys to Honda's global factory network. Timing refers as much to synchronizing internal organizational changes – for instance bringing new products on-line, new production capacity – as to predicting external events. Flexibility means the ability to respond to environmental changes, to move with the flow of markets and tastes at the same pace as they change.

The key point is how complex the interplay of different factories and markets on a global scale can be once you have embarked upon operating a global local corporation. That complexity has to be matched with a corporate organizational framework that fits closely. Market destabilization and internal rigidities sabotaged previous attempts to shift from a separate subsidiaries model of multinational enterprise to world car and global sourcing strategies. Their success was premised on a stable global economic environment – from convergence of market tastes to stable exchange rates – that has not existed for many years now. The unstable global market environment of the 1980s and 1990s puts in sharp relief why *global local flexibility* will be the winning strategy for multinational enterprises into the next century.

THE GLOBAL LOCAL CAR

How do you design a single car to sell all over the world, yet which also caters to different market needs? There is a seemingly unbridgeable dualism here. The convergence in global tastes forecast during the 1970s, when it came, simply didn't go far enough to enable Western producers to sell the same car on a large scale, for any length of time, in both North America and Western Europe, the traditional testing grounds for the 'world car'.

Japanese firms now have a head start in this quest because the quality and cost attributes of their cars have won consumer loyalty across the West, often for vehicles basically designed to satisfy Japanese tastes during the 1970s, American tastes during the 1980s, and Japanese tastes again during the 1990s. This way the Japanese have been pulling a certain convergence of tastes along in their wake. There has also been a certain convergence in engineering, around precisely the mechanical configuration that Honda pioneered in Japan: front-wheel-drive vehicles with transverse-mounted engines, which save space and weight and have good handling characteristics.

But there are still many differences between the world's major markets. For instance:

- different aesthetic expectations: from the bulky American look to the Japanese 'bio' style epitomized by Mazda's '121' model;
- different road conditions: from the straight low-speed highways of North America to the high-speed curves of Germany to the traffic jams of Tokyo;
- different uses for cars: for instance, the 5-door and estate-car variants are popular in Europe, for shopping, for family, but have not been so in Japan, where they have been tainted with commercial vehicle status;
- different expectations about how long a model should be manufactured before it is replaced: Japan's innovation-oriented four-year cycles seem too fast in Europe, where consumers don't like it when their new car quickly looks out of date.

Let's look at how Honda is approaching the question of global product design.

The American Decades, 1970s and 1980s

As we saw in Chapter 2, during the early 1970s Honda switched its design focus from Japan to target North America. That was consistent with a long-standing Honda policy of aiming at the world's most difficult markets first, the theory being that if they could be conquered, success elsewhere would follow as a matter of course. At that time the United States was seen as the key: if Honda could sell cars there, it could sell them anywhere.

Importantly, however, this didn't mean dropping the mechanical configuration we noted above even though the norm in North America remained longitudinal engines powering the rear wheels. (Though as we noted in Chapter 2, Honda's manufacturing flexibility was such that by the late 1980s it was mounting longitudinal engines only in the Legend, and rear-wheel drives only in the NSX.) However, exterior and interior design were increasingly aimed at the North American consumer.

The Accord became the core American model, first in sales, then in sales and production too as the new factories came on line. But in 1989 that began to cause difficulties in Japan, and Honda was hit by a classic 'world car' type problem. The Accord was selling so well in the United States that it had become the country's single best-selling model. Simultaneously, the sharp rise of the yen's value against the dollar in the mid 1980s made the export of cars from Japan to North America increasingly less viable financially. If the yen rose any higher than its eventual settling mark, Honda was prepared to abandon all Accord production in Japan and shift it entirely to Marysville and the soon-to-open East Liberty plant. The pressure was clearly on to think of the Accord entirely in terms of North America.

Following the design dictum 'don't mess with success', in 1989 Honda introduced a new Accord model that had only subtle modifications in style, and indeed looked quite similar to the previous version. The plan worked, North American sales continued to rise, and the always dangerous period of changing a best-selling model had passed. Back in Japan, however, 1989 marked the high point of a booming economy with booming car sales, and what the market wanted was novelty, innovation, cars that looked *different* (one result was the 'bio' style). Along came Honda with a car that to Japanese eyes was essentially, well, dull. The new Accord was widely panned in Japan as evidence that Honda was losing its touch.

At the same time a second, related difficulty emerged. The 2-door coupé version of the Accord had also been designed with North American consumers in mind. But the car had been given quite similar design characteristics to the sporty Prelude model. The two cars overlapped too much, the Accord was less expensive, and Prelude sales were hit badly, production (at Sayama) tumbling from 166 000 in 1987 to 69 000 in 1991. Not until the 1991 introduction of a radically restyled Prelude was the problem solved.

Here was Honda coming face to face with two classic problems of simultaneously designing cars for different markets. The problems are recurrent, signifying a real difficulty to be overcome. For instance, in 1992 Honda's American and Japanese designers were reported to be in dispute over a new Integra model. They both agreed it should be 'sporty', but they defined sporty in subtly different ways, which each team wanted reflected in the design of the automobile.

What about Europe? Where did the concentration on design for North America and Japan leave the third major market? With two difficulties:

- *A model range made up of cars designed for Japanese and American markets*. There were continuing problems sustaining a clear and full range of cars for Europe with a clear Honda style. That tended to happen only fleetingly before various new models were being replaced, withdrawn, added, in an effort to find the right mix. The model range looked more like a series of niche cars, and even as one found favour it was likely to be replaced by a quite different-looking, and targeted, model replacement, designed with needs on the other side of the world in mind. A classic case was the 1992 replacement of the CRX 'hot hatchback' sporty car, which had developed a minor cult reputation in some European countries, by a completely different car concept, when the older version clearly had more years of market-life in it.
- *Cars not built with Europe in mind mechanically or interior-wise*. Again there was a mix of Japan- and America-oriented cars with little commonality to define them as Hondas and frequently found wanting in Europe as far as their driving characteristics were concerned (seats and suspensions in particular were frequently criticised as too 'soft' for European driving conditions).

True, by the early 1990s these problems were being tackled, with the presentation in Europe of a clearer range from Civic up to Legend and NSX by way of Accord and Prelude. Even then, the Rover-built Concerto still seemed an odd car out. Indeed it had always seemed an odd car in some European markets, with its dull grey plastic interior combined with a fast high-tech engine, a combination that defied European efforts to decide what category to place it in: was it a family car? sports car? car for retired people? Also characteristically, along came a new Prelude in 1991 with no shelves or compartments in the front for the driver to put belongings: another car that simply didn't seem to have been thought out with the European consumer in mind.

Making the 1990s a Global Local Decade?

How are challenges like these being tackled? Some Japanese firms announced they would build different cars for the different markets. Some analysts, as we have said, argued that the mass-market cars produced in each region could be cross-exported to perform niche roles in the other major markets. In a third strategy, as we saw in Chapter 3, Honda itself began to centralize production of Accord-niche derivatives at Marysville.

But Honda's most innovative and significant solution so far came in 1992 and 1993 with the introduction of a new Accord model. By the early 1990s it had become clear that designing for the hardest market first by no means brought automatic success in the rest, and anyway, which market was the hardest changed every few years: that was the real lesson of the 1989 Accord's Japanese flop. Linked to this realization came a new concept of 'total car behaviour', in which the way that the package of features of a car work together should be matched to particular market targets. As this approach emerged, Honda engineers knew they still fell behind some European companies in creating appropriate overall images: 'safe cars', 'prestige cars', 'environmentally-oriented cars'.

The goal would be to match variations in the design of a basic and single global model to the appropriate 'total car behaviour' for each market, and with that to get precisely the right mix of commonality and variation in the car that would both provide sufficient economies of scale in shared designs and parts and match market differences. (We saw some of the dangers of getting this combination all wrong in the Honda Legend/Rover 800 project.)

The seeds of the breakthrough at Honda had already been planted in Japan. From the early 1980s Honda had built different-looking versions of the same underlying car to sell to its different sales outlets in Japan: the Civic getting a Ballade twin, the Accord later getting an Innova and other offshoots. This might be described as a process of *horizontal spin-off*. A related process of *temporal spin-off* was also adopted. Thus the 1993 Today version shared 40 per cent of parts with its predecessor. Rover had also become adept at both types of product spin-off. By the early 1990s the Accord had already branched out into the mainstream car made primarily for North America, an upmarket Vigor offshoot for Japan and North America, plus an Accord Inspire, and an Innova, with various engines and body shapes, designed to fit niche roles in Japan. Now this same theme of deriving different models with strong commonality from a common base was to be expanded worldwide, in a process of *geographical spin-off*:

- a larger-bodied and larger-engined Accord version specifically for North America, and manufactured only there, from 1993;
- a smaller-bodied and smaller-engined Accord version for Japan in 1992, sold as Innova (Japanese Accord-badged sales would be of the larger American version, henceforth imported from Marysville);
- two separate Accord versions for Europe, branching directly out of the Japanese version (Innova) introduced in 1992: the European version of Accord for Swindon, with a different roof, for instance, to match European styling; and the Rover 600, also piggybacking onto the Innova but with a Rover-designed exterior body and trim that differed significantly from the Accord.

The key to making this approach work is to retain the same powertrains and major mechanical parts, keep the same body frame, and keep many other parts the same too (exterior lights, for instance). But the exterior bodies, hence the styles, can vary, and likewise the interiors, seats and suspensions, to suit differing fashions and driving conditions. That means essentially reversing one traditional solution to the problem of meeting diverse needs with basically the same car, which was to keep the same bodies but to vary trim like lights and bumpers (the problem here was that the cars still looked too much alike).

Honda will no doubt argue that it is designing and making unique cars for each market. To be unique, however, by no means implies being entirely different. Where do we draw the line? This is a similar question to the one we looked at in Chapter 2, of whether the Japanese companies really change car models every four years or just freshen them up: we saw that Honda does neither. Likewise the Honda Accords spun off for each geographical market will be neither entirely the same nor entirely different from each other, and yet they will be both the same and different: that's why the idea works. As in all dualist puzzle-solving, in building a true global local car what counts is to achieve the right combination of opposites, of similarity and difference.

There are still problems ahead, and we can't say that the new version of the global local car represented by the 1992–1993 Accord model change is the definitive one:

- *Can model replacements be timed correctly for each market?* If it makes more sense to move to a six-year cycle in Europe, we could envisage the European version of a car skipping over a Japanese model replacement, and coming in the middle of the next. There are myriad such time–geography problems to manage in coordinating the spin-off process. Fragmentation of model replacements in time as well as in space would be a major departure from the rhythmic Japanese four-year cycle that enables planning to proceed smoothly and R&D workloads to be paced evenly.
- *Can the Honda strategy of the late 1980s – export of niche variants from single sources – be continued?* For instance, can derivatives of the American Accord (for example, Marysville coupés and station-wagons) be successfully sold alongside the different-looking European Accord in Europe without reverting to the fragmented model range of the past?

Here, then, lie some of the new questions for the 1990s as the global local car takes shape. The key to it all is going to be organizational speed, timing and flexibility, the ability to respond quickly, at the right moment, and with sufficient variation to meet local needs: and all the while, mass-producing cars at sites across the globe.

GLOBAL LOCAL RESEARCH AND DEVELOPMENT

How will the global local corporation organize its research and development activities on a world scale? The main question here is actually where R&D will be located. At one extreme all activities could be retained at home base, with instructions passed down to overseas operations from on high. At the other extreme all activities necessary to bring a new model on line could be recreated in each region of the world. It's the second *impression* that Honda has been trying to leave.

Needless to say, what we're in fact interested in is how Honda has combined these opposites.

There are four key points to bear in mind. The first is simply the importance of R&D for a product-led firm like Honda. The second is the fact that R&D actually consists of diverse activities, from basic research to market research to design and to model development-cum-engineering; and we noted in Chapter 2 how the research process, for instance, is managed quite differently from development activities. The third point is that, in the Japanese model, and Honda is no exception, parts makers are tightly integrated into model design and development, and some of them undertake basic research too. Fourth is the issue of spatial organization: if all these different R&D activities are to be integrated – between firms, and with manufacturing too – geographical proximity would appear *prima facie* advantageous.

How has Honda dealt with the main problem which these points raise for location of R&D: what is the best way to maximize integration and maximize dispersal at the same time? The global organization of R&D at Honda is intimately related to the evolution of Honda's global local car. The world-wide R&D map Honda has developed so far looks like this (see also the Box 11.1):

- Keep basic research and fundamental product research – new engines, new mechanical and electronic components – entirely in Japan. That allows economies of scale in these areas. The global local car does not vary from region to region along these lines, so global centralization makes sense.
- Establish parallel market research and design studios in North America, Europe and Japan, to create a strong current of new ideas related to consumer demands from the hottest overseas markets (hence the California and Germany locations). Initially these are outposts of Honda R&D in Japan rather than being closely connected to local manufacturing operations.
- When output levels permit, and new model derivatives are to be made overseas, set up parallel development activities aligned with manufacturing (hence located at Marysville). Increasingly link the local market research and design activities to the development facilities (for example, California to Marysville). What is fundamental here is that the specific R&D activities thus decentralized from Japan correspond directly to the differences between the versions of the global local car.
- encourage parallel parts-maker R&D too, for development activities

Box 11.1   Research and Development: The Accord Station-wagon

One of the key tests of Honda's 'self-reliance' in North America is its independently functioning R&D and Engineering activities, 600 employees in the former, 200 in the latter by the mid-1990s.

Honda has therefore made a great deal of the Marysville-made Accord station-wagon, trumpeted as a car designed and made in America. The clear public impression is of a vehicle designed and developed, with its manufacturing engineering planned and installed, entirely in California and Ohio. Let's take a closer look, and with that at the nature of global local research and development.

Honda planned to introduce a replacement Accord model, following the regular four-year cycle, in mid-1989, to be introduced simultaneously at Sayama and Marysville. For years the sales and marketing people in North America had been clamouring for a mini-van, a popular and profitable market segment pioneered by Chrysler, but Honda had kept holding back, not wanting to enter last along a well-worn path without something really innovative. While a mini-van is now planned for 1994, a temporary solution came in early 1988 when Japan gave the go-ahead for the American operation to design, develop and engineer its own station-wagon version of the Accord. Design took place in California, development and engineering (including prototype production) at Marysville. Production commenced in 1990.

The process bore all the hallmarks of a Honda development project. It was overseen by a Sales–Engineering–Development (SED) group with its headquarters in California. Horizontal communication with the factory people at Marysville ensured that the vehicle would physically fit on to existing equipment in welding, painting, and final assembly: that meant a rear compartment of limited size, with a sloping back window. Criticism of difficult-to-assemble wiring harnesses led to redesign.

The concept behind the car was 'classy and sporty', distinct from the full-sized lumbering vehicles the Big Three made, which mini-vans were replacing anyway. The sloping rear window fits that image, and the structural pillars at the back are thin, to deemphasize the rear compartment.

But the station-wagon was exactly the same as the Japanese-designed 4-door Accord from the front seats forward. The American team had learned to work on a derivative: changing bodywork, interior, trim, but not touching mechanicals, electronics and so on. Ambitious enough, but certainly not a whole new automobile.

As a derivative from an existing model, the station-wagon is not so different in principle from a local variant of a global local car. The process of designing and making it in North America offers real insights into what global local R&D will look like in the 1990s.

Source: Author's research.

especially, in North America and Europe. But again concentrate on those components that differentiate versions of the global local car, like exterior body and trim, seats and suspensions. Fifty-nine parts makers for the 1993 Accord undertook the relevant R&D in North America. That speeds up the development process enormously over sending parts back to Japan for testing. Parts-maker R&D for components that are common across the globe can be retained in Japan (for example, brakes, gearboxes, steering, electronics).

- Because parts makers overseas may not be as well-equipped for R&D as they are in Japan – in North America because transplant parts makers are too small to warrant full R&D facilities, in Europe because smaller domestic parts makers have little R&D experience – it may be better to operate a more centrally coordinated R&D process overseas than in Japan. That means Honda building facilities that the parts makers can also utilize (for example, testing) and training guest engineers from parts makers in Europe and North America.

Unsurprisingly, this model of global local R&D raises its own set of problems. The whole process now becomes fragmented across the globe. Here lies the importance of mastering satellite technology to link computer-assisted design facilities across the world: judicious use of high technology to overcome distances eases problems. Likewise, sites like those in Europe close to major international airports (Heathrow, Frankfurt) ease the necessary flows of people back and forth.

What is so very striking about the way that Honda's strategy for global local R&D has developed is the high degree of complementarity between (i) variations in the global local car (that is, what's shared, what's different locally), (ii) variations in the types of parts locally sourced (see Chapter 4) and (iii) which R&D activities are localized. Here we begin to see a a clearer picture of the global local corporation emerging as a coherent whole, an enterprise that retains some activities at home base but decentralizes others: the process governed in a carefully coordinated way in which the centralization/decentralization combination runs in parallel for R&D, car design, models made, parts sourcing and manufacturing.

GLOBAL LOCAL TECHNOLOGY TRANSFER

Can the Japanese manufacturing system and its associated management techniques really be operated abroad? This question perplexed many observers a decade ago. We can't speak for every Japanese company, but we can say that Honda's production system and its management techniques definitely can, and do, work in North America and Europe. Let's look at the numbers, and then examine the process of global technology transfer at Honda: diffusion of methods beyond Honda, cultural factors, the advantages of operating in the West, and the emergence of global learning networks within the company.

The Productivity Question

What we really want to know is: are the Honda factories in North America and Europe as good as the ones in Japan? Is their productivity as high? Before we delve into this question, let's sound two cautionary notes. First, in fact productivity isn't really what counts, it's cost per vehicle that is the key (and even that isn't the whole story since relative market prices also vary across markets and that too affects profitability). Hypothetically, lower wages and higher market prices could compensate for significantly lower productivity in the United Kingdom, making Swindon more profitable than a higher-productivity (but higher-wage, lower-market-price) American plant. If the Swindon factory had the same productivity, then its profitability could be much greater than higher-cost, lower-market-price sites. The global local corporation has a lot of juggling to do beyond simple productivity comparisons.

The second caveat is that it may be less important to compare productivity across sites within the global local corporation – Honda's factories in Japan versus North America versus Europe – than between Honda and its rivals in each region. We already noted in Chapter 2 Honda's high productivity in Japan, level with the leader Toyota. No one doubts that Honda in North America and Europe is in a similar position regarding local rivals. The transplants – Honda in North America in particular – have become the targets to which domestic companies aspire.

These points notwithstanding, there is every reason for Honda to maintain a keen interest in relative productivity levels because they provide a measure of weak points in the global local network of factories. The problem for us is that Honda is not willing to tell the world – and its rivals – just what levels it has reached, so we don't have the accurate measures readily available that we might prefer.

But we can and must still try to get an idea of how Japan, North America and Europe compare. Admitting this to be a rough exercise, we can make the following basic assumptions:

- we measure gross productivity, including all employees and all activities (not just production work in the more commonly measured assembly plants), because that better reflects overall costs;
- we assume hours worked per person per year across the world are similar (which at Honda is actually almost the case because of its unusually low hours worked in Japan);
- we assume levels of in-house versus outsourced production are the same in each region;
- we exclude Honda-badged vehicles manufactured by other companies (in Japan and Europe);
- we assume the varying complexities of the vehicles made in the different regions balance each other (for example, in Japan some very simple cars and some very complex cars are made, whereas in Swindon one medium-complex car is made);
- we assume the absence of a stamping-plant at Swindon is compensated by the manufacture of more engines than cars.

On this clearly approximate basis we arrive at the rounded figures given in Table 11.1. Honda's gross productivity figures turn out to be the same across the globe.

Table 11.1 Rough Measures of Gross Productivity at Honda Across the World

	Annual Production	Employees	Production per employee
Japan	1 250 000	25 000	50
United States	500 000	10 000	50
United Kingdom	100 000	2000	50

Now relax some assumptions: in Japan there is more R&D work (though 5 per cent of Honda's American employees work in R&D, not so different from the 8 per cent in Japan). The cars made in Japan are on average somewhat more complex. Even so, it is unlikely that Marysville, Alliston, Anna, East Liberty and Swindon fall far behind Sayama, Suzuka and the others in productivity. All are new state-of-the-art factories, which perhaps compensates for their less-experienced workforces. Another approach to the productivity numbers confirms our analysis. Using the same method adopted in Table 2.2, in which Toyota and Honda in Japan each produce 7.6 units per 1000 hours worked, Mazda makes 6.25, Nissan 5.7, and Mitsubishi 5.4, we find that Honda in North America comes in at approximately 6.5, behind Honda in Japan but above several Japanese rivals in Japan.

Innovation Diffusion Beyond Honda

To what extent is the process of manufacturing technology-cum-organization transfer from Japan diffusing beyond Honda itself into the West's domestic automobile industries? Here there's a stark contrast between North America and Europe. In the former, we saw how Honda has established virtually a parallel automobile industry, with its network of transplant parts makers, and with its domestic purchases biased towards non-traditional automotive industry suppliers. That means that direct diffusion of new manufacturing methods outwards from Honda is restricted, barely reaching into the traditional supply chain of the Big Three. To make things worse for the domestic parts makers, the Big Three have themselves turned to purchasing parts from transplant parts makers.

In Europe, by contrast, a decade of Honda collaboration with Rover has helped that firm reorganize itself technologically, and provided lessons in organizational innovations too. Moreover, Honda has plugged into a large section of Rover's traditional parts-maker base and into several other European domestic firms too. That means that these firms – existing firms with existing markets – will be in a position to transfer what they learn from Honda, and Japanese parts makers they collaborate with, to the benefit of their other customers too, just as Rover is aided by Honda. The domestic parts industry in Europe is therefore in a better structural position than its North American counterpart to innovate with direct aid and encouragement from Honda.

Moreover, the diffusion of Honda's know-how is becoming increasingly widespread, now involving not only directly-related companies like Rover and parts-makers, but other assembly companies too. While Chrysler, for instance, sought to learn from Honda by studying it, BMW went a step further, in hiring top American managers for its new South Carolina factory directly from Honda. The goal was explicit, to teach BMW how to make cars 'the Honda way', knowledge which will surely find its way back to Europe.

Technology Transfer and Culture

We have hinted throughout this book – and now let's make it explicit – that the idea of 'Japanization' is pretty much worthless for understanding the process of social and cultural change that is accompanying global technology transfer at Honda. What Honda wants to implant overseas is, first, the hard technology, second, the way people use it, and third, the managerial structures that keep the whole organized. This process has a physical side, an organizational side, and a mental side too.

We haven't discovered a shred of evidence that a social and cultural Japanization of production workers is the way to do it. At managerial level the matter is more complex, because of the many interactions necessary between Western and Japanese counterparts (which Western production workers don't have). But at this level we've found that diffusion of some Japanese-style personal interactions has caused problems, not helped matters.

There are large Japanese teams running the technical side of production at Honda in North America and Europe, as the local employees only gradually become proficient at what Honda considers to be a very difficult method of operating a company. For Honda, the Japanese presence is vital because of the two kinds of 'glue' which hold the organization together, neither of which can be quickly taught to local employees. First, there's the organization of manufacturing itself, meticulously planned, with internal control devices – like producing in lots of 60 – so that it should function as much as possible on 'auto-pilot'. Second, and more difficult, there's the culture, the ideas, that form a framework for people (a) to be able to suggest ideas for making the production system better, and (b) to be able to swiftly react exactly as they should, and autonomously, to resolve problems that arise. These glues replace a great deal of the typical Western managerial system that combines a top-down hierarchical command structure with rule-books and reference manuals. But it is correspondingly harder to get the Honda Way adopted abroad, because it really has to be implanted in people's brains: culture change is far from superficial.

There are twin lessons to be learned from Honda's experience in North America. First, developing the glues in the factories has meant Americanization, not Japanization. Second, that in turn doesn't mean adopting traditional American managerial approaches. Instead, it means incorporating a new culture and social structure, reinterpreting the Honda Way in terms judiciously selected from the elements that make up American culture and ideology, terms which are able to mesh closely with the production system Honda wants to implant and to motivate the people to play the roles Honda wants of them. In this regard Honda may have been blessed with particular insight precisely because of its stress in Japan on non-traditional ideas like individuality and breaking down status barriers.

What is interesting about Europe is that the cultural elements that can play those same roles are not so clear. To begin with, Honda wants to pound out of its workforce all the elements of British cultural tradition that stand in the way of flexibility and worker innovation. What's going to follow? Here is a very interesting question indeed.

Rover stands at the same crossroads: what would a 'Rover Way' look like? The conclusion we arrived at when we looked at Rover in Chapter 10 is that if Japanization has any meaning, it is to do with adaptation and the skilful creation of new behaviour, not imitation of Japanese cultural practices, and that goes for Honda's worldwide operations too. Paradoxically, then, true Japanization does not mean adopting Japanese behaviours in a concrete sense, but an approach aimed at finding fruitful combinations of the cultural dualist opposites.

Better in the West?

Let's speculate a little, and invert the old view that Japan had so many innate advantages over the West as to be invincible. Are there not advantages to operating in the West instead of in Japan?

We will leave aside all the important changes happening in Japan during the early 1990s, from general cultural evolution to economic instability, that have made Japan itself less attractive. And we will leave aside too the undoubted advantages of setting up greenfield sites in the West (though Marysville hardly seems so new now). We want to get to the principles behind the question. Does the Western environment actually have strong points for Honda compared to Japan? Is Honda actually better off operating in the West than in Japan? Our study has indeed revealed several such advantages:

- *Mass consumption markets:* North America and Europe are both far bigger markets than Japan. While Europe is admittedly still broken up into separate national markets, these are converging under the impetus of Europe's domestic and American-owned car makers, and of the Japanese themselves. Honda is a mass producer, and its production system seems well-suited to simple levels of variation within its model range, without the customized tailoring to the individual consumer associated (in the West) with Japan. The sales levels possible in the West – as the Accord has shown – allow Honda to reap enormous advantages from churning out single models by the hundreds of thousands from each factory.

- *Easier market penetration:* sales and marketing systems in the West are far more open to newcomers than is the case in Japan. As a latecomer itself, Honda has continued to suffer the consequences in Japan, as have the Big Three American firms. Assuming political barriers can be overcome, it's much easier, and less expensive too, to increase market share in the West.

- *Pick of the workforce:* Honda has been able to recruit from scratch, to carefully choose its workers, in the West. Working for a Japanese manufacturer is still viewed as prestigious in the West, whereas in Japan, labour shortages have increased the difficulties of securing the right kind of factory workforce at the right kind of price.

- *Individualism:* this was supposed to be the big cultural disadvantage in the West compared to Japanese groupism. Perhaps so, from a dualist perspective. But the lesson of Honda is that what counts is to achieve the right combination of individualism and groupism. In Japan Honda has had to knock individualism into workers who might otherwise prefer to blend anonymously in with colleagues; which is why Honda looks so Western to the Japanese. In the West, while people do understand authority, it is also taken for granted that there is an innate right to ask questions, to take individual responsibility and credit for problems and their solutions. Western workers, then, may be less conformist, more innovative, less threatened by being different, potentially more productive as a result, than their Japanese counterparts. What Honda is doing in North America and Europe is to provide the right group framework for Western individualism to flourish, and that's something its Western rivals had long neglected.

- *Design:* Honda's Japanese designers have proved to be among the more innovative and adaptable in the world. But in terms of concepts for cars, in terms of the sophistication of users, it is the Europeans, Germany in particular, that remain ahead of Honda in the game: so far anyway. There is much still to be learned by being physically located in the West.

- *Spatial organization:* Western road infrastructures are a breath of fresh air for Japanese companies. There's no need to build up a Toyota City style tightly concentrated manufacturing complex to avoid logistical paralysis in North America and Europe, with all the added costs and problems which that might eventually cause. The North American just-in-time region is spatially concentrated up to a certain point, but it is widely dispersed at the local scale too, so that Honda can tap into existing communities rather than have to build its own new city. In Europe Honda seems to be going the same way.

Advantages like these mean that it is not so speculative to suggest that – in a few years, say – Honda's production system might work better in the West than in Japan itself. Certainly, what we've already seen is that Honda has decided it is at least as able to meet the needs of Western consumers (versus its Western competitors) as it is to meet the needs of Japanese consumers (versus its Japanese competitors).

The idea a decade ago was that 'Westernization' of Japanese ideas implied some kind of hybridization, and that that in turn meant a watering down. What we're saying is that the opposite may be true. The lesson of Honda is that 'Westernization' may improve the Japanese model: the right kind of skilfully adapted 'Westernization', that is. Put another way, in creating the global local corporation Honda wants to capitalize on the best of the Japanese environment and capitalize on the best of the Western environment too. The focus is not on the contradictions, dualist-style, but on how to combine the differences to best effect.

Learning, Global Local Style

We can take this argument a step further. We've tended to think recently that learning is a one-way street: that the West needs to learn from Japan. And there's no doubt that's how it has started off with Honda.

Lots of Western staff have visited Japan. It is important to pitch these visits at the right level for maximum effect. It is easy to send high-level managers and other top people, but it is far more effective for those who actually guide the production process to make the trip. For instance, nearly half of Honda's transplant parts makers in North America sent every one of their original team leaders to Japan for training courses. By 1990 the first small team of Honda's Americans had moved with their families to Japan for periods of up to three years to deepen their understanding of engineering, research and development processes, the goal being to increase the independent capabilities of the Americans at Marysville in the medium term. And let's not forget how we've seen Honda's Japanese staff transplanted to North American and Europe in large numbers, teamed up with shadows, with great effort going into teaching Westerners the Honda Way for the long stretch.

But what's really worth noting is that there are already moves at Honda to make the learning process move in other directions too. The ultimate goal is a *global learning network* with no necessary primacy of one direction for knowledge transfer over another.

To begin with, there's the flow back to Japan. A great advantage for Honda of having a large Japanese staff stationed in North America is the build-up of a significant cadre back in Japan with several years' experience of working in California, Ohio, or Ontario. That process gives fresh, Westernized, impetus to thinking in Japan. Rather than the overseas appointment signalling disfavour – as it used to in Japan – at Honda it becomes a positive advantage to career prospects. The Americans on long-term secondment to Japan will carry the same knowledge of the American production facilities with them to Japan. So great is the influence of Honda North America in Japan now that Japanese Honda engineers working in Europe complain that the European viewpoint is swamped by North American ideas, and they can hardly get themselves heard in Japan.

We've also seen the budding of horizontal networks for global learning about manufacturing and human resources strategies in the links between Rover and Marysville. Naturally there can be jealousies to overcome, with competition inside the corporate structure making it hard at first for some in Japan to swallow that Rover doesn't want to learn more about Sayama or Suzuka as far as human resources are concerned. Now the Americans want to learn more from the British too, weaving further strands in the nascent global learning network.

Horizontal learning means spreading the innovations that are developed in each factory, with carefully organized study visits, and with people at appropriate (that is, low) hierarchical levels taking part. And the process needn't be limited to personal visits. By the early 1990s, for instance, the Americans were busy making videos and developing training modules to increase their technical competence, which they expected might later be used at Honda facilities around the world. Japanese staff were already talking of developing ways to ensure that manufacturing innovations developed in North America could be passed back to Japan.

So the global local corporation can seize the opportunity not only to utilize the different environments in which it operates to complement each other, but to systematically swap and learn the innovations developed independently within each local production complex. Moreover, the very process of comparison and exchange itself can lead to further fertilization of the innovation process. Innovations developed to combat a particular problem where it is most keenly felt can then be diffused to other factories, across the globe, where solving that problem had perhaps only had low priority. The blossoming of networks of innovation diffusion operating horizontally across the globe is definitely a trend to watch for in the 1990s.

Japanese Management Techniques and Globalization: From Impediment to Necessity

Reliance upon Japanese management techniques – from human resources management to manufacturing methods – was until quite recently expected to prevent the Japanese from operating abroad. The paradox is that Honda has turned those very methods into the fundamental underpinnings of its global local corporation, the world's most advanced type of multinational manufacturing enterprise. Once you separate general principles out from their concrete manifestations in Japan, strategies like human-using-to-capacity and just-in-time relations between parts makers and assemblers become central elements for providing the manufacturing flexibility needed to make the global local corporation function.

The central lesson here is to stop confusing the ideas behind Japanese management techniques with the exact way Japanese firms implement those techniques in Japan. It's the whole approach to problem-solving that matters, and not necessarily the particular solution appropriate in one place (though lessons may of course be learned). Producing in fixed lots may be right for Honda, but not for every car maker. Developing systems of auto-control over production, however, may be a very useful principle.

What It All Means

What a difference a decade makes. The early 1990s seem utterly unlike the early 1980s. What Honda's creation of a global local corporation shows most emphatically is that all sorts of recent ideas – from the characterization of 'reluctant' multinationals, to the impossibility of just-in-time outside Japan, to how Japanese culture limits international transfer of human resource management, and to the looming Japanization of Western industry – have simply gone out of the window. Let's summarize some key conclusions on these issues:

- there is no innate (environmental) reason why firms operating in the West should have productivity levels inferior to those in Japan;
- in fact there are several advantages to operating in the West compared to Japan: there are clear Western strengths to be played to;
- adaptation is fundamental, mimicry must be avoided;
- while some in the West interpret the new ideas they see at transplant operations (for instance, single status) as Japanization, what is actually happening is a thoroughgoing Westernization of Japanese management techniques, with innovation of new Western ideas at the transplants.

Needless to say, this perspective has significant implications for managers, engineers and workers at Western companies. That's what Rover has discovered. The keys are to play to your own strengths, to learn lessons and fit together pieces based on your own trajectory.

The process of change has to be managed with great skill, effort, thoughtfulness, because there's no easy blueprint to adopt. Moreover, change will have to be fundamental. It is not just a question of engineers learning and implementing new manufacturing and logistical techniques. Instead, the very ideas that make the new system work have to be implanted in people's brains. Almost everybody is going to have to utterly change what they do, how they do it, and how they think about how they do it. This is not a novel idea these days, but it is important to note how clearly the Honda case confirms it.

That is a tall order indeed. Whose responsibility is it? Not government's, not trade unions', not workers': it is management's responsibility. The lesson of Honda is that good management and managers have to be placed at the very top of the agenda.

GLOBAL LOCAL MANAGEMENT

We have now sketched out the physical organization of Honda's global local corporation, from the manufacturing–sales nexus, to model design, to R&D, and to technology transfer. It is time to turn to the management of this ever-more complex organization. Who is going to manage it, and how? What kinds of coordinating structures are necessary to make it function smoothly?

The Global Local Manager

If there is a new breed of global local manager emerging, who is best suited to the task: the Japanese, the Americans, the Europeans? In theory, perhaps the Europeans, because they're generally more experienced at dealing with other cultures and other languages. But in practice the first cadre of the new breed at Honda are of necessity Japanese, precisely because that's where the global local corporation's roots are, and because it is the Honda Way, developed in Japan and best understood in Japan, around which Honda's global local corporation is being constructed.

But the Japanese were hardly ready for the task. They originated in a culture not exactly well-known for its easy acceptance of foreigners. And normal business practice held that working abroad, and wanting to work abroad, often spelled the death of a managerial career, partly because it meant being isolated from the so-important personal networks, and partly because of sheer cultural prejudice against any 'foreignness'.

Honda has embarked upon a deliberate strategy to change all that. With large numbers of Japanese staff stationed abroad, often for several years at a time, before circulating back to Japan, it has created within its managerial ranks a substantial group with experience in the West (so far, as we have just pointed out, mostly in North America). The result is that Honda's Japanese organization has been infused with 'foreignness'. Only first-hand experience of a different society will enable people to understand the boundedness of Japan, and permit a loosening of ties – in thought – with Japan: and that's the prerequisite of thinking in a global local way.

Honda has pioneered the idea that a posting in the West is a positive advantage from a career viewpoint. It has become systematic strategy to run almost all the top management through North American posts before they are promoted in Japan: and not just at an early stage in their careers – 'for the experience' – but in high-level postings. By 1991 two of the top three 'troika' managers at the pinnacle of the company had previously been posted to North America, between them having spent a total of thirteen years there. The third member, President Kawamoto, was perhaps the last of the generation that had not worked abroad. Until his unexpected early retirement in 1992, one of the troika, Soichiro Irimajiri, President of Honda R&D and the man responsible for 'translating' the Honda Way for the Americans, and closely personally associated with the success of the American operations, was widely expected to be the next company president. (That retirement, incidentally, would appear to have been related to the continued tension between R&D and manufacturing at Honda, as noted in Chapter 2. Irimajiri's background was in manufacturing at Suzuka, and in North America. The episode highlights that coordination of R&D with manufacturing need not be a smooth process.)

There are sound reasons for sending large numbers of Japanese abroad for extended periods. At first sight employing large numbers of local managers from the start might seem a more sensible way to promote localization. But in fact at Honda the whole process is deeper than that, with global learning both from and to Japan expected to take place on a substantial scale.

Not only are the Japanese managers much improved as managers by their Western experience, but in the meantime they play a vital role in the infusion of the Honda Way to North America: a two-way exchange of knowledge as we saw above when we looked at technology transfer. The transplantation of a sufficiently large cadre of Japanese human resources deeply imbued in the Honda Way reduced the risk of watering it down, and has given thousands of Westerners the chance to learn directly by daily contact with Japanese. This fits into the organizational structures characteristic of Honda. With minimal pyramidal hierarchy and with minimal rule-books to guide behaviours, personal contacts, group decision-making and the development of an implicit knowledge – from corporate philosophies down to details of what to do in particular situations – become fundamental to making the system work. Learning all that is unavoidably a slow process for Western managers and engineers.

That is not to say that Japanese staff necessarily make very good managers in the West. We have mentioned some of the difficulties they have faced, sometimes in ceding control, sometimes in adopting Western behaviours in their dealings with Western counterparts. Indeed, the adoption of a managerial division of labour such that it is Western managers who tend to be in charge of Western subordinates leaves as the biggest source of intercultural friction the personal-level interactions between Western and Japanese managers.

The system of managerial rotations through a Western posting is also not without problems. Take Europe, for instance. Some of

Honda's Japanese engineers stationed in Europe view Europe very favourably compared to Japan in terms of the development of the individual person, and argue that Europe has much to contribute to improving Honda's corporate organization. However, it has been difficult for the Japanese to get the hang of the differences between European markets and the subtle complexities of each (even by the early 1990s, within Europe Honda still seems to be aiming for the top market in the brave expectation that the rest will follow).

Although there is a need for more people in Japan with European experience, the current system of rotating people back to Japan after stints of three to five years actually creates the problem that just at the moment when the Japanese engineer has – sometimes with great difficulty – begun to understand and to make the most of European society, he finds himself recalled to Japan and replaced by somebody who has to start all over again: hampering the full establishment of a 'European culture' within Honda either in Japan or in Europe.

These Japanese engineers have learned to appreciate some of the freedoms enjoyed by Western counterparts, to enjoy family life more, to run a private life without the corporate interference characteristic of Japan. So it is very interesting to note that Honda still appears to be treating its Japanese global local managers *without* the distance from their 'personal' affairs and (Western-defined) respect that is the norm in the West. Japanese managers and engineers are sometimes shipped around the world at very short notice, with families left alone – sometimes abroad – quite unexpectedly, all in the interest of personnel flexibility. People who fall out of favour on their way up the managerial ladder are still being demoted to parts makers, but now on a global scale (for example, from Honda in Europe to a North American parts maker). When personal lives don't meet standards in the eyes of superiors, temporary demotion to boring jobs may now also mean a post on the other side of the globe. And despite the advent of global technologies and global interfacing links, the managerial approach of 'going to where the problem is, talking to the people involved directly' has so far been retained at the global level, with all the human stress that that involves.

What, then, of the Western–native global local manager? The hot question is what roles Westerners will be allowed to play in the medium term. Will they find themselves high up the corporate ladder in Japan? What behaviours will they need to adopt?

One interpretation of the large Japanese staffs abroad would be that the Japanese are jealous of their power and decision-making and don't want to see it ceded. We have steered clear of suggesting such a view at the corporate level. But there's no doubt that this happens at an individual level, with Western managers feeling frozen out of decision-making in some cases, not allowed to be sufficiently independent of Japanese shadows in others. What we can say is that it probably isn't in Honda's medium-term interest to allow this kind of behaviour to persist. There's far more to be gained from incorporating the Westerners more fully than from freezing them out, and doing so would fit all we've learned about Honda so far. On the other hand, incorporation needn't go so far as to promote Americans into the top levels of the corporate hierarchy in Japan: that too would fit what we've learned so far.

There is an important cultural conundrum here that points up a key difference between production workers and managers in the global local corporation. For production workers we've seen how Honda has developed Westernized human resources strategies in North America and Europe. But there is a key difference at manager and engineer level: Japanese managers have been sent over to the West in droves, to work closely with Western counterparts, which indicates that Honda has a choice about whether to employ Western or Japanese engineers and managers, because they are more mobile. (To make the point crystal-clear, it simply wouldn't be viable economically or politically to bring over thousands of production workers from Japan.)

But if it is the case that the Japanese managers are bringing Japanese habits with them, and Honda is bringing the same expected flexibility and corporate overview of their behaviour from Japan too, how can Westerners compete for promotions unless they are also prepared to adopt those habits, habits they might not normally countenance? If they can't compete, won't there be a permanent gap that will eventually cause ruptures and resignations as promotions are blocked? Could there be a two-tier system? The question we are raising here – and we can't fully answer it yet – is that of the Westernization of the Japanese manager versus the Japanization of the Western manager. It is a significant question to follow in the years ahead.

Intimately linked to these questions is the issue of corporate ideas, philosophies, cultures, and the ultimate evolution of the Honda Way into a managerial approach that has both similarities across the globe and also local interpretations, local variations, and even locally different forms (that is, implicit knowledge versus slogans versus written manuals versus videos). That issue is also sure to remain to the fore during the 1990s as the global local corporation both deepens its local roots, with increasingly autonomous decision-making, and also deepens the complexity of its global linkages.

A Framework for Global Control?

In Chapter 2 we noted how, in Japan, every few years have seen Honda revamp its organizational structure as it has grown bigger, often with the aim of shaking things up to keep 'big business disease' at bay. Honda is adopting the same approach at the global level, and we can see the same rejigging of combinations of opposites with each shake-up: group and individual decision-making, vertical and horizontal organization, top-down control and autonomy, centralization and decentralization.

The early 1990s have indeed marked an important watershed in the development of Honda's global management structures, as Honda moves to create a framework for global control that at once mirrors and guides the physical shape of the global local corporation we have been discussing above. Familiar language is resurfacing, now at the global level: how to avoid big business disease, how to overcome tendencies towards bureaucratic slowness. And again, it was the appointment of a new president, Mr Kawamoto, in 1990, that inaugurated a new bout of organizational restructuring.

Within Japan, the ascendency of Kawamoto brought the installation of a top troika, consisting of the top R&D engineer from Japan (Kawamoto himself) together with a manufacturing and a marketing specialist possessing many years' overseas experience, as we noted above. There were the beginnings of the abandonment of the famous 'joint boardroom', with its college of equal top managers who had few individual responsibilities, but that was leading to increasingly unwieldy consensus decision-making: from now on there would be more individual responsibilities, and private offices too for those that wanted one.

We've seen the same kind of reorganization before at Honda. Individual responsibility means fewer meetings and more impetus to get out of the boardroom to visit factories and sales outlets: it is a renewal of the individual and the diagonal tendency against the collective and horizontal. And yet these managerial changes were portrayed by outside observers in typical dualist terms. The joint boardroom had been seen to epitomize Honda's ('groupist') Japaneseness, and journalists in particular revelled in labelling its dissolution as a turn to American-style management (even interpreting it as Honda belatedly realizing that American is best after all!). That's nonsense. We've seen throughout this book how Honda puts opposites together. It's quite wrong to automatically interpret any shift of emphasis, any change of tack, as evidence that Honda is adopting radically different policies.

At the global level, Kawamoto's arrival meant recombining centralization and decentralization. The various product areas – automobiles, motorcycles, power products – became fully separate divisions. At the same time, control over automobile operations was pulled into the centre for a year and subjected to tight management by the troika as they studied them and sorted out their future direction. Then, by 1992, control was decentralized again on a regional basis, with Japan, North America and Europe to be increasingly equal geographical divisions, and the global local corporate centre distancing itself for the first time from the company headquarters for Japan; indeed speculation centred on whether Honda was now capable of moving its corporate headquarters to the United States.

So Honda continues its regular revisions of corporate organization. The goal is not to find a single perfect structure for the long term, but to keep trying to match up management organizational structures to the evolving form and functioning of the physical corporation. Sometimes the latter gets ahead of the former. At that point the firm slows down and loses direction, and it's time for fresh leadership from the top, for new direction. Staying flexible, fighting off bureaucracy, dealing with complexity, these are the watchwords, and they will continue to be, with management structures subject to regular revisions to ensure that Honda's global local corporation is both an organization that follows when it is led, and has leadership providing it with real direction.

PLAYING GLOBAL LOCAL POLITICS

In recent decades, our understanding of the political issues associated with multinational enterprises has been conditioned by the idea of the ladder we discussed in Chapter 1 in which a firm either proceeds from exports to CKD production overseas to full-fledged local subsidiaries, or goes straight to the last stage by purchasing an existing local firm. The key political issue has concerned respectively either how far up the ladder the multinational would go, or what foreign takeover would imply for the 'independence' of local firms.

But we also took note in Chapter 1 of claims that a new type of multinational enterprise is emerging in the late twentieth century: a post-national firm, a stateless corporation, that operates in a borderless world. Honda is uniformly cited as exemplary of the new type by its advocates. But is Honda now moving beyond politics, as the new argument would suggest? What's happened to the old-style politics?

The first point to make is that in creating the global local corporation Honda has by no means been able to ignore the nation-state and its political borders. To refresh our memories:

In North America:

- American politics was far from irrelevant to the Japanese transplant investments: the most we can say here is that in Honda's case its role was less clear, given Honda's early move to establish North American production. On the other hand, Honda's corporate philosophy of investing in countries where products are sold smacks of keeping in tune with political currents. It's just that Honda doesn't wait for local politics to come to a boil, but tries to stay ahead of the game.
- Honda clearly benefited from the VRA in the United States during the 1980s, which provided a useful insurance policy for Marysville by increasing automobile prices, and a fillip to profits as well.
- Honda has not been able to avoid the highly charged controversy over whether its automobiles 'really are American', 'really are Canadian'; indeed the matter came to a head in 1992, almost a full decade after production began at Marysville.
- There was controversy over Honda's hiring practices in the mid-1980s that appeared to exclude racial minorities, women and older workers.
- Honda has continually stressed the 'full-fledged' nature of its operations in North America, because of the importance of the public perception that it operates a fully American company.
- Honda has been able to take advantage of the protection of national governments in host countries too. Just as one branch of the United States government argued that Canadian Hondas should count as Japanese cars, another branch stoutly defended American Hondas in Europe as definitely not Japanese in origin.
- Honda uses its North American base to supply markets around the world where political pressures restrict supply from Japan, markets

from the European Community to Israel. Exports to Japan and elsewhere have been loudly trumpeted in the United States as beneficial to the US economy, again reflecting the importance of the domestic political context.

In Europe:

- Honda's approach to the European market has been more constrained by politics than in North America. There are clear differences in political context between the two world regions: in the shape of the coalitions ranged against the Japanese, and in their underlying strength.
- The resulting virtual exclusion of all Japanese sales in some European countries has obviously affected market penetration. A high-level political accord between the European Community and Japan was needed to set the terms for increasing Japanese sales over the 1990s.
- Honda's link to Rover has been infused with politics, from British concern over the foreign takeover of a national asset, to Honda's reference to the Rover case as evidence that it is not seeking to destroy but to help the car industry in Europe.
- Local content has played a key role again, with Honda announcing high levels of local content, and the British government undertaking responsibility to ensure it. The British government is then in a position to protect Honda's exports to the rest of Europe.
- Once more, at every turn Honda stresses the Europeanness of its operations, as it does in North America, revealing just how important it thinks public perceptions to be.
- Finally, let's not forget that racism lurks continually behind the scenes in both North America and Europe, and on all sides.

In short, for Honda, politics is also a global local phenomenon. And if it doesn't always break out openly, that's because Honda has carefully prepared for it, taking into account national policies, trade agreements, the role of public opinion, in very many aspects of its strategic decision-making.

But can we approach the question of the post-national, stateless corporation and the borderless world from another standpoint? Perhaps what its proponents really mean is that the multinational enterprise of the future needs a uniform corporate culture, with no single national culture – especially the headquarters and country of origin – imposing its perspective and its will. Managers should therefore sever their ties to the nation-state. On the face of it there would seem to be more to this idea – that national cultures have to be jettisoned – than to the thesis of a strictly borderless world. But in fact here we have no more than the dualist opposite to the national company: the non-national company. That is not Honda's goal at all.

Far from wanting to lose its original national identity as a Japanese company to adopt a post-national, stateless character, Honda is in fact trying to gain several new identities: American, Canadian, British, European even. And that means more than just 'acceptance' by the host country as a local corporate citizen. Adopting a new citizenship also means adopting new habits and practices within the corporation, real habits and real practices, in tune with the national culture: that's exactly what we saw in North America, and that's the question we posed for Honda (and Rover) in Europe.

In fact what we're seeing with Honda is a new species of *multinational* enterprise. That's why we insist upon calling it not simply a global corporation but a global *local* corporation.

What about the traditional politics of multinational enterprises? While we have argued the case for a new type – the global local corporation – what seems to have happened is that politics, along with many of our attitudes, has been left behind, stuck in the old mould. Paradoxically then, a company that is creating a novel type of organization pretends that it isn't, pretends that it is just like the old multinationals (the best ones, of course). That is how to interpret Honda's claims to be truly American, truly European, all the claims about self-reliance, about how the full gamut of activities is carried out in each place, and so on. Of course, what we've discovered is that these claims tell only half the story: one half of a dualist opposite. The other half is the permanent insertion of these North American and European branches into a constantly evolving global manufacturing network.

There's no suggestion that the global local corporation is unique in having to play world politics as best it can. That is the point though: it's pretty hard to see a stateless corporation operating in a borderless world when we closely examine one of its supposed leading exponents, Honda. We are still awaiting the emergence of a full political comprehension of the global local corporation; for a few years yet, we'll be seeing Honda having to make do with the old ideas, despite the uncomfortable fit with its actual practices.

LOOKING FORWARD

It is time to draw in the threads of our complex analysis. Our argument is that Honda has created a new form of multinational enterprise. The global local corporation is distinguished by successful global-scale organization on all operating dimensions at once, including manufacturing, parts sourcing, technology diffusion, product R&D, trade between regions, well beyond the traditional multinational links of finance and top management.

We've concentrated our investigation on the story of the rapid and massive investments that launched Honda into global local status during the 1980s and early 1990s. The next few years probably won't see the same kind of expansionary evolution (though Swindon may expand, and there will be smaller third-world manufacturing investments, especially in Asia and Latin America). What we'll see instead is consolidation and deepening of the existing physical structures, as Honda learns how to extract more and more out of the factory network it has built up across the world.

There therefore remain a series of questions to be posed, issues to follow as the operations of Honda's global local corporation evolve into an ever more intricate grand ballet organized on a global scale. These questions set the agenda for the 1990s.

- How will the global local car evolve? Are the latest Accord-based innovations the end-point? What other combinations of similarity and difference are possible? Will various strategies for how to create a global local car eventually coexist at Honda? The complex relationship between models variously badged Civic, Integra, Concerto and Domani, which has sprung out of the original Civic-Ballade link, suggest no simple structure, as horizontal, temporal, and geographical spin-off processes are increasingly inter-woven.

- Relatedly, how will the process of model changeover evolve? There has been much talk of extending the habitual four-year cycle to reduce costs. The product spin-off process at Honda, however, points to something far more complicated, revolving around a capability to reduce costs by introducing what appear to be new models or separate models, without re-engineering an entire new car. Hence the 1993 Today shares 40 per cent of parts with its predecessor. The 1992 Domani shares 60 per cent of parts with other models, including Civic, from which it is derived. The point is that the very nature of the model replacement cycle is in question.

- How separate can Honda's global headquarters become from Japanese operations? Does it matter where in the world they are located? While perhaps spatially mobile in principle, are there not other factors at play which will in fact leave the global headquarters located in Japan?

- How will patterns of parts sourcing eventually evolve at the global level? Can they be made coherent with the permutations of the global local car? Already there is growing evidence that a deep restructuring of parts sourcing in Japan is underway, in part related to the growing complexity of the model replacement cycle, in part related to a cost-cutting rationalization drive (with parts sourcing operations in North America and Europe to a certain extent now more advanced than in Japan).

- How far can decentralization of R&D proceed? Precisely how will it be organized geographically to fit in with the evolving global local car?

- What new engineering challenges will arise? How will the currently daunting task of resolving the puzzle of lean-burn engines that increase pollution be tackled?

- When North American and European operations mature, what kinds of manufacturing process innovations will develop there (in technology, organization and the roles of people), and which ones will then flow back to improve Japanese operations? Will we soon be studying the 'Westernization of Japan' via intra-corporate links as horizontal and diagonal innovation networks develop across the globe?

- How far will the 'Westernization' of the Japanese global local manager proceed? How far up can the Western manager get, and what kinds of behavioural changes are going to be required? Here lie some vital questions involving not only social interactions but the very personalities of the people implicated.

- What will a mature Honda Way for Europe look like? Will Rover try to adopt a parallel 'Rover Way', drawing upon Western culture and ideology?

- How will the new understanding of cutting-edge multinational enterprises filter into worldwide political discussion? Will the global local corporation continue to be measured against past multi-national behaviour? Will it continue to present itself in terms from the past, or will a more accurate understanding be developed and diffused?

- How will Honda deal with society's questions over the future of the car? How will Honda try to market its cars, with what concepts? While pulling out of F-1 car racing 20 years ago led to concentration of resources on ecological engines (CVCC), and the 1992 pullout from F-1 led to new resources devoted to electric vehicles, now the situation is more complex, with an attempt to keep racing cars, but now only in North America (on the Indy car circuit). That suggests increasingly subtle awareness of wider issues involved in global local marketing.

- What will the full international division of labour within Honda's global structure look like? By the mid-1990s exactly which activities will remain in Japan, and which will be decentralized? Here there are several *qualitative* questions to be answered: what *kinds* of cars, what *kinds* of parts, what *kinds* of capital equipment, what *kinds* of research and development, will be located in Japan, North America and Europe? The hypothesis to test here is the critical one that the 'top-end' (high-tech, high-skill, high-value-added, control-point) activities on all fronts will remain in Japan. But this thesis must be recognized as inspired by one type of experience with multinationals based in the West.

This is only a beginning. There are many other significant questions too that we can't tackle here, especially concerning social change, work life, the role of labour unions and government policies, and how technology transfer works within chains of parts makers.

What we see at Honda so far is less a single and stable new organizational model than a trajectory, a case of continuous change. This means that prediction is dangerous, as is any assumption that present patterns will continue unchanged. Indeed the very idea behind the global local corporation is to retain the flexibility to respond to evolving circumstances in its world markets that means it will regularly defy predictions. We need to keep our eye constantly on the cutting edge of Honda activities, because it is hard to foresee reaching a point where we know enough to stop. We have come a certain way along the path in this book. I hope we've caught up with Honda to a certain extent. But the story will continue to develop, as a new type of global local corporation now unfolds, built on the foundations we have been examining.

The perspective adopted here does seem to give us the tools to continue the analysis fruitfully. We should have learned to approach problems a little like Honda does. That doesn't mean we are now in a position to safely predict future corporate policy, for reasons we have just mentioned, but it does mean that we should no longer be so surprised, no longer make ultimately foolish predictions of the kind that used to characterize the Western view of Japanese firms.

Our method has been both complex and straightforward. Complex because we've preferred to attempt a total overview of Honda rather than isolate fragments of the story, like human resources, technologies, relations with parts makers, or localization in one world region, for closer examination of each. Straightforward because in the idea of dualist puzzle-solving we've found a useful way to get to grips with Honda's strategic decision-making and its management philosophy on all these fronts. That's meant a conceptual leap forward, moving away from the old dualist ideas, a move requiring innovation on our part just as on Honda's.

The extent of this leap can be seen by going back to where we started, only a decade ago (or at the start of this book). At that point it was still widely believed that Japanese manufacturing firms would remain confined to Japan, that they couldn't survive as multinational enterprises, that their culture prevented them from operating their manufacturing systems overseas; at best, it was thought, if they did go abroad they would either flounder or be obliged to attempt a thorough cultural Japanization of their new operating environments.

With Honda in the lead, all these ideas have been turned on their heads. A medium-sized car maker has pointed the way forward by creating a major new multinational organization, has transferred its production system overseas, has adapted Western culture where appropriate, and has discovered that operating in the West actually has advantages over Japan.

Is Honda unique? What lessons does it hold for its competitors? In this book we have separated Honda from its rivals in order to subject it to a thorough yet manageable analysis. A next step forward would be to draw lessons from very detailed comparisons with other global companies, especially Japanese ones. Let's end with some pointers for that ambitious task.

Honda has been a pioneer for the car industry, but there have been other Japanese manufacturing firms involved too in the decisive shift away from the 'reluctant multinational' image, among them firms in other sectors like Sony and Matsushita. And another pioneer Japanese firm in the car industry must be mentioned, Nissan. Nissan arrived in North America soon after Honda, and opened its own factory in Europe before Honda did.

A full comparison with Nissan would be intriguing indeed, because Nissan's version of the global local corporation appears to differ in significant respects from Honda's. A big difference is that Nissan handed over a substantial degree of control of its American and European operations at an early stage to local managers drawn directly from other local car makers. In Europe Nissan recognizes a trade union, in North America it was involved in a bitter struggle with the United Automobile Workers, in which one-third of its employees wanted to join the union even though management was overtly hostile. And that's just a start. Detailed study would doubtless throw up a host of fascinating and revealing similarities and differences between Honda and Nissan.

What about Toyota? Here's where we see just how important the Honda model is, because in North America, after its first involvement in the joint venture with General Motors (NUMMI) in California, the firm most people take to be Japan's leading car maker decided to create a close copy of Honda's North American operations, including its two Kentucky assembly lines and engine plant making Accord-sized models, its smaller factory in Canada to make Civic-sized models, its decision not to recognize the United Automobile Workers (unlike NUMMI) and the building of a station-wagon and coupé for export. A familiar pattern?

Western companies too have sought to learn from Honda. We have looked at the Rover case. Another fascinating example is the oft-troubled Chrysler, which undertook a detailed study of Honda's management techniques in the late 1980s, implemented much of what it learned, and by the early 1990s was being hailed as having achieved its own corporate turnaround. As we have seen, the highly successful BMW, perhaps Europe's premier car maker, is also set to learn all it can, having hired top American managers from Honda to help it establish its own new transplant. Honda has thus formed an 'innovation pole' for car makers the world over, both successful and troubled manufacturers.

As with all pioneers and leaders, we can't expect other companies to mimic Honda exactly. Indeed they shouldn't. And yet there are so many lessons to be learned from Honda, from its management style and problem-solving philosophy, from what it has achieved in turning itself into a global local corporation. A host of people in many different positions could do worse than take Honda's innovations into account, from managers and engineers, to workers and labour unionists, to small business owners and to government officials and politicians. I hope we've made it a little easier to seriously consider what the advent of the global local corporation might imply for them.

Notes

1. Honda President Tadashi Kume, cited in Jon Lowell, 'Far East outlook . . . clear sailing', *Ward's Auto World*, April 1989, pp. 31–3. Passage from p. 32.
2. Honda Motor Co., *Guide to Honda 1992*, p. 14.
3. Honda President Nobuhiko Kawamoto, cited in Rick Johnson, 'Making the best of tough times', *Automotive News*, 16 December 1991, pp. 2i, 7i. Passage from p. 2i.

Index

AP Technoglass 101–2
Asahi Glass 101–2, 115, 264
Austin Rover *see* Rover

Bellemar Parts Industries 99, 101, 117–20, 122
Belletech 102
Bertrand Faure 264
best-of-both-worlds solutions *see* puzzle-solving
Big Three 27, 73, 89, 95–7, 123, 146, 198, 213, 214, 219, 221, 253, 306, 322
   see also Chrysler; Ford; General Motors
Blanchester FCM 120
BMW 3, 77, 83, 180, 267, 268, 319, 340
Bosch 237
British Leyland (BL) *see* Rover
Bush, President George 96–7

Capitol Plastics 100
company philosophy (Honda) 5, 45
   Americanization 147, 157–9, 160–7, 181, 269, 296, 320, 327–8
   British culture and 244, 251, 252, 260–1, 269, 321
   Honda Way 15, 44, 147, 157–60, 183, 248, 279, 296–7, 320, 323–4, 328, 337
   national cultures or global uniformity? 272, 330–1, 334–5
   role as organizational 'glue' 44, 320, 328
   role of metaphor in 44–6, 59
   transfer outside Japan 278–9, 320–1, 328
   see also 'Japanization'; puzzle-solving; Rover; training

Chrysler 3, 57, 66, 81, 96, 319, 340
culture, corporate *see* company philosophy
currency fluctuations 27, 100, 102, 145, 232, 303, 307, 309

Daihatsu 74, 222
Diamond Star Motors 75, 123, 127
domestic parts makers (and Honda)
   capacities of (in Europe) 221, 246, 261–2
   changes expected of 143–5
   innovation diffusion and 143, 319
   Japanese intervention in 138–9
   joint ventures, in 124, 144, 264
   location 131–3
   North America, bypassed in 120, 244, 319
   parts supplied by 99–105, 107–8, 264
   problems due to 112, 135–6, 142–5
   see also European motor industry; North American motor industry; *individual company names*
dualisms
   autonomy (for worker) *v.* task specification 50, 194, 254–7, 259
   autonomy *v.* authority 15, 16–17, 42–4, 199, 254–7, 259, 272, 280, 284–5
   centralized (organization) *v.* decentralized 28–9, 42–4, 112, 141–2, 213–14, 316, 331
   conflict (in parts sourcing) *v.* cooperation 21, 122
   confrontation (in labour relations) *v.* cooperation 22, 261
   direct labour *v.* indirect labour 187–8